The Holy Quran for Educating the Child

With illustrative stories and psychological explanations

Part I

Dr. Ofer Grosbard
Clinical Psychologist

The Holy Quran for Educating the Child
With illustrative stories and psychological explanations
Part I

Ofer Grosbard

Ttanslation: Chaya Galai

ISBN: 978-965-92829-0-6

Table of Contents

Preface

1. How "The Holy Quran for Educating the Child" began:

In spring 2007 a group of fifteen Bedouin students studying for graduate degrees in educational counseling attended a course on Developmental Psychology given by our lecturer Dr. Ofer Grosbard.

One day I went up to him and said: "May I tell you the truth. What you are teaching us is not going to be of help to us."

"Why do you say that?" Ofer asked.

I said that when I become an educational counselor, a parent may come to me one day and say, "A demon has entered into my child" or some similar statement from the same cultural background. "Do you think that what you have taught us here will be of any use to me then?"

"Then what would be helpful to you?" Ofer asked.

I replied with one word: "The Quran."

He asked me to explain. I said that, in the appropriate context, quotation of a verse from the Quran has enormous impact on Muslims.

Ofer brought a copy of the Quran to our next lesson. He divided the chapters among us and asked us to locate the educational-therapeutic verses. It transpired that there are many of these in the Quran. The verses exhort individuals to take responsibility, learn the truth, respect others etc. Ofer asked us to compose a brief story taken from everyday life for each verse to illustrate how a parent or teacher can utilize the verse to convey a message to the child. Together we collected more than three hundred stories, and Ofer added to each a simple and brief educational-psychological explanation.

This is how **"The Holy Quran for Educating the Child"** came into being.

Bushra Mazarib

The student who set the project in motion

1 | Loss, Illness and Tragedy

1. What should you say to a girl who feels guilty about her father's death?

{ أَيْنَمَا تَكُونُوا يُدْرِككُّمُ الْمَوْتُ وَلَوْ كُنتُمْ فِي بُرُوجٍ مُّشَيَّدَةٍ وَإِن تُصِبْهُمْ حَسَنَةٌ يَقُولُوا
هَٰذِهِ مِنْ عِندِ اللَّهِ وَإِن تُصِبْهُمْ سَيِّئَةٌ يَقُولُوا هَٰذِهِ مِنْ عِندِكَ قُلْ كُلٌّ مِّنْ عِندِ اللَّهِ
فَمَالِ هَٰؤُلَاءِ الْقَوْمِ لَا يَكَادُونَ يَفْقَهُونَ حَدِيثًا } (النّساء: 78)

Wherever you are, death will catch up with you, even if you live in formidable castles. When something good happens to them, they say, "This is from GOD," and when something bad afflicts them, they blame you. Say, "Everything comes from GOD." Why do these people misunderstand almost everything? (The Women: 78)

Samira, a fourth-grade pupil, excelled in her studies and everything else at school until about five months ago when her father took her for tests to a nearby hospital. A vehicle traveling in the opposite lane crossed into their lane and crashed head on into them. Her father was killed instantly, and she, who was sitting in the back, sustained only light injuries. When Samira returned to school a month later, both her personality and her behavior seemed to have changed significantly. She had become a very quiet child, participating neither in the lessons nor the school activities, and her grades fell drastically. When an announcement is made about a parents' meeting or when the pupils are requested to obtain their parents' permission for an activity outside the school, she bursts into tears. When anyone tries to calm her down, she is reminded of her father and blames herself for causing his death. "Because of me we went for tests that day," she keeps repeating. "There's no happiness, no point in living and no hope without my father who I killed," she sobs bitterly. The teacher began to worry that Samira might harm herself, and decided to refer her to the school counselor.

Samira went to meet the counselor and told her story. When she started crying, the counselor opened the Quran at Verse 78 of the Surah 'Women' and asked Samira to read aloud slowly and clearly: **"Wherever you are, death will catch up with you, even if you live in formidable castles."** How do you understand this verse? the counselor asked. "That it is God who decides about life and death, and no one can run away from what God decides." That's good, said the counselor. What does it say about you? "That I'm not to blame," said Samira with a slight smile as she dries her tears. "That it's God's will and I'm not to blame," she repeated. The counselor smiled back at her.

Explanation: Children (girls possibly more than boys) often feel guilty for something that they were not responsible for and that was out of their control. Samira thinks that she killed her father, because according to her logic she was responsible for the fact that they went for tests that day. It is difficult for her to think that what happened was out of her control, and what is out of her control is also not her responsibility. Of course, this can be explained to her in various ways. She can be told that her father could have been involved in a road accident at another time and place. She can be told that children always ask their parents to take them places, but this doesn't mean that the child is responsible for the road and for the driving. Maybe she could be told how much she would like things to be dependent on her, because in that case she could have saved her father. However, there is no stronger and more calming statement than the verse in the Quran which emphasizes that it is God who determines people's fates and not the girl Samira. From now on she will no longer have to carry around the terrible burden of guilt.

It should be pointed out that we will not use this sentence in all instances of manslaughter, and certainly not in cases of murder. In a situation of negligence, for example when a driver kills someone while under the influence of alcohol, and certainly in the case of premeditated murder, we will not make use of this sentence that places the responsibility on God. In these cases, we will refer to verses in the Quran that talk about a person's responsibility for his actions and his fate.

2. Is loss an excuse for aggression?

{ إِلاَّ الَّذِينَ تَابُواْ وَأَصْلَحُواْ وَبَيَّنُواْ فَأُوْلَئِكَ أَتُوبُ عَلَيْهِمْ وَأَنَا التَّوَّابُ الرَّحِيمُ } (البقرة: 160).

As for those who repent, reform, and proclaim, I redeem them. I am the Redeemer, Most Merciful. (The Cow: 160)

Rami, a tenth-grade student is considered a particularly troublesome child. At school he respects no one, treats everyone with contempt, and is aggressive to the people around him. He also causes problems for his parents. He steals the family's car, cruises around and commits traffic offenses. Rami's parents are very worried, especially his mother whom he doesn't listen to and responds rudely to.

Rami hasn't always behaved like this. He used to be a somewhat quiet and introverted child until his cousin, whom Rami felt very close to, unexpectedly committed suicide. Since then, Rami has become a pampered child, sleeping during the day and awake at night, neglecting himself and his studies and exploiting his parents. They continue to feel sorry for him, while he threatens that if he doesn't get what he wants, he will commit suicide. The parents feel torn. On the one hand, they are afraid he will harm himself, and on the other, they are afraid that if they give in to all his requests, he will also become a lost child.

Rami has recently started to smoke without shame in front of his father and to hit his little sister. All requests to him to change his ways have made absolutely no impact.

The parents approached Rami's homeroom teacher whom Rami respected in the past. The teacher spoke to Rami about his falling grades and his behavior, but this made no impact. The teacher then opened the Quran and read to Rami verse 160 from the Surah, The Cow: **"As for those who repent, reform, and proclaim, I redeem them. I am the Redeemer, Most Merciful."**

Explanation: Without his cousin Rami is not the same child. It seems there was something in their close relationship that enabled Rami to contain his feelings and function properly. After the loss of his cousin, Rami possibly felt guilty and angry at himself that he didn't take care of him. Possibly he blames the environment for not taking care of him, and possibly he is angry with his cousin for having left him, and it is also possible that he has transformed his mourning and the depression he feels into anger and aggression towards the world. In any event, an attempt should be made to talk openly to Rami about his feelings, and to enable him, if he wishes, to express his pain and his anger. Only when he expresses his pain will be able to begin the process of gradually releasing himself from it. This therapeutic process will not be possible, however, without setting clear limits for Rami, and in this respect the quote of the appropriate verse from the Quran is vital for his recovery.

3. How should one behave towards an orphan?

} فِي الدُّنْيَا وَالآخِرَةِ وَيَسْأَلُونَكَ عَنِ الْيَتَامَى قُلْ إِصْلاَحٌ لَّهُمْ خَيْرٌ وَإِنْ تُخَالِطُوهُمْ
فَإِخْوَانُكُمْ وَاللّهُ يَعْلَمُ الْمُفْسِدَ مِنَ الْمُصْلِحِ وَلَوْ شَاءَ اللّهُ لأَعْنَتَكُمْ إِنَّ اللّهَ عَزِيزٌ حَكِيمٌ
{ (البقرة: 220)

...upon this life and the Hereafter. **And they ask you about the orphans: say, "Bringing them up as righteous persons is the best you can do for them. If you mix their property with yours, you shall treat them as family members." GOD knows the righteous and the wicked.** Had GOD willed, He could have imposed harsher rules upon you. GOD is Almighty, Most Wise (The Cow: 220).

Hussein, a fifth-grade pupil, is a mediocre learner but is a sociable child who excels in art. His father was killed in a car accident about a year ago. They live in an adjacent apartment to Hussein's uncle, who has taken the family under his wing. The uncle does not allow the mother to go out to work, saying that it is unacceptable in their society. He has taken all the money that the father left, and has told the mother and her son that he will give them what they require. Recently the uncle has demanded that Hussein leave school in order to help support the family. The mother is passive and doesn't say a word, but Hussein doesn't agree; he wants to continue going to school. The uncle curses him and beats him because of this. Hussein has already run away several times and sleeps on the street. Recently Hussein came crying to the school counselor's office, told her everything that had happened, and showed her the signs of the beatings he received from his uncle.

The counselor invited the uncle for a discussion. He was full of excuses and of stories about Hussein's bad behavior. The counselor listened to the uncle without interrupting, and when he finished, she read him just one sentence, Verse 220 from the Surah, 'The Cow': **"And they ask you about the orphans: say,**

'Bringing them up as righteous persons is the best you can do for them. If you mix their property with yours, you shall treat them as family members.' GOD knows the righteous and the wicked."

The uncle remained silent. He clearly understood the severity of his actions. The school counselor did not content herself with this, and suggested that she visit the uncle at home, accompanied by a respected religious figure, and that together they would work out how to help him obey the Quran's commandments regarding the treatment of orphans.

Explanation: Not everything in life is easy. We have to honor commitments that we have not willingly chosen. Looking after an orphan child, a relative, is one of these commitments we have to fulfill with all our hearts. No society can allow itself to leave these children without care, not because of moral considerations or because of the future of the society, but rather because a child who is not looked after can become a burden to society in a variety of ways. He is liable to be incapable of earning a livelihood, or to become involved in crime etc. Family members sometimes feel guilty that they do not take care of their orphan relative in the same way they would like their children to be taken care of if, God forbid, some tragedy were to occur. These guilt feelings are healthy and positive, and motivate the relatives to take care of the orphan. Sometimes, however, the relative feels no commitment and no guilt feelings, but rather uses the situation to exploit the orphan and his family. In such cases, the Quran and the divine commandment do the work that no therapist or authority figure can. Quite simply, the person is told how to behave with the member of his family, the orphan, who should not be discriminated against in any way. Hussein, like any other child, needs a good father who can take care of him and love him, otherwise it will be difficult for him to develop properly. This is the direction the Quran points to.

4. How do you encourage someone who has experienced a tragedy?

﴿ لَتُبْلَوُنَّ فِي أَمْوَالِكُمْ وَأَنفُسِكُمْ وَلَتَسْمَعُنَّ مِنَ الَّذِينَ أُوتُوا الْكِتَابَ مِن قَبْلِكُمْ وَمِنَ الَّذِينَ أَشْرَكُوا أَذًى كَثِيرًا وَإِن تَصْبِرُوا وَتَتَّقُوا فَإِنَّ ذَٰلِكَ مِنْ عَزْمِ الْأُمُورِ ﴾
(آل عمران: 186)

You will certainly be tested, through your money and your lives, and you will hear from those who received the scripture, and from the idol worshipers, a lot of insult. If you steadfastly persevere and lead a righteous life, this will prove the strength of your faith. (The family of Imran: 186)

Ranin, a sixth-grade pupil, comes to school every day with new clothes, new shoes and a purse full of money. She is attractive, well-groomed and keeps herself aloof from her classmates. They, in turn, tend to keep away from her. One day the teacher came into class and found Ranin sitting alone looking very sad, and the pupils whispering, "she deserves it. Now she'll feel what we felt."

Teacher: Sit down all of you and be quiet. Tell me what happened?

Ahmad: Teacher, didn't you hear? Ranin's house together with the shop burned down last night and nothing is left.

Teacher: Ranin, is this true?

Ranin: Yes teacher (starts crying).

Teacher: It's not so terrible Ranin (goes up to her and hugs her). Ranin, it happens.

Ranin: But teacher, now we're poor. There was no insurance on the house and the shop. My father forgot to renew the inSurahnce on the property.

Teacher: Ranin, you have to be brave and strong. It hurts terribly now, but in time you and your family will feel better. Time heals all pain. There are many poor people in the world who live and work, and succeed nicely in their lives. You have your whole life ahead of you Ranin. Do you know Verse 186 from Surah 'Ali-Imran'? Do you know it pupils? I want to read it to you as it is written (the teacher opens the Quran and recites): **"You will certainly be tested, through your money and your lives, and you will hear from those who received the scripture, and from the idol worshipers, a lot of insult. If you steadfastly persevere and lead a righteous life, this will prove the strength of your faith."** You and your family Ranin were tested with your property and you heard many insults. But remember, God loves the sufferers who don't give in, but who continue and succeed.

Ranin: (Still crying) I want God to love me too.

Explanation: Children are like this; they can't hide their malicious joy. Especially, as in this case, that Ranin used to mock her poorer classmates. The teacher did the right thing by not mentioning this to Ranin and by being warm and supportive to her. To say to Ranin, "you deserve it" or "now you will suffer like we suffered" are statements of revenge that are of no help to anyone. Even to reprimand the pupils for poking fun at Ranin would not be beneficial. On the contrary: the teacher's supportive reaction teaches the pupils to be more humble. Life is a wheel and even those on the bottom, as Ranin is now, can learn and advance and attain success. But the teacher went beyond this. She gave Ranin and the pupils a gift, a most important verse from the Quran which talks about the need to be strong and to persevere even in the most trying times, and that even when everyone is making fun of you, you should continue to toil and to hope for a better future.

5. What should you say to a girl who feels guilty about the death of her brother?

{ الَّذِينَ إِذَا أَصَابَتْهُم مُّصِيبَةٌ قَالُواْ إِنَّا لِلّهِ وَإِنَّا إِلَيْهِ رَاجِعونَ * أُولَـئِكَ عَلَيْهِمْ صَلَوَاتٌ مِّن رَّبِّهِمْ وَرَحْمَةٌ وَأُولَـئِكَ هُمُ الْمُهْتَدُونَ } (البقرة: 157-156)

When an affliction befalls them, they say, "We belong to GOD, and to Him we are returning." These have deserved blessings from their Lord and mercy. These are the guided ones. (The Cow: 156-157)

Bushra is a seventh-grade pupil, an attractive, pampered girl, whose school grades are mediocre. During the spring recess, the family went for a weeks' vacation to a hotel at the sea. This was a real vacation, a different atmosphere of sea and sun, and everyone in the family was having a wonderful time.

One afternoon they were playing in the sea, making up various competitive games. As it got darker, Bushra suggested to her brothers a race to see who could get out of the water and reach the beach first. Bushra put all her energy into the race and didn't look behind her. When she reached the shore panting, she saw her brothers running behind her. She was happy to have beaten them. Suddenly she heard a loud scream. Her younger brother shouted that one of her brothers was missing. Bushra dashed along the beach, screaming to her parents and the lifesaver. When they finally got the brother out of the water, he was dead.

Bushra blamed herself for the terrible tragedy. Had she not suggested a race to her brothers, she said, she wouldn't have left them and her brother would not have drowned. Bushra felt that the loss was driving her crazy. I didn't know it was a "game of death", she said.

At the end of the school vacation, all the children returned to school, but Bushra refused. "How can I go back without my brother?" she said. "I'm embarrassed to meet everyone," she added, "and to hear them say that I killed my brother." Bushra remembered how she used to help her brother with his homework, and really believed there was no reason to continue learning, because she had no one to help.

The school counselor and the teacher decided to take action. They spoke to Bushra and her family and tried to cheer them up. They said that it was God's will and that everyone returns to Him, that he is responsible for death and Bushra was not to blame. The counselor asked Bushra to read aloud Verse 156 from the Surah, 'The Cow': **"When an affliction befalls them, they say, 'We belong to GOD, and to Him we are returning.' These have deserved blessings from their Lord and mercy. These are the guided ones."**

Maybe it really wasn't my fault, Bushra murmured for the first time. After all, we were playing and how could I have known that the sea would suddenly pull him down. Mom and Dad also didn't know. It seems that it really was God's will.

Explanation: In life, people are liable to encounter various tragedies, some they are responsible for, others they are not responsible for, and sometimes those they are partially responsible for. The Quran consistently exhorts people to be responsible for their actions and not to impose blame on others. This verse deals with tragedies that are not our fault and that we are incapable of preventing. In these cases, there is no need for a person to punish himself with unnecessary guilt feelings and feelings of depression. Rather, the person needs to understand that it is God's will. This is the case with Bushra. A small child, only in seventh grade, who was given the responsibility of looking after her brothers, without being aware of the vagaries of the sea, and its unpredictable and dangerous way of behaving. Does she have to blame herself all her life? Possibly her parents are responsible for what happened. Small children should not be allowed to go far into the sea without adult supervision. It is reasonable to assume that had the parents looked after their children better, the tragedy would not have happened. The parents thus cannot say the verse from the Quran, but Bushra can and should say it, because she is not responsible.

2 | Husbands and Wives

1. How can we encourage husbands and wives to concede to one another?

{ وَإِن طَلَّقْتُمُوهُنَّ مِن قَبْلِ أَن تَمَسُّوهُنَّ وَقَدْ فَرَضْتُمْ لَهُنَّ فَرِيضَةً فَنِصْفُ مَا فَرَضْتُمْ
إَلاَّ أَن يَعْفُونَ أَوْ يَعْفُوَ الَّذِي بِيَدِهِ عُقْدَةُ النِّكَاحِ وَأَن تَعْفُواْ أَقْرَبُ لِلتَّقْوَى وَلاَ تَنسَوُاْ
الْفَضْلَ بَيْنَكُمْ إِنَّ اللّهَ بِمَا تَعْمَلُونَ بَصِيرٌ } (البقرة: 237)

And if ye divorce them before consummation, but after the fixation of a dower for them, then the half of the dower (is due to them), unless they remit it or (the man's half) is remitted by him in whose hands is the marriage tie; and the remission (of the man's half) is the nearest to righteousness and **do not forget liberality between yourselves. For Allah sees well all that ye do.** (The Cow: 237)

Rami and Rima have been married for eighteen months. They are in love, support one another and are generally acknowledged to be a perfect couple. But it seems that the Evil Eye has visited their home; their relationship, based on love and respect, has begun to collapse. One day Rima went to visit Rami in his law office. When she opened the door, she was shocked to see Rami embracing his secretary. She fled, distressed and weeping. Rami followed and tried to explain but to no avail. Rima refused to listen, accused him of infidelity and demanded a divorce. Then she went home, packed her belongings and returned to her parents' house.

Rami tried to talk to her and asked her to calm down and rethink the situation, because, he claimed, she was doing him an injustice. She had misunderstood the situation, he said. Rima asked him to leave her alone and swore she would never return to him because he was a liar and a cheater. Rami tried again in every possible way to appease her and to explain the incident but again in vain. She was deaf to his pleading and demanded only one thing – a divorce.

A month later, Rima was in the shopping center when she saw Rami's secretary. The girl came over to her and asked for an opportunity to explain what had happened. She begged until finally Rima agreed to sit down in a café with her. The secretary told Rima that what she had seen was a comradely embrace, a hug of support and commiseration. "What do you mean, commiseration?" Rima asked. The secretary told her that on that same day, someone had telephoned to tell her that her best friend had been killed in an automobile accident while on a trip abroad. When Rami saw her weeping, he hugged her in a gesture of comfort.

At first Rima did not believe the story but the secretary swore it was true and even supplied proof. Now Rima regretted not having given Rami the opportunity to explain and didn't know what to do. She knew she had insulted him and hurt his pride. Would he ever want to talk to her again?

Rima is a proud woman and it was not easy for her to admit her mistake and to apologize. She felt that to apologize was a sign of personal weakness and would enable others to exploit this fact against her. She did not know what to do. She thought about it all weekend and then consulted her mother for help in finding a solution. Her mother pondered and then replied: **"Do not forget liberality between yourselves. For Allah sees well all that ye do".** Rima understood the message and apologized to Rami for having done him an injustice. He found it hard to believe his ears, since he knew her well and was aware that she did not like apologizing. He forgave her and she has not told him to this day what impelled her to change her attitude.

Explanation: people do not like to concede and prefer to be the winners in any situation. They are reluctant to apologize since to do so hurts their pride and undermines their conviction of being in the right. But without concessions and forgiveness there can be no family life and no orderly society, because nobody is perfect and we all make mistakes. The Quran says: "the remission.... is the nearest to righteousness" and lauds concession. Give in, remit, says the Quran, because not in every case is one party entirely right and the other wrong; only concession, yielding, enables life to continue smoothly. When you give up your pride, Rima's mother was saying to her, you are doing something great. We know that only those who are truly strong can give in.

That Quran verse saved Rami and Rima's marriage.

2. What can we say to a quarreling couple?

{ يَسْأَلُونَكَ عَنِ الْأَنفَالِ قُلِ الْأَنفَالُ لِلَّهِ وَالرَّسُولِ فَاتَّقُوا اللَّهَ وَأَصْلِحُوا ذَاتَ بَيْنِكُمْ وَأَطِيعُوا اللَّهَ وَرَسُولَهُ إِن كُنتُم مُّؤْمِنِينَ } (الأنفال: 1)

They ask thee concerning (things taken as) spoils of war. Say: "(Such) spoils are at the disposal of Allah and the Messenger: **So fear Allah, and keep straight the relations between yourselves**: obey Allah and His Messenger, if ye do believe." (The Spoils: 1)

The teacher noticed that Lama, an eighth-grade student, had been behaving strangely for some time. She didn't concentrate in class, when she was addressed, she did not answer and she appeared to be in a world of her own as if she were living in a bubble. The teacher sent Lama to the counselor and Lama told her that her parents quarreled all the time. All the past week there had been shouting and they had even come to blows. At night, she said, she often awoke with a start in fear, covered in cold sweat. She was afraid that her parents might divorce.

The counselor scheduled a meeting with Lama's parents. She told them how Lama was suffering because of their incessant quarreling and how their tense relationship was affecting both her studies and her relations with her friends. She advised the parents to try to solve their problems quietly and without violence and to foster understanding for the sake of their children. "You must maintain family unity as the Quran commands us," she said. She opened the Quran at Surah 8, Verse 1, and read out to them: **"So fear Allah, and keep straight the relations between yourselves."** The parents realized that it was the will of Allah that they make peace and decided to make an effort to stop quarreling for the sake of the family.

Explanation: In every culture there are disputes between couples and it is not always easy and simple to solve them. In non-religious societies, divorce is rife because each of the partners is concerned with his or her own emotions; when they quarrel bitterly there is no unifying authority which can help them solve their problem. But in this case, the Quran imposes its authority and commands the couple to make peace. Lama's parents are believers who are in awe of Allah and so they obey the command and make peace. When Allah commands, all mutual recriminations and incessant quarreling must cease. Now, when each is responsible for his or her own action and ready to forgive the other and act compassionately, the couple can open a new page and improve their relationship. In other words, the Divine authority elevates the couple from a state of mutual recriminations to one of mutual responsibility.

3. What can we say to someone who refuses to accept a gesture of peace?

﴿ وَإِن جَنَحُوا لِلسَّلْمِ فَاجْنَحْ لَهَا وَتَوَكَّلْ عَلَى اللَّهِ إِنَّهُ هُوَ السَّمِيعُ الْعَلِيمُ ﴾ (الأنفال: 61)

But if the enemy incline towards peace, do thou (also) incline towards peace, and trust in Allah: for He is the One that Heareth and Knoweth (all things). (The Spoils: 61)

One day Naim yelled at his wife, Fatma and cursed her. Then, as the neighbors watched, he threw her out of the house with her belongings and ordered her not to return. Fatma telephoned her father who came and took her to his house.

After several days Naim began to feel lonely. He could not manage the household and children without her and so he went to Fatma's father and asked him to send her back. Her father threw him out and said: "Never come back. I want you to give my daughter a divorce. I have always treated Fatma with respect. She was my most pampered child and now you have insulted her in front of the neighbors."

Naim appealed to several of the village notables and asked them to help him bring Fatma home. He promised never to act like that again. The notables approached the father and asked him to agree to send Fatma home if only for the sake of her children. Her father refused. The mukhtar said to Fatma's father: " If Naim has regretted his actions and wants to make peace with your daughter, give him that opportunity and let Allah's will be done. You certainly are familiar with Surah 8, Verse 61, which says: **"But if the enemy incline towards peace, do thou (also) incline towards peace, and trust in Allah."**

Explanation: everyone knows that making peace entails risks. Who can guarantee that the other party's intentions are sincere? Who can guarantee that Naim will not repeat his conduct? He may have promised a number of times in the past to treat his wife with respect but failed to keep his word. However, the Quran tells us that if we err, it is better to incline towards conciliation and peace and not war. Since all peace-making entails risk, we must place our trust in Allah so that if we are led astray, He will help us. The Quran does not recommend that we behave foolishly and close our eyes to the facts. But in those cases where an individual gains the impression that the other party may be inclined towards a peaceful solution, it is not worth missing the opportunity. However, if Naim again behaves badly and again asks for forgiveness, Fatma and her father should not fall into the trap and delude themselves, as do many abused women, who return to their husbands again and again, sometimes until they meet a bitter end.

4. How much should one spend on a wedding?

{وَلَا تَجْعَلْ يَدَكَ مَغْلُولَةً إِلَىٰ عُنُقِكَ وَلَا تَبْسُطْهَا كُلَّ الْبَسْطِ فَتَقْعُدَ مَلُومًا مَّحْسُورًا}

(الإسراء: 29)

Make not thy hand tied (like a niggard's) to thy neck, nor stretch it forth to its utmost reach, so that thou become blameworthy and destitute. (The Night Journey: 29)

"The summer season is at hand, the season of joy and blessing," the imam declared as he began his Friday sermon. He added: "It is the season of joy, weddings and celebrations and each of us wants the whole world to share our joy. So, we invite all our relatives, neighbors, friends and acquaintances to the celebrations we hold in our homes. I see no need to preach to you about the obligation incumbent on all of us to entertain all those who come to our homes. But it is my duty to remind you of the verse:" **"Make not thy hand tied (like a niggard's) to**

thy neck, nor stretch it forth to its utmost reach, so that thou become blameworthy and destitute."

"We have all heard of families who become bankrupt after paying for a wedding and we have all heard of weddings which shamed the celebrants. We must remember that Allah hates profligates who do not guard their money for the future and are forced to spend the rest of their lives in poverty. Allah also hates misers who spend their lives guarding their money, thereby stifling themselves and their families. Allah wants you to find the golden mean between profligacy and miserliness."

Explanation: A wedding is undoubtedly a significant event in the life of a family and of the couple and is usually celebrated only once in a lifetime. Hence, many families spend all their money on lavish and impressive weddings and go into debt which they spend years repaying. It is wrong to do so. There are enough important matters on which it is worth spending money rather than wasting it in order to impress others. Perhaps the young couple want to study, perhaps they need to purchase a home or to save money to guarantee security for their future. There is no shortage of important goals. The imam was right to instruct his congregation to seek the golden mean. It is possible to hold a modest celebration which shames nobody but does not entail uncontrolled squandering of money.

5. What is the importance of preparations for married life?

{ قُل لِّلْمُؤْمِنِينَ يَغُضُّوا مِنْ أَبْصَارِهِمْ وَيَحْفَظُوا فُرُوجَهُمْ ذَٰلِكَ أَزْكَىٰ لَهُمْ إِنَّ اللَّهَ
خَبِيرٌ بِمَا يَصْنَعُونَ * وَقُل لِّلْمُؤْمِنَاتِ يَغْضُضْنَ مِنْ أَبْصَارِهِنَّ وَيَحْفَظْنَ فُرُوجَهُنَّ وَلَا
يُبْدِينَ زِينَتَهُنَّ إِلَّا مَا ظَهَرَ مِنْهَا وَلْيَضْرِبْنَ بِخُمُرِهِنَّ عَلَىٰ جُيُوبِهِنَّ وَلَا يُبْدِينَ زِينَتَهُنَّ
إِلَّا لِبُعُولَتِهِنَّ أَوْ آبَائِهِنَّ أَوْ آبَاءِ بُعُولَتِهِنَّ أَوْ أَبْنَائِهِنَّ أَوْ أَبْنَاءِ بُعُولَتِهِنَّ أَوْ إِخْوَانِهِنَّ أَوْ
بَنِي إِخْوَانِهِنَّ أَوْ بَنِي أَخَوَاتِهِنَّ أَوْ نِسَائِهِنَّ أَوْ مَا مَلَكَتْ أَيْمَانُهُنَّ أَوِ التَّابِعِينَ غَيْرِ أُولِي
الْإِرْبَةِ مِنَ الرِّجَالِ أَوِ الطِّفْلِ الَّذِينَ لَمْ يَظْهَرُوا عَلَىٰ عَوْرَاتِ النِّسَاءِ وَلَا يَضْرِبْنَ

بِأَرْجُلِهِنَّ لِيُعْلَمَ مَا يُخْفِينَ مِن زِينَتِهِنَّ وَتُوبُوا إِلَى اللهِ جَمِيعًا أَيُّهَ الْمُؤْمِنُونَ لَعَلَّكُمْ تُفْلِحُونَ ﴾ (النور: 30-31)

Say to the believing men that they should lower their gaze and guard their modesty: that will make for greater purity for them: and Allah is well acquainted with all that they do.

And say to the believing women that they should lower their gaze and guard their modesty; that they should not display their beauty and ornaments except what (must ordinarily) appear thereof; that they should draw their veils over their bosoms and not display their beauty except to their husbands, their fathers, their husbands' fathers, their sons, their husbands' sons, their brothers or their brothers' sons, or their sisters' sons, or their women, or the slaves whom their right hands possess, or male servants free of physical needs, or small children who have no sense of the shame of sex; and that they should not strike their feet in order to draw attention to their hidden ornaments. And O ye Believers! turn ye all together towards Allah, that ye may attain Bliss. (The Light: 30-31)

Majdi, who is in the eleventh grade, constantly leers at the girls and makes suggestive comments to them. Salma, his classmate, sees other girls dressed in the latest fashion and envies them. Salah is shy and scared to talk to the girls in his class while Huda is afraid that someone might read her thoughts and punish her.

Explanation: these are a few examples of the dilemmas faced by adolescent boys and girls who are in great need of guidance and direction. They see their bodies changing rapidly and are not yet accustomed to their new appearance. They have new sexual urges, and sense social pressure from their peer group on various subjects. Intellectually speaking, they feel much cleverer than in the past. These boys and girls are undergoing far-reaching changes on the physiological, social, emotional and intellectual spheres. They are confused and seek guidance. Surah 16, Verse 64, says: **"And We sent down the Book to thee for the express purpose, that thou shouldst make clear to them those things in which they differ, and that it should be a guide and a mercy to those who believe."** Indeed, young people need guidance and if they do not receive it from the Quran, they will obtain inappropriate advice elsewhere. Thus, it is recommended to equip them with knowledge regarding marital life and not to hide anything from them. It is often a question of life and death, for example, where sexually-transmitted diseases are concerned.

It is recommended that they be divided into separate groups of boys and girls and that the lesson begin with Verses 30 and 31of Surah 10 which refers to the importance of modest conduct, for both boys and girls. Once they understand the importance of restraint and purity, other subjects can be discussed without embarrassment and without fear.

6. How should one treat one's husband or wife?

{ وَمِنْ آيَاتِهِ أَنْ خَلَقَ لَكُم مِّنْ أَنفُسِكُمْ أَزْوَاجًا لِّتَسْكُنُوا إِلَيْهَا وَجَعَلَ بَيْنَكُم مَّوَدَّةً وَرَحْمَةً إِنَّ فِي ذَٰلِكَ لَآيَاتٍ لِّقَوْمٍ يَتَفَكَّرُونَ } (الروم: 21)

And among His Signs is this, that He created for you mates from among yourselves, that ye may dwell in tranquility with them, and He has put love and mercy between your (hearts): verily in that are Signs for those who reflect. (The Romans: 21)

Sami and Rim are a young couple who have been married for one year. They squabble constantly and once, after a quarrel, Rim returned to her parents' house. This infuriated Sami and he decided not to bring her back. He refused to listen to her or to hear how she felt or to appease her. Rim, for her part, was very hurt by Sami's conduct because he did not enquire about her or bother to come to see her.

Rim's parents tried to persuade her to return home, talk to Sami and make peace with him, but she refused. She wanted Sami to come to her and plead with her to return. Her parents talked to Sami and asked him to come but he refused. Finally, the mother turned to a family guidance counselor for advice on how to solve the problem. The counselor asked Rim and Sami to come for a session and gave them permission to give full rein to their emotions and tell him what bothered each of them about the other. Then he asked each of them to list the qualities they loved in the other. "Not everything in life is perfect," he said, "and you can live together if each of you understands and loves the other." Finally, he opened the Quran at Surah 30 and read them Verse 21: **"And among His Signs is this, that He created for you mates from among yourselves, that ye may dwell in tranquility with them, and He has put love and mercy between your (hearts): verily in that are Signs for those who reflect."**

When Rim and Sami returned home, they recalled the injunction of "love and mercy" which the Quran commands and acted accordingly.

Explanation: This precious verse from the Quran should perhaps be inscribed on the wall in the offices of family counselors. It expresses the essence of a healthy relationship between man and woman: love and mercy. And if couples inscribed this same verse on the wall of their bedroom, they could solve many of their problems thereby. Does it not also describe the essence of modern Western psychology, which echoes basic tenets in the Quran? Does not the phrase **"And he has put love and mercy between your hearts"** constitute a clear statement of the need for symmetry in marital relations? Equality of emotion must precede all other forms of equality between man and woman.

7. What can we say to a woman whose husband's family mistreat her?

{ وَاصْبِرْ عَلَىٰ مَا يَقُولُونَ وَاهْجُرْهُمْ هَجْرًا جَمِيلًا } (المزمّل: 10)

And have patience with what they say, and leave them with noble dignity. (The Enwrapped: 10)

Samira is a good wife, mother to five children. She has been married for twenty years and lives in peace and happiness with her husband and children. But there is a permanent sad look in her eyes. As the teacher of one of her sons I always asked myself what was troubling her.

I received my answer by chance. Samira's son was absent from school for a week and I decided to visit the family to discover the reason for his absence. One evening I went to the child's house, climbed the stairs and knocked on the door. The boy opened the door and Samira greeted me warmly, but, although she smiled, her expression was still melancholy. We talked and she told me that from the first day of her marriage she had been suffering. Her sisters-in-law harassed her and gossiped about her at every opportunity; she kept her silence and forgave them. But a week ago something terrible had happened. One of her sisters-in-law accused her of informing the police that her brother-in-law had been involved in a fight in the village the previous week. It was a lie, said Samira, but her oldest brother-in-law then burst into her house and demanded that her husband divorce her. He did this without trying to clarify the truth. "Luckily for me, my husband refused. He wanted to prove my innocence and asked to hear the recording of the telephone call to the police so as to identify the voice. He also asked for a printout of the conversation so as to ensure that I was not the one who called the police. I would never have done such a thing," Samira said with great pain. "It is against all the norms and values I was raised on."

Since then Samira has been depressed. She and her children do not leave the house. She cries all the time and does not know what to do. I advised her not to take note of her sisters- and brothers-in-law, to keep her distance from people who are envious of her. Then I opened the Quran which I always carry with me and read her Verse 10 of Surah 73: **"And have patience with what they say, and leave them with noble dignity."**

Samira was cheered and thanked me.

Explanation: Samira's fate has not been a happy one. In some societies it is easier to keep one's distance from undesirable relatives but in others the individual is forced to spend his life not only alongside a spouse but with the spouse's family as well, and is condemned to a life of endless squabbling. That is Samira's story. Her sisters- and brothers-in law permit themselves to interfere in her life, to accuse her and to pressure her husband to divorce her. This is by no means a simple situation. In traditional societies the relationship with the spouse usually replaces previous family ties and loyalty now belongs to the spouse. Samira's husband did well to demand facts and not insinuations and not to bow to pressure. He would have done better to defend his wife against her sisters-in-law and to put them in their place. In any event, the teacher did right in coming to see the family because of her concern for her pupil and in giving Samira good advice from the Quran – not to quarrel, to tolerate in silence the remarks of those who wanted to harm her and to keep her distance from them.

8. What can we say to a woman whose husband abuses her?

{ فَتَوَلَّىٰ عَنْهُمْ وَقَالَ يَا قَوْمِ لَقَدْ أَبْلَغْتُكُمْ رِسَالَةَ رَبِّي وَنَصَحْتُ لَكُمْ وَلَٰكِن لَّا تُحِبُّونَ النَّاصِحِينَ } (الأعراف: 79)

So Salih left them, saying: "O my people! **I did indeed convey to you the message for which I was sent by my Lord: I gave you good counsel, but ye love not good counselors!"** (The Elevations: 79)

Samira and Amira, are good friends who grew up in the same neighborhood and are in the same ninth-grade class. They confide in one another and support one another in good times and bad. One day Samira told Amira that she was in a relationship with the neighbor's son and loved him. Amira was stunned and tried to dissuade Samira. "You know he's a delinquent and a drug-trader," she said. But nothing she said had any effect, and Samira was as stubborn as a mule. "Nobody can change my mind," she announced. A week later Amira noticed that Samira's eye was swollen and bruised and asked her what had happened. Samira told her that she had fallen and hurt her eye. Amira shouted at her that she was endangering her life by staying with that boy. Samira accused her of being envious of her for having a boyfriend and of hating her. Amira was very hurt, wept and did not know what to do.

She tried to defend herself but eventually summoned up strength and said to Samira: "I want to quote to you a verse from the Quran. Try to understand what it means and then we'll talk," she said, and read out:" **"O my people! I did indeed convey to you the message for which I was sent by my Lord: I gave you good counsel, but ye love not good counselors!"**

Then, for the first time, Samira was taken aback, began to think and burst into tears.

Explanation: Amira utilized the verse from the Quran in which the Prophet spoke to the people in order to underline her arguments. She knew that she was right and her friend was misguided, and so did not hesitate to use the quotation to save her. Indeed, Samira was infatuated with a boy who did not have her best interests at heart and could do her great harm. As to why she was she attracted to a delinquent, and moreover without her parents' knowledge – we cannot answer that question. Regrettably, she is not alone in her behavior. She may have been led to act like that because her father was a weak figure and she was seeking a strong man. Perhaps the reverse is true: her father was violent towards her and she was repeating her experiences by choosing a violent mate. In any event, she was displaying masochistic tendencies, thereby inviting violence. This is the sad story of many women whose husbands batter them until their lives are at risk but who refuse to leave the abusive partner. In cases where it is abundantly clear to the onlooker that someone is acting in self-destructive fashion and is not accepting advice, this verse is highly appropriate.

9. What can we say to a man who is unfaithful to his wife?

{ وَالَّذِينَ هُمْ لِفُرُوجِهِمْ حَافِظُونَ * إِلَّا عَلَىٰ أَزْوَاجِهِمْ أَوْ مَا مَلَكَتْ أَيْمَانُهُمْ فَإِنَّهُمْ غَيْرُ مَلُومِينَ * فَمَنِ ابْتَغَىٰ وَرَاءَ ذَٰلِكَ فَأُولَـٰئِكَ هُمُ الْعَادُونَ } (المؤمنون: 5-7)

Those who safeguard their chastity, except from their spouses, or their dependents for they are free from blame. But whoever seeks anything beyond that these are the transgressors. (The Believers: 5-7)

Ali was tired of explaining that he did not want to marry Sausan. He felt nothing towards her, neither love nor attraction. He was twenty-nine and she a girl of nineteen who did not understand him. He liked her as a cousin or a friend but found it hard to imagine her as his wife. In the end Ali gave in and married Sausan. Now she is heavily pregnant and cannot accompany him when he goes out. In the past he avoided going out with her because of her head covering and now her heaviness and exhaustion are additional factors.

One day Ali is invited to the wedding of a friend from work and asks Sausan to accompany him but she is feeling ill and refuses. He attends the wedding alone. He is uncomfortable sitting at the table with his friends and their wives and goes out to the balcony to smoke a cigarette. Suddenly a woman comes out and asks him for a light. He lights her cigarette and that is how he becomes acquainted with Amal. When they part at the end of the evening they promise to stay in touch.

Their friendship grows closer and they begin a sexual relationship. Sausan senses that Ali has changed and become distant and cool. He is indifferent towards her and their newborn baby. When she tries to discuss this with him, he leaves the house, slamming the door angrily. Then she weeps because she has driven her husband away.

One day she decides to confide in her mother. "I think he has another woman," she says. Her mother replies: "We will send your brother to follow him. Then you can get all that nonsense out of your head."

Sausan's brother tails Ali and sees him meeting Amal. He tells his mother and sister. That same day Sausan's family summon Ali for a discussion and tell him they have proof he is cheating on his wife, which is forbidden by their religion. Ali replies that he sees nothing wrong in his actions. "I live with a wife I did not choose. My family chose her. From the outset I didn't want this marriage and I love Amal."

Then Sausan's mother opens the Quran and reads him the beginning of Surah 23: **The believers must eventually win through… Those who safeguard their chastity, except from their spouses, or their dependents for they are free from**

blame. But whoever seeks anything beyond that these are the transgressors.

Explanation: There is no way of telling how Ali and Sausan's relationship will develop. But when a marriage is arranged through pressure, the chance of such an outcome is greater. An age difference creates distance between the couple, particularly in the case of young people where a gap of only a few years can be significant. A disparity in the degree of religious observance can also create difficulties. Ali was not interested in Sausan and agreed to marry her because she was his cousin and his family were exerting pressure. But nonetheless Ali is an adult and responsible for his actions and Sausan's mother was right to put him in his place with the help of the Quran.

3 | Adolescent Girls

1. Is it important for girls to study?

{ كُتِبَ عَلَيْكُمُ الْقِتَالُ وَهُوَ كُرْهٌ لَّكُمْ وَعَسَى أَن تَكْرَهُوا شَيْئًا وَهُوَ خَيْرٌ لَّكُمْ وَعَسَى أَن تُحِبُّوا شَيْئًا وَهُوَ شَرٌّ لَّكُمْ وَاللَّهُ يَعْلَمُ وَأَنتُمْ لاَ تَعْلَمُونَ } (البقرة: 216)

Fighting may be imposed on you, even though you dislike it. **But you may dislike something which is good for you, and you may like something which is bad for you. GOD knows while you do not know.** (The Cow: 216)

Mona is a pleasant and well-groomed twelfth-grade student, and is considered as having the potential and the ability to progress in whatever field she chooses. She has recently been studying hard and preparing day and night for her matriculation examinations. Lo and behold, a boy arrived at their home about a week ago asking for her hand in marriage. Mona was overjoyed and expressed her wish to get engaged to the boy as soon as possible. "Why in fact should I finish my studies?" she said. She reminded her parents about other girls they know who had left school because they had got engaged. These girls said that in any event they wouldn't need their studies after the wedding and while raising their children. Mona asked to leave school.

Her parents refused. They claimed that what she has to do now is to prepare for her matriculation examinations, and that she is too young for these other matters. They also said that Mona should have a profession in life, not only because acquiring education confers respect on her, but also in order for her to contribute to the family's livelihood. Mona was not convinced. It was clear that she was in love, and as they say: love is blind.

In her distress, Mona went to the school counselor and told her what had happened. She asked the counselor to speak to her parents, because she is in love with the boy. To her surprise, the counselor picked up the Quran, opened it at Surah 'The Cow', and asked Mona to read aloud Verse 216: **"But you may dislike something which is good for you, and you may like something which is bad for you. GOD knows while you do not know."** Mona was silent. "What do you think?" the counselor asked her. Mona hesitated for a while and then said, "yes, I know it's important that I study, and that it's good for me. This is what I will do, even though it's so hard to give up on my beloved. God will take care of me and compensate me in the future. But then I'll already have a profession."

Explanation: Adolescence is without doubt a difficult age. In this short time-span fateful decisions are made, which often affect a person for the rest of his or her life. What should I study? Who should I marry? And when these important decisions are all being made at the same time – it becomes doubly difficult. Mona lets herself get carried away. She already sees herself running her home and raising her children. After all, this has been her life's dream. Will she be able at this stage to also appreciate more "boring" activities such as studies? Will she be able to understand that a profession for life is of primary importance? What if, Heaven forefend, she gets divorced from her husband, or if Heaven forefend her husband dies, or if he is unable to provide for the whole family and she needs to work in order to supplement the family's income. Mona finds it hard to think about these things when she is in love. Her parents have done the correct thing by providing her with direction and not allowing her to make mistakes that will be difficult to correct at a later stage. For indeed, when Mona is married and has children, it will be far more difficult for her to study. As the Arab proverb says: the man with a profession is the king of the castle. Mona can be queen of the castle on condition that she has a profession she can work in.

2. How should one behave towards women?

﴿وَلاَ جُنَاحَ عَلَيْكُمْ فِيمَا عَرَّضْتُم بِهِ مِنْ خِطْبَةِ النِّسَاء أَوْ أَكْنَنتُمْ فِي أَنفُسِكُمْ عَلِمَ اللّهُ
أَنَّكُمْ سَتَذْكُرُونَهُنَّ وَلَكِن لاَّ تُوَاعِدُوهُنَّ سِرًّا إِلاَّ أَن تَقُولُواْ قَوْلاً مَّعْرُوفًا وَلاَ تَعْزِمُواْ
عُقْدَةَ النِّكَاحِ حَتَّىَ يَبْلُغَ الْكِتَابُ أَجَلَهُ وَاعْلَمُواْ أَنَّ اللّهَ يَعْلَمُ مَا فِي أَنفُسِكُمْ فَاحْذَرُوهُ
وَاعْلَمُواْ أَنَّ اللّهَ غَفُورٌ حَلِيمٌ﴾(البقرة: 235)

You commit no sin by announcing your engagement to the women, or keeping it secret. GOD knows that you will think about them. Do not meet them secretly, unless you have something righteous to discuss. Do not consummate the marriage until their interim is fulfilled. You should know that GOD knows your innermost thoughts, and observe Him. You should know that GOD is Forgiver, Clement. (The Cow: 235)

Miada is a neat, cheerful high-school student who enjoys talking and laughing with everyone around her. Recently she talks a lot about romance and love, proudly displays a new bracelet and ring to her friends, which she says she received from her boyfriend who is crazy about her. He wants to marry me, she says, but she isn't thinking about it yet. Miada says that many boys want her, but that she will definitely get engaged soon to her boyfriend.

One day she noticed that her friends were looking at her and whispering, as were the boys. It transpired that her boyfriend was going around telling everyone that he meets her secretly and that she is madly in love with him. He says that she writes him letters, buys him presents, and believes him that he really loves her. "She's building castles in the air because I told her how much I love her," he told everyone. Miada felt that everyone was laughing at her and relating to her completely differently from in the past.

In her distress, Miada went to talk to the school counselor and told her that she does indeed talk to her boyfriend for hours on the telephone and that she meets him secretly. He tells her the whole time that he is dying to meet her and doesn't stop buying her presents. The last time they met he phoned her and said that he wanted to see her urgently because he had a surprise for her. He hinted that he wants to talk to her parents and ask them for her hand in marriage. Miada agreed that he would fetch her from school and told her mother that she had an extra lesson at school and would return later. The boyfriend drove her to a far-away place and tried to rape her. She was afraid to tell anyone, because she didn't want them to know she had met him secretly. The counselor spoke to Miada about her prohibited actions and how she is endangering both her reputation and that of her family, as well as the possibility of finding a good husband. She then opened the Quran at Verse 235 of the Surah, 'The Cow', and asked Miada to read aloud: **"You commit no sin by announcing your engagement to the women, or keeping it secret. GOD knows that you will think about them. Do not meet them secretly, unless you have something righteous to discuss."** If he really loves you, this is the way he should behave, the counselor said. Miada was stunned. She understood that the boy she loves and in whom she had placed her trust, had betrayed her and sold her in order to increase his status. She asked the counselor to copy the verse. "I don't want to talk to him," she said, "I just want to show him the verse from the Quran, so that he will understand what he did."

Explanation: It is not by chance that Miada behaves in a way that is different from what is acceptable in her society. Something seems to be bothering her inside. Often, girls who behave in this way are desperately looking for love they didn't receive at home. Girls who feel rejected in their families often try to prove to themselves in unacceptable ways that they are wanted and loved. They are thus likely to develop romantic fantasies about boys who offer them marriage etc. The school counselor acted correctly by first explaining to Miada the seriousness of her actions, and making use of the Quran for this purpose. She might also decide to involve Miada's parents in such a serious matter that concerns the whole family. Or, she might decide it is preferable to deal with the matter herself and not inform the family. It all depends on the likelihood, in her opinion, that Miada's parents will be positive and not destructive partners in the process of her development. First, however, Miada has to develop acceptable behavior norms. Only then can the counselor begin to understand Miada's inner pain, and what in her past and her family background led her to behave in the way she did. Without setting clear limits to protect her, there will be little value in clarifying Miada's inner feelings.

3. Is it permissible for parents discriminate against girls?

{ فَاسْتَجَابَ لَهُمْ رَبُّهُمْ أَنِّي لاَ أُضِيعُ عَمَلَ عَامِلٍ مِّنكُم مِّن ذَكَرٍ أَوْ أُنثَى بَعْضُكُم مِّن
بَعْضٍ فَالَّذِينَ هَاجَرُواْ وَأُخْرِجُواْ مِن دِيَارِهِمْ وَأُوذُواْ فِي سَبِيلِي وَقَاتَلُواْ وَقُتِلُواْ لأُكَفِّرَنَّ
عَنْهُمْ سَيِّئَاتِهِمْ وَلأُدْخِلَنَّهُمْ جَنَّاتٍ تَجْرِي مِن تَحْتِهَا الأَنْهَارُ ثَوَابًا مِّن عِندِ اللّهِ وَاللّهُ
عِندَهُ حُسْنُ الثَّوَابِ } (آل عمران: 195)

Their Lord responded to them: "I never fail to reward any worker among you for any work you do, be you male or female - you are equal to one another. Thus, those who immigrate, and get evicted from their homes, and are persecuted because of Me, and fight and get killed, I will surely remit their sins and admit them into gardens with flowing streams." Such is the reward from GOD. GOD possesses the ultimate reward. (The Family of Imran: 195)

Samir and Samira are two twins in a rural family. Last year they completed their high-school studies. Samir's average grades were lower than his sister's, not for any physical or intellectual reason, but rather because he is a pampered child and always relies on his sister to do his school work for him. In the matriculation examinations his sister couldn't help him, and thus his grades dropped. This year, because of the family's difficult economic situation, it was decided that only one of the children could continue with university studies.

The mother insisted that the son continue his studies, because the daughter will get married and go to live with another family. The son, on the other hand, will continue living with his parents, and his studies will benefit the whole family. The father disagreed. He felt that the most deserving child should continue his or her studies, irrespective of whether it is the son or the daughter. The mother was very angry with her husband and threatened to leave home if he stuck to his opinion. The father did all he could to persuade the mother. Finally, he recalled Verse 195 of the Surah, 'Ali-Imran' that says: **"Their Lord responded to them: 'I never fail to reward any worker among you for any work you do, be you male or female - you are equal to one another'".** He quoted this verse to his wife and added: "If God rewards each person for his work, who are we to do the opposite?" The mother felt shamed, apologized to her daughter, and wished her success in her studies and in her life.

4. Should girls excel in their studies?

{ فَاسْتَجَابَ لَهُمْ رَبُّهُمْ أَنِّي لاَ أُضِيعُ عَمَلَ عَامِلٍ مِّنكُم مِّن ذَكَرٍ أَوْ أُنثَى بَعْضُكُم مِّن بَعْضٍ فَالَّذِينَ هَاجَرُواْ وَأُخْرِجُواْ مِن دِيَارِهِمْ وَأُوذُواْ فِي سَبِيلِي وَقَاتَلُواْ وَقُتِلُواْ لأُكَفِّرَنَّ عَنْهُمْ سَيِّئَاتِهِمْ وَلأُدْخِلَنَّهُمْ جَنَّاتٍ تَجْرِي مِن تَحْتِهَا الأَنْهَارُ ثَوَابًا مِّن عِندِ اللّهِ وَاللّهُ عِندَهُ حُسْنُ الثَّوَابِ } (آل عمران: 195)

Their Lord responded to them: "I never fail to reward any worker among you for any work you do, be you male or female - you are equal to one another. Thus, those who immigrate, and get evicted from their homes, and are persecuted because of Me, and fight and get killed, I will surely remit their sins and admit them into gardens with flowing streams." Such is the reward from GOD. GOD possesses the ultimate reward. (The Family of Imran: 195)

Nur is a sixth-grade pupil. She is talented, as all the teachers know, but hardly participates in class. When you ask her a question, you can see she knows the answer, but she sits quietly and never raises her hand in order to demonstrate her ability. The teacher invited Nur's mother to discuss the issue with her.

Teacher: Nur doesn't make any effort. She doesn't want to succeed, even though she is capable of doing so and is a talented pupil. I would like to know what the source of the problem is.

Mother: I have a daughter older than Nur who got married at 17. She also was an excellent student, but her father didn't want her to study, and married her off before she had completed her schooling. For a long time, I tried to persuade him, but he always tells me that I also got married at 16. Nur therefore says there is no reason to make an effort because her father will marry her off and she'll have to stop her studies. She says, "all my effort will be wasted. I'll succeed, and nothing will come of it in the end."

Teacher: (Invites Nur to join the discussion) Listen Nur, you know what I'm discussing with your mother. About the fact that you are capable but don't make an effort, and don't try in any way to show what you know. Your mother told me about your sister who got married at 17 and left school. But you should know that God sees you and is protecting you. I want to read you Verse 195 of the Surah 'Ali-Imran: **Lord responded to them: 'I never fail to reward**

any worker among you for any work you do, be you male or female - you are equal to one another.' Do you understand what the Quran tells us?

Nur: That God gives people the reward they deserve, whether they are boys or girls, and that we give birth to each other and are made from the same material.

Teacher: You see how clever you are and how well you understand? I am sure that if you invest and make an effort, you will go far. Together, you and your mother will try to persuade your father, and remember that God helps people who wish to study. You have to be able to exploit the opportunities and not to despair. I am also here at your side for anything you want. We can also talk to a respected religious figure if necessary, and he can talk to your father. But you must never give up. And always remember the verse: **Their Lord responded to them: 'I never fail to reward any worker among you for any work you do, be you male or female - you are equal to one another.'**

Explanation: The issue of studies is problematic. Many families do not let their daughters continue their studies, and designate them the role of being a mother at home. The family's intentions are good – to protect the women and their honor, and sometimes the question of benefit to the family enters the picture, as we saw in the first example. The loss, however, is great. A society that produces weak and passive women instead of strong women loses something, because stronger women can contribute a great deal to society, and especially to their families and their children. A mother who studies and who has gained knowledge will raise stronger and more capable children. A weak mother who has never moved from the four walls of her home and who has never encountered the wider world, will transmit her fears to her children. In many places, the practice of marrying off the girls at a young age and not allowing them to develop and to study comes from family tradition, but not from the Quran. Furthermore, giving preference to boys over girls with regard to studies does not come from the Quran. In this important verse, the Quran emphasizes that women and men are created from each other, from the same material, and that God will determine reward according to their actions and not according to their sex. A girl who studies, who perseveres and succeeds in her studies is as worthy of reward as a boy who learns and succeeds. We can only hope that Samira will succeed in her studies, and that Nur, her mother, her teacher and respected religious figures will manage to persuade the father to allow her to progress just as boys do.

5. Are girls permitted to go on school trips?

هُوَ الَّذِي يُصَوِّرُكُمْ فِي الأَرْحَامِ كَيْفَ يَشَاء لاَ إِلَهَ إِلاَّ هُوَ الْعَزِيزُ الْحَكِيمُ (آل عمران: 6)

He is the One who shapes you in the wombs as He wills. There is no other god besides Him; the Almighty, Most Wise. (The Family of Imran: 6)

The ninth-grade students were in a joyous mood. After an exhausting examination period they were all going on a trip to Eilat. Everyone had already paid, except for Amal.

Teacher: Amal, don't you want to go on the trip?
Amal: (Angrily) There's nothing to do in Eilat.
Teacher: I noticed at the beginning that you were very excited about the trip. What happened?
Amal: (Starts crying).
Teacher: I'm here for you. Would you like to tell me what happened?

Amal: (Dries the tears) My father won't let me go. I'm a good girl. He always acts like this and I don't do anything. I'm destroyed. It's all because I'm a girl and he's scared for me.

Teacher: Tell me about your father.

Amal: My father is a good-hearted person. But he is influenced by others and is scared of pressure from the environment. He always says that he can't be different from other fathers and from his family.

Teacher: I want to pay a visit to your home tomorrow afternoon. Please tell your father that I want to talk to him, but don't tell him about what. Tell him you don't know.

Amal: All right.

(The following day, the teacher went to Amal's home. The parents received her very well.)

Teacher: I wanted to talk to you about the fact that Amal is not going on the trip.

Father: I'm not letting her go on the trip because she is a girl, and you know the stories about girls in our society. You live here.

Teacher: Listen, sir, I know that you have educated your daughter very well. And God said: **"He is the One who shapes you in the wombs as He wills. There is no other god besides Him; the Almighty, Most Wise."** God created all of us in the same way. We are all human beings, boys and girls. You are no greater than God and not more forgiving than God.

Father: (Lowers his head) All right, she can go, and the responsibility is on her. You should know that I'm doing this because I love her and want to protect her, and God is great.

Explanation: There are many cases like this. Parents don't allow their daughter to go on trips because they don't believe she can manage by herself, and think that boys are liable to exploit their innocent daughter. This, of course, is not confined only to school trips, but generally to various assignments that the parents tend to impose on their son and not on their daughter, on the assumption that the girl doesn't have sufficient resources to deal with them. But this is precisely what causes the girl to feel that she is unable to manage with her own resources. How then can she trust herself and manage by herself if she has never been given any opportunity to prove herself? If the parents are interested in raising a strong daughter who trusts herself and can afterwards be of help to her husband and her family, they have to allow her to do things from a young age. She can be given easier tasks in the beginning, and as she proves herself, she can take on more complex tasks. A woman like this will, in the future, be a blessing to her family.

6. Is it permissible for a teacher to discriminate against girls?

{ يَا أَيُّهَا النَّاسُ اتَّقُواْ رَبَّكُمُ الَّذِي خَلَقَكُم مِّن نَّفْسٍ وَاحِدَةٍ وَخَلَقَ مِنْهَا زَوْجَهَا وَبَثَّ مِنْهُمَا رِجَالاً كَثِيرًا وَنِسَاء وَاتَّقُواْ اللّهَ الَّذِي تَسَاءلُونَ بِهِ وَالأَرْحَامَ إِنَّ اللّهَ كَانَ عَلَيْكُمْ رَقِيبًا } (النساء: 1)

O people, observe your Lord; the One who created you from one being, and created from it its mate, then spread from the two many men and women. You shall regard GOD, by whom you swear, and regard the parents. GOD is watching over you. (Women: 1)

Menar, an industrious and well-mannered tenth-grade student arrived at the school counselor's office. She spoke softly and the counselor found it difficult to understand what she was saying.

Counselor: Menar, please speak louder. I can't understand a single word.

Menar: I'm scared to talk. I want help and I want everything I say to remain a secret between us.

Counselor: Menar, this is my obligation as a counselor to every student in the school.

Menar: I'm still scared.

Counselor: What do you feel?

Menar: Even when I'm not speaking, I feel I'm chocking. I'm a very good student, but I feel miserable in my class. It's not only me, it's all us seven girls. The teacher doesn't treat us with respect. He ignores us, even though we are quieter than the boys and also better students. He is very strict with us, and we feel as if we are not part of the class.

Counselor: Why didn't the other girls come with you?

Menar: They are frightened. They sent me instead of them, and if you agree they will come as well.

Counselor: I'll speak to them.

Menar: I'm scared that you will insult the teacher and that he'll take revenge on us through our grades. That is why we are keeping quiet.

Counselor: Don't worry. I have my ways of speaking to him.

The counselor decided not to involve other people. She prepared a lecture, which she gave to the class in the presence of the above teacher. The subject of the lecture was "The status of women in the religion". The counselor began her lecture by reading from the Quran: "O people, observe your Lord; the One who created you from one being, and created from it its mate, then spread from the two many men and women." She asked the students how they understand this verse, and a discussion developed on the importance of relating equally and with respect to girls and boys in the class and in the family. The counselor read them other verses from the Surah 'Women' that regard the woman with respect and defend her rights. The counselor thus managed to convey the important message to the teacher and the students, without any confrontation with the teachers, the parents or the principal.

Explanation: Menar's story is not unique. Many girls suffer from discrimination in class. Many girls are also discriminated against at home in favor of their brothers. These attitudes cause girls to be less ambitious and to invest less in developing their capabilities. They say to themselves that ultimately no one will appreciate their efforts, and sometimes even the opposite: their learning success will be used against them. God granted many girls ability in order for them to use it, each in her own area, for the benefit of their family and their society. Sometimes, however, this ability is wasted and no one appreciates it. Every parent and teacher is thus obliged to encourage the girls, no less than the boys, to succeed in their studies. Sometimes they even need extra encouragement, because they come from families and from backgrounds that don't encourage studying. In these cases, the teacher should help them to realize their inherent potential. The counselor did the right thing by not entering into a confrontation with the environment on such a sensitive subject, but rather found a way to make use of the Holy Quran to transmit this important message. Again, it needs mentioning that a strong woman makes a strong man, strong children and a strong family.

7. What should one say to a girl who has been sexually abused by her father?

} حُرِّمَتْ عَلَيْكُمْ أُمَّهَاتُكُمْ وَبَنَاتُكُمْ وَأَخَوَاتُكُمْ وَعَمَّاتُكُمْ وَخَالاتُكُمْ وَبَنَاتُ الأَخِ وَبَنَاتُ
الأُخْتِ وَأُمَّهَاتُكُمُ اللاَّتِي أَرْضَعْنَكُمْ وَأَخَوَاتُكُم مِّنَ الرَّضَاعَةِ وَأُمَّهَاتُ نِسَآئِكُمْ وَرَبَائِبُكُمُ
اللاَّتِي فِي حُجُورِكُم مِّن نِّسَآئِكُمُ اللاَّتِي دَخَلْتُم بِهِنَّ فَإِن لَّمْ تَكُونُواْ دَخَلْتُم بِهِنَّ فَلاَ جُنَاحَ
عَلَيْكُمْ وَحَلاَئِلُ أَبْنَائِكُمُ الَّذِينَ مِنْ أَصْلاَبِكُمْ وَأَن تَجْمَعُواْ بَيْنَ الأُخْتَيْنِ إِلاَّ مَا قَدْ سَلَفَ

إِنَّ اللَّهَ كَانَ غَفُورًا رَّحِيمًا { (النساء: 23)

Prohibited for you (in marriage) are your mothers, your daughters, your sisters, the sisters of your fathers, the sisters of your mothers, the daughters of your brother, the daughters of your sister, your nursing mothers, the girls who nursed from the same woman as you, the mothers of your wives, the daughters of your wives with whom you have consummated the marriage - if the marriage has not been consummated, you may marry the daughter. Also prohibited for you are the women who were married to your genetic sons. Also, you shall not be married to two sisters at the same time - but do not break up existing marriages. GOD is Forgiver, Most Merciful. (Women: 23)

Ruba is a ninth-grade student, full of the joys of life, a good student and liked both by her classmates and her teachers. At the end of the winter vacation, Ruba returned to class and it was obvious everyone that her appearance and her behavior had changed significantly. She had become very thin, hardly spoke, didn't participate in lessons or in school activities. The students and the teachers tried to find out what had happened to her. The homeroom teacher invited her for a individual discussion, but Ruba just looked at the floor and didn't say a word, and it was clear that beneath the silence Ruba was concealing some kind of severe pain. The teacher invited the parents. Only the mother arrived. She said that the change in Ruba's behavior was also noticeable at home. She isolates herself in her room, locks the door and refuses to come out and eat. Therefore, the mother brings her food to her room. When the mother goes out, Ruba clings to her and wants to go with her. The mother also wanted to have her examined by a doctor because she had lost so much weight, but Ruba refused to be examined. Now, the mother tells the teacher, she is afraid that she is going to lose her daughter.

The teacher suggested that the school counselor should become involved.

The counselor met several times with Ruba. As the trust between them grew, Ruba told the counselor that her father had abused her sexually. He threatened her that if she told anyone about it, he would kill her. Since then she feels contaminated and worthless, and has no desire to do anything except lie on her bed and cry. When the counselor heard this, the first thing she did was to open the Quran at Surah 'Women', Verse 23, which she read to Ruba: **"Prohibited for you (in marriage) are your mothers, your daughters, your sisters…"** Do you understand what this is saying? she asked Ruba. It is saying that you are not to blame for anything, and therefore you don't need to blame yourself and be depressed. Your father is the grown-up and the person responsible, and it is his job to protect you. He betrayed the trust, and instead of protecting you, he exploited you. All the responsibility is on him and not on you. This was the first time that Ruba smiled.

Explanation: Incest is a phenomenon that exists in all societies, and in all societies, it is forbidden, both according to the religion and the laws of the country. The Quran particularly emphasizes this. When a girl is sexually abused, she usually becomes depressed and tends to blame herself for what happened. She is liable to think to herself: Maybe I tempted my father or my brother or a relative? The truth is that a daughter cannot tempt her father. His role is to protect her and take care of her and to remember that she is his daughter. Therefore, the first thing that therapists usually tell a girl who has been sexually abused is that she is not to blame and is not responsible for what happened. It is her father who is responsible. The counselor did the right thing to use the Quran to reinforce the statement that Ruba is not responsible. In this, as in other cases, the therapeutic value of a single verse from the Quran is worth many words.

8. What can we say to a girl who engages in sexual relations before marriage?

{وَمَا لَكُمْ أَلاَّ تَأْكُلُواْ مِمَّا ذُكِرَ اسْمُ اللّهِ عَلَيْهِ وَقَدْ فَصَّلَ لَكُم مَّا حَرَّمَ عَلَيْكُمْ إِلاَّ مَا اضْطُرِرْتُمْ إِلَيْهِ وَإِنَّ كَثِيراً لَّيُضِلُّونَ بِأَهْوَائِهِم بِغَيْرِ عِلْمٍ إِنَّ رَبَّكَ هُوَ أَعْلَمُ بِالْمُعْتَدِينَ} (الأنعام: 119)

Why should ye not eat of (meats) on which Allah's name hath been pronounced, when He hath explained to you in detail what is forbidden to you, except under compulsion of necessity? But many do mislead (men) by their appetites unchecked by knowledge. Thy Lord knows best the transgressors. (The Livestock: 119).

Ramzia has a friend called Aliya, who is in a relationship with a young man without thinking about the consequences of her behavior. Ramzia has warned Aliya many times that she is liable to become pregnant and then she will face great problems. Aliya replies that she has nothing to be afraid of because she is taking precautions. Recently Aliya suggested introducing Ramzia to her boyfriend's friend. "You can have a good time together. Take it from me, it's fun. I enjoy myself and I'm not scared of anything. My boyfriend says he wants to marry me and that's why I don't have a problem about having sex with him. We'll get married in the end anyway." Ramzia is not convinced. She explains to Aliya that what she is doing is forbidden, that God sees and knows everything and **"Thy Lord knows best the transgressors"**. When Aliya hears the familiar verse from the Quran she is alarmed. For the first time she understands that she had exceeded the limit.

Explanation: many young people do forbidden things and are content because their parents know nothing about it. They forget that Allah sees and knows everything. They take drugs, gamble, steal and sometimes engage in pre-marital relations.

Modern societies generally permit the young to engage in pre-marital sex but traditional and religious societies do not. Aliya, who lives in a traditional society, is endangering her future and perhaps even her life. The boyfriend may not keep his promise to marry her. She may be vilified for having violated family honor etc. Her conduct is very risky, bordering on self-destructive and suicidal. Perhaps Ramzia would do well to confide in the school's educational counselor or some other educational figure she trusts. That person should try to help Aliya without giving the story away to Aliya's relatives who might harm her for violating family honor. This is what the friends of young people with suicidal tendencies should do. Their tendencies should not be kept secret but should be reported to the proper educational authorities so as to help them and protect them. Aliya will be angry with Ramzia but Ramzia's actions may save her life. It is hard to give advice in such complex situations and each case should be considered separately.

9. How should one treat a girl who dresses in unacceptably immodest fashion?

{ قُلْ أَغَيْرَ اللّهِ أَبْغِي رَبّاً وَهُوَ رَبٌّ كُلِّ شَيْءٍ وَلاَ تَكْسِبُ كُلُّ نَفْسٍ إِلاَّ عَلَيْهَا وَلاَ تَزِرُ وَازِرَةٌ وِزْرَ أُخْرَى ثُمَّ إِلَى رَبِّكُم مَّرْجِعُكُمْ فَيُنَبِّئُكُم بِمَا كُنتُمْ فِيهِ تَخْتَلِفُونَ } (الأنعام: 164)

Say: "Shall I seek for (my) Cherisher other than Allah, when He is the Cherisher of all things (that exist)? Every soul draws the meed (reward) of its acts on none but itself: **no bearer of burdens can bear the burden of another.** Your goal in the end is towards Allah: He will tell you the truth of the things wherein ye disputed." (The Livestock: 164)

Manar comes to the school counselor in tears.
Counselor: Good morning

Manar: Good morning. I am Manar from the eighth grade and I've come because I heard that you help everyone.

Counselor: Please, tell me what is bothering you.

Manar: What troubles me most is my parents. They don't like anything I do. They complain all the time and say that what I do is not fitting. "Look at yourself, you are a disgrace", they say all the time.

Counselor: Is there a reason why they act like that?

Manar: It's because of my friend, Nur. She's a good friend, listens to me and supports me. But my family doesn't like her because she dresses shamelessly. She chooses whatever clothes she fancies.

Counselor: Have you told your parents that she's a good close friend?

Manar: A thousand times. They don't listen. I'm burning up inside, it's a vicious circle. I love my friend and I love my parents and I don't want to lose any of them.

Counselor: I'd like to meet your parents. Do you agree?

Manar: Yes, yes. I want a rest from all this.

Two days later the counselor met with Manar's parents. She told them about her conversation with Manar and said she knew they didn't want Manar to stay in contact with her friend.

Mother: Yes, yes. Can't you see how she dresses? Like in Europe.

Counselor: It's no crime for your daughter's friend to be different from her. There are differences in this world. She is a good friend to your daughter, worries about her, helps her and that is what is important. I want to read you something so that you will understand: **"No bearer of burdens can bear the burden of another".**

"What do you understand from this verse," she asked the parents. They had understood correctly. "Each individual is responsible for his own sins and actions and not those of others," they said. "If that is so, you should support your daughter and understand her better so as not to burden her with issues which are not relevant to her."

Explanation: the counselor was right to separate the various components of the friend's personality – she is a good girl who cares for her friend but dresses immodestly. Not everything in life is black and white. In fact, very little in life is black and white and nobody is perfect. Parents should remember that they are not perfect either and the truth is not always entirely on their side. And since nobody is perfect, we should forgive and not expect our friends to be perfect and without flaws.

With regard to immodest dress, one can ask whether it is the responsibility of the dresser not to wear revealing clothes or the responsibility of the onlooker to exercise restraint and understand that various people regard clothes in different ways. The truth, as always, lies between. People are responsible for the way they dress and girls should not dress provocatively in order to attract attention. But the onlooker too should remember that there are no limits to conservatism just as there are no limits to permissiveness. One may demand that a girl cover herself completely as is customary in some places in the world or one can also demand a little less than that, perhaps much less, each according to taste, customs and religion. The most important thing to remember is that the responsibility never lies entirely with the women but also with the men who observe them. Otherwise we face an absurd situation whereby women are expected to dress in a manner which is convenient for men. The Quran puts it well: **"No bearer of burdens can bear the burden of another"** which reminds us that each of us, both men and women, should be responsible for his or her own burden.

10. How can we encourage wearing of school uniforms?

{ يَا بَنِي آدَمَ خُذُواْ زِينَتَكُمْ عِندَ كُلِّ مَسْجِدٍ وكُلُواْ وَاشْرَبُواْ وَلاَ تُسْرِفُواْ إِنَّهُ لاَ يُحِبُّ الْمُسْرِفِينَ } (الأعراف: 31)

O Children of Adam! Wear your beautiful apparel at every time and place of prayer: eat and drink: but waste not by excess, for Allah loveth not the wasters. (The Elevations: 31)

Maram, a ninth-grade student, does not usually wear uniform to school. When she comes into the building, she tries to hide so that the principal won't see her. When she is caught, she starts making excuses: "My uniform is dirty and, in the wash, I spilled food on it this morning…" The principal is tired of all these stories. She has summoned Maram's parents several times to ask them how they can permit their daughter to go to school dressed like that. She wears revealing clothes which are not suited for school and inappropriate for their culture and second, she openly resists wearing the uniform. The mother told the principal that Maram likes buying clothes and there are arguments around this issue. She covets any new and fashionable garment she sees, her mother says. She simply pursues fashion and squanders money. The principal recently decided to summon Maram and her parents again. She knows what to quote to Maram: **"O Children of Adam! Wear your beautiful apparel at every time and place of prayer: eat and drink: but waste not by excess, for Allah loveth not the wasters."** In other words, Maram may come to school in clean tidy uniform and be well-groomed but she must not exaggerate when buying new clothes and wearing them to school.

Explanation: The purpose of school uniforms, and sometimes work uniforms as well, is to blur individual identity to some extent and to encourage identification with a place or role. That is why each army has its own uniforms. In the army, differences between individuals are undesirable, and what is important is carrying out missions as ordered. Some boys and girls feel inner resistance to uniforms because they experience them as obliteration of their unique identity. These are usually the boys and girls who want to emphasize their uniqueness and are afraid of being swallowed up by the group. The establishment cannot accept this because all the other pupils would immediately ask: Why is it that he is not obliged to wear a uniform and I am? The principal was right to compare the school to a mosque and to quote the verse which permits us to dress well and appropriately in order to preserve our unique identity but without overstepping the mark in order to be conspicuous, as Maram does.

11. Is it fair to burden a young girl with maternal tasks?

{ وَالَّذِينَ آمَنُواْ وَعَمِلُواْ الصَّالِحَاتِ لاَ نُكَلِّفُ نَفْساً إِلاَّ وُسْعَهَا أُوْلَـئِكَ أَصْحَابُ الْجَنَّةِ هُمْ فِيهَا خَالِدُونَ } (الأعراف: 42)

But those who believe and work righteousness - **no burden do We place on any soul, but that which it can bear** - they will be Companions of the Garden, therein to dwell (for ever). (The Elevations: 42)

Sara is in the sixth grade. Until recently she was an outstanding student, responsible, quiet and polite. Her class teacher was surprised when Sara's grades dropped significantly over a few months. She was often absent, and the teachers reported that she was not preparing her homework. The teacher called Sara to her home room to talk to her. She asked about the reason for the frequent absences, low grades and failure to prepare homework. Sara gave the same reply to each question: "Don't know." Then she started crying and ran out.

The teacher summoned Sara's parents for an urgent meeting. She told them about their daughter's grades and asked about her absences and failure to do homework. The parents glanced at one another and said nothing. The teacher was puzzled by their expression but persisted. "I want to help Sara. What's wrong with her? Tell me?" They remained silent. "Is she sick or is something troubling her?"

And then the mother said: "The truth is that I have two boys at home aged one and three. I work all week and I leave them with their grandmother. When she is not available, I leave Sara at home to look after them. When I come home from work, the household chores are waiting, so Sara continues to look after the babies. I ask her to do her homework when her brothers have gone to sleep but sometimes, she falls asleep before them and doesn't have time to do her homework...that's the whole story."

"The whole story..." cried the surprised teacher. "Your poor daughter! Do you know that you are burdening her with too much responsibility and work and not allowing her to live or study. She needs leisure time for herself to spend with girls her own age. You must find another solution for the boys. Look at her and you'll see that she is exhausted and frustrated. She is a human being and she too deserves to be a child and a girl and a pupil and not a mother at her early age. Do you know verse 42 in Surah 7? I want to read it to you: **"No burden do We place on any soul, but that which it can bear."** Remember that your children are your responsibility and not Sara's."

Explanation: Sara's sad story is the story of many young girls, sometimes, but not always, from poor families, who are burdened in childhood with maternal roles because there are many children in the family and the mother is unable to tend all of them or because the mother works, or simply doesn't want to work hard. Sometimes this was the mother's fate as well in childhood and she is continuing the tradition and imposing the same bitter fate on her daughter. The girls miss out on childhood years and instead of having fun and playing with their friends, they act as mothers at an early age. They are liable to drop out of school and remain uneducated. An uneducated mother who is not acquainted with the world will sometimes find it hard to raise successful children, capable of becoming useful members of society. Thus, the children too pay the price of the mother's lack of education. In other words, imposing maternal roles on a young girl can cause great damage. The child forfeits her childhood and education, and the coming generations pay the price. Hence, the Quran commands us not to burden our children, both boys and girls, beyond their capacities. Girls must be permitted to grow and develop and when the time arrives for motherhood, they will meet the challenge more successfully because they will be mature, educated and capable.

12. What can we say to a teacher who has something against girls?

﴿ أَلَمْ يَأْتِهِمْ نَبَأُ الَّذِينَ مِن قَبْلِهِمْ قَوْمِ نُوحٍ وَعَادٍ وَثَمُودَ وَقَوْمِ إِبْرَاهِيمَ وَأَصْحَابِ مَدْيَنَ وَالْمُؤْتَفِكَاتِ أَتَتْهُمْ رُسُلُهُم بِالْبَيِّنَاتِ فَمَا كَانَ اللَّهُ لِيَظْلِمَهُمْ وَلَٰكِن كَانُوا أَنفُسَهُمْ يَظْلِمُونَ ﴾ (التوبة: 70)

Hath not the story reached them of those before them? The people of Nuh, and 'Ad, and Thamud; the people of Ibrahim, the men of Madyan, and the Cities overthrown. To them came their Messengers with Clear Signs. **It is not Allah Who wrongs them, but they wrong their own souls.** (The Repentance: 70)

Nur, an eighth-grader, complained to the school counselor several times about the history teacher.

Nur: Good morning, I am Nur. I came to see you a week ago and it's happened again. I'm tired of that teacher!

Counselor: I've talked to him about your complaint that he discriminates against the girls and shouts at them although they are quiet and good students.

Nur: Yes, yes. Then he shouted at me for complaining about him. He said I turn everything into a big issue.

Counselor: He says that he doesn't discriminate but that you girls annoy him.

Nur: What does that mean? It's not true.

Counselor: I set up a meeting with him. Don't worry, I'll solve the problem.

Nur: I'm relying on you.

The counselor set up a meeting with the teacher. At first, he refused to come, saying that it was a waste of time and he had examinations to check. The counselor was surprised that an educated teacher should behave like that. She insisted and finally he came and sat down with an angry expression.

Counselor: Good morning.

Teacher: Good morning. Believe me, I have no time. Let's get this over quickly.

Counselor: Calm down. We are having a conversation, that's all, about the eighth-grade class you teach.

Teacher: Last time you told me the girls were complaining about me. Yes, I have a problem. I don't trust them. They cause problems and because they are girls, they want me to treat them nicely and delicately. But they behave badly. I blame them and I blame Allah for making them girls and making us their slaves. I won't change my mind and treat them differently. It's too hard for me.

Counselor: Believe me, if you want to change, nothing will be difficult. Start and I'll help you. Allah has done nothing and the girls have done nothing. It's you who are responsible. Open your heart and see how

> all the teachers want to help you and love you. Treat the girls the way you treat boys. There is no need for pity. I know you believe in the Quran and I want to read you Verse 70 of the 9th Surah which I believe with all my heart. **"It is not Allah Who wrongs them but they wrong their own souls."**

The counselor stayed in contact with the teacher to encourage him to persevere in his new attitude.

Explanation: this important verse from the Quran is appropriate for those people who blame others and Allah, but never themselves. This teacher has difficulty with women. Neither the women nor Allah are responsible for his difficulty. He must accept responsibility for himself and change his attitude towards girls. If he undergoes psychotherapy, he will be able to understand why he holds such opinions about women (for example, he believes that he is their slave). Perhaps he had problems with his mother or women in general in his past. But now he is an adult and responsible for his actions. He can no longer blame others. Does this teacher treat his own daughters like that? We hope not. We hope he treats them equally to his sons. We have already noted that not only does the Quran command the faithful not to treat others unfairly but that fair treatment is also the precondition for building a healthy society, in which women can make their contribution both as mothers and as working women. The teacher's attitude undermines society because it makes his female students feel inferior and unable to believe in their own capabilities. The counselor was right not to show anger towards the teacher but to treat him with warmth and understanding and to try to help him. She herself is a woman and by her actions she is showing him how wrong he is in his attitude to women. The way of the Quran is love.

13. What can we say to a girl who is occupied with romantic matters instead of studying?

{ قُلْ يَا أَيُّهَا النَّاسُ قَدْ جَاءَكُمُ الْحَقُّ مِن رَّبِّكُمْ فَمَنِ اهْتَدَى فَإِنَّمَا يَهْتَدِي لِنَفْسِهِ وَمَن ضَلَّ فَإِنَّمَا يَضِلُّ عَلَيْهَا وَمَا أَنَاْ عَلَيْكُم بِوَكِيلٍ } (يونس: 108)

Say: "O ye men! Now Truth hath reached you from your Lord! those who receive Guidance, do so for the good of their own souls; those who stray, do so to their own loss: and I am not (set) over you to arrange your affairs." (Jonah: 108)

Nasrin was an outstanding student until the beginning of the ninth grade when everything changed. Her mother told her class teacher in despair that the girl was spending hours in front of the mirror, grooming her hair and face and was totally preoccupied with fashion. She had also begun to spend hours in front of the TV set watching romantic films or fashion programs. If her mother commented that the girl had homework to prepare, she started shouting: "I've done the reading! I've done the work! What do you want of me?" and fled her room.

Her mother began to examine who her friends were and discovered that her best friend did not attend school because she was betrothed and would be marrying next year. Nasrin wanted to be betrothed and to marry like her friend and had stopped studying hard at school. "You are ruining your future and causing damage you will never be able to mend," her mother cautioned her. "Wherever you go they will ask for your high school diploma and without it you won't be able to find work." But Nasrin replied that study didn't interest her.

Her mother took out the Quran, opened it at Surah 10, Verse 108 and read out: **"Those who receive Guidance, do so for the good of their own souls; those who stray, do so to their own loss: and I am not (set) over you to arrange your affairs."** "I can't force you to study," she said. "You must worry about yourself and you are the one who bears responsibility for your actions."

Explanation: many young people find it hard to concentrate on studies during adolescence because they are flooded with urges and thoughts about contacts with the opposite sex. It is just then, however, that their high school studies are vital for their future advancement. Despite the difficulties, both boys and girls are expected to focus on studies for the sake of their future. How can Nasrin concentrate on studies when she spends her time watching TV and romantic movies? Perhaps her parents should be more authoritative and restrict her TV viewing to a shorter period during the day. Perhaps they should curb her incessant preoccupation with fashion. Imposing such restrictions, coupled with explanations based on the Quran, may help create order in Nasrin's life. With the aid of the Quran, Nasrin's mother has transmitted an important truth to her: if she does not take responsibility for herself, nobody will do it for her.

14. What can we say to a girl who is arrogant?

{ لَا جَرَمَ أَنَّ اللَّهَ يَعْلَمُ مَا يُسِرُّونَ وَمَا يُعْلِنُونَ إِنَّهُ لَا يُحِبُّ الْمُسْتَكْبِرِينَ }
(النحل: 23)

Undoubtedly, Allah doth know what they conceal, and what they reveal: verily He loveth not the arrogant. (The Bees: 23)

Nada, a twelfth-grader, is a beautiful girl and always wears expensive clothes since she is the only daughter of a prosperous family. Her father owns a number of businesses and pampers her. He has bought her a new car which she drives to school every day. In class she behaves as if she is better than everyone else and boasts that her father is the richest man in the village.

Nada does not make friends with her classmates, does not talk to them because they do not belong to her social class and looks down on them.

Nada's conduct annoys her classmates and they have discussed it with their teacher. He invites her for a talk and tried to explain to her how her classmates feel. He tells her it is not worth her while to cut herself off from everyone and to arouse envy and anger. He adds that Allah loves the modest. Then he asks her to open the Quran and to read Verse 23: **"Undoubtedly, Allah doth know what they conceal, and what they reveal: verily He loveth not the arrogant."**

Nada thinks things over and several days later comes back to her teacher and tells him that she understands that her conduct was wrong and that she needs to follow a different path so that people will like her. She begins to approach her classmates and talk to them and makes some good friends.

Explanation: we know that often arrogance disguises a sense of inferiority. It is not evident outwardly but felt deeply within. Often people who are arrogant towards others are trying to compensate for their sense of inferiority. In any event, Nada is the loser thereby because the people around her do not like her and she is isolated in her arrogance. Sometimes such an attitude can be infuriating because it indicates contempt. Her classmates were right to appeal to the teacher for help instead of taking revenge on her in various ways. The teacher first gave her a brief lesson in understanding her classmates' feelings. He explained to her the effect her conduct was having. Then he utilized the Quran to convey the clear message that God does not like the arrogant. It is likely that without the Quran verse, the teacher would not have succeeded in persuading Nada to change her ways. One verse from the Quran can have a greater impact than the combined protracted efforts of a number of teachers.

15. What should a girl say to a young man who urges her to have extra-marital sex?

﴿ وَلَا تَقْرَبُوا۟ الزِّنَىٰٓ إِنَّهُۥ كَانَ فَاحِشَةً وَسَاءَ سَبِيلًا ﴾ (الإسراء: 32)

And do not come near adultery. It is immoral, and an evil way. (The Night Journey: 32)

The ninth-grade class set out on an annual trip to Eilat. Ali is infatuated with Yasmin and has been trying very hard to persuade her to have sexual relations with him. Yasmin refuses because of her beliefs and the moral code she has been raised on. She tries to evade him in every possible way. She is infatuated with him but does not want to betray her code of values and engage in pre-marital sex. He pleads and she refuses, then he asks for an explanation and each time she ponders what to say. Finally, she looks in the Quran. When he pleads again, she says: "You always say you believe in God and respect Him. God says: **"And do not come near adultery. It is immoral, and an evil way."**

Ali is ashamed and replies: "I am really sorry for what I have done. From now on I will remember that sentence and remind myself and my friends that fornication is wrong."

Explanation: in adolescence young people begin to experience sexual urges and are preoccupied with sexual thoughts. When Yasmin tries to explain to Ali that what he is asking for is an abomination and a grave transgression, he is not persuaded and continues to pester her. Boys sometimes promise girls to marry them if they will agree to sexual relations. The girls are won over but the boys often regret their promises. Girls are also sometimes offered various enticements in order to yield. But the Quran, with its great authority, pacifies Ali and frees Yasmin of the incessant pressure. Yasmin was right to resort to the Quran for help and it was there that she found the solution to her predicament.

16. What can we say to a boy who annoys and pesters a girl?

{ قُل لِّلْمُؤْمِنِينَ يَغُضُّوا مِنْ أَبْصَارِهِمْ وَيَحْفَظُوا فُرُوجَهُمْ ذَلِكَ أَزْكَى لَهُمْ إِنَّ اللَّهَ خَبِيرٌ
بِمَا يَصْنَعُونَ } (النور: 30)

Say to the believing men that they should lower their gaze and guard their modesty: that will make for greater purity for them: and Allah is well acquainted with all that they do. (The Light: 30)

Fatma is an eleventh grader, an outstanding student. One day she comes to see her class teacher with tears in her eyes. "Tell me why you are crying," says the teacher and offers her a seat. Fatma says that she wants to move to another class. "But why?" the teacher asks. "You are an outstanding student and all the teachers and pupils like you." Fatma says that one of the boys in the class keeps pestering her. The teacher asks for an explanation and Fatma tells her that he torments her in various ways. "The way he looks at me and behaves and the gestures he makes. I can't concentrate in class. All the pupils see it, and I can't bear it any more. So, I want to change classes."

The teacher asks Fatma if the boy pesters her outside school as well, and Fatma says that during break, in the courtyard, he follows her and harasses her. "You see," says the teacher, "moving won't help. And apart from that, it would be better if he moved rather than you. Why should you suffer? He is the one who deserves to be punished. Don't worry, I'll talk to him."

The next day she summons the boy and tells him that Fatma has complained about him. At first he pretends not to understand what she is talking about but when the teacher takes out the Quran and asks him to read out Verse 30: **"Say to the**

believing men that they should lower their gaze and guard their modesty: that will make for greater purity for them: and Allah is well acquainted with all that they do", he admits that he has been annoying Fatma. "Allah does not love boys who torment girls," she explains. "Please don't do it anymore." The boy looks at her and says: "No problem, I won't do it again."

Explanation: many girls suffer in various places, including school, from being pestered by boys. These problems are more common in adolescence. Teachers must ensure that girls can study quietly and safely and enjoy full protection. They have the right to benefit from all the activities the school offers, for example to go on trips without fear. A society in which girls are not secure is an immoral society in which nobody is safe. The teacher was right to deal with the problem immediately and to comment that it was not Fatma who should be punished and moved but the boy who was bothering her. And in fact, the boy admitted his wrongdoing immediately after hearing the Quran verse. This teacher undoubtedly made appropriate and impressive use of the Quran in this case.

17. What can we say to a girl who has been raped or forced into prostitution?

﴿ وَلْيَسْتَعْفِفِ الَّذِينَ لَا يَجِدُونَ نِكَاحاً حَتَّى يُغْنِيَهُمُ اللَّهُ مِن فَضْلِهِ وَالَّذِينَ يَبْتَغُونَ الْكِتَابَ مِمَّا مَلَكَتْ أَيْمَانُكُمْ فَكَاتِبُوهُمْ إِنْ عَلِمْتُمْ فِيهِمْ خَيْراً وَآتُوهُم مِّن مَّالِ اللَّهِ الَّذِي آتَاكُمْ وَلَا تُكْرِهُوا فَتَيَاتِكُمْ عَلَى الْبِغَاءِ إِنْ أَرَدْنَ تَحَصُّناً لِّتَبْتَغُوا عَرَضَ الْحَيَاةِ الدُّنْيَا وَمَن يُكْرِههُّنَّ فَإِنَّ اللَّهَ مِن بَعْدِ إِكْرَاهِهِنَّ غَفُورٌ رَّحِيمٌ ﴾ (النور: 33)

Let those who find not the wherewithal for marriage keep themselves chaste, until Allah gives them means out of His grace. And if any of your slaves ask for a deed in writing (to enable them to earn their freedom for a certain sum), give them such a deed if ye know any good in them; yea, give them something yourselves out of the means which Allah has given to you. **But force not your maids to prostitution when they desire chastity, in order that ye may make a gain in the goods of this life. But if anyone compels them, yet, after such compulsion, is Allah Oft-Forgiving, Most Merciful (to them).** (The Light: 33)

Suha is in the ninth grade, child of a one-parent family. Her father died three years ago and her older brother Ahmed took over as head of the family. Suha comes to school in a despondent mood, unwilling to study. She often cries and is terrified of all males. She keeps her distance from the boys in the class. On one occasion, when the teacher wanted her to sit beside a boy, Suha started crying and ran out of the class. The teacher was upset at this incident and sent her to the counselor. The counselor invited Suha for several sessions. After a few meetings the girl began to trust her and told her that her older brother was forcing her to spend the night with men who gave her money. The counselor opened the Quran and read Suha Verse 33: **"But force not your maids to prostitution when they desire chastity, in order that ye may make a gain in the goods of this life. But if anyone compels them, yet, after such compulsion, is Allah Oft-Forgiving, Most Merciful (to them)."**

"First, I want you to know that, according to the Quran, you are not to blame because these actions were forced on you," she explained. "I am telling you this because many girls in your situation feel guilty and responsible and all their lives feel that they are unworthy and do not deserve to marry, bear children and raise a family. So, remember that you are guilty of nothing and your brother deserves to be punished severely for forcing his sister into such acts. If it is forbidden to treat a slave like that, how much more so a sister!"

The counselor summoned the brother and read the verse to him as well so that he would understand how grave his actions were. Then she telephoned the police and reported the story.

Explanation: in the world of psychology, it has long been accepted that girls who have been raped (through incest, sexual slavery or forced prostitution or assault) should be convinced that they are not to blame. The attacker is the sole transgressor. This is important because many women who have undergone sexual attack feel guilty and responsible. They think that perhaps they gave out some message to the attacker, perhaps by dressing provocatively, perhaps through hidden thoughts etc. Even if this is true, it can in no way justify rape. These girls may bear a sense of guilt and low self-esteem all their lives, feelings which undermine their ability to develop healthy relationships with the opposite sex or to raise a family. But the Quran states explicitly that Allah will forgive women who were forced into sexual relations. This is a therapeutic statement of the first order!

4 | Dishonest Conduct

1. What can we say to a girl who steals?

{ وَلاَ تَأْكُلُواْ أَمْوَالَكُم بَيْنَكُم بِالْبَاطِلِ وَتُدْلُواْ بِهَا إِلَى الْحُكَّامِ لِتَأْكُلُواْ فَرِيقًا مِّنْ أَمْوَالِ النَّاسِ بِالإِثْمِ وَأَنتُمْ تَعْلَمُونَ } (البقرة: 188)

And do not devour your wealth among yourselves through falsehood, and offer it not as bribe to the authorities that you may knowingly devour a part of the wealth of other people with injustice. (The Cow: 188)

Warod was only in the fifth grade but was already considered disruptive and problematic and squabbled with all her friends. Her classmates complained that she took things without permission – pens, food or money – but she denied this vehemently.

One day, in sports lesson, while all the other pupils were on the sports field, Warod asked permission to go to the toilet, but instead ran to her classroom. One of the pupils saw her going through her classmates' schoolbags and reported this to the teacher. In the past, pupils had complained after the sports lessons that articles had vanished from their bags, but the teacher had not taken the complaints seriously. Now the story was clear. She summoned Warod for a talk but the girl responded with indifference, shrugged her shoulders and said she knew nothing about it. Even when the teacher asked her about a toy belonging to another pupil which was found in her possession, she claimed to know nothing about it. Then the teacher took out the Quran and asked Warod to read out Surah 2, Verse 188: **"And do not devour your wealth among yourselves through falsehood."**

Then she asked Warod what she had understood from this verse. This time Warod went pale, stammered and said she understood that it forbidden to steal and cheat. "From now on we are opening a new page," said the teacher. "We all forgive you, but on condition that from now on you do not do such things." Warod looked at the teacher and said quietly: "I promise."

Explanation: There are various reasons why children are impelled to steal. Sometimes something is lacking in their lives, sometimes they are envious of another child and often they have everything but still steal. Thus, the children of the rich are sometimes caught pilfering in supermarkets when they could obviously buy anything they want. In such a case, the child steals in order to feel that he has gained something, not necessarily something material but perhaps a good feeling. These children lack parental love and steal in order to overcome their sense of emptiness. We do not know why Warod steals, but unless she is stopped and limits are set it is impossible to talk to her and find out what is troubling her and making her behave like that. Her teacher has tried to talk to her but without success. Warod denied wrongdoing. The Quran verse her teacher quoted persuaded Warod that Allah sees and knows everything. She cannot tell Him tales and pretend not to understand. Thus, the Quran has helped her teacher to set limits for Warod. Now she or the counselor can talk to her about what is really troubling her and try to understand why she has been stealing. Without the Quran quotation, they could not have done so.

2. Is it always possible to repent?

{ إِلَّا الَّذِينَ تَابُوا مِن بَعْدِ ذَٰلِكَ وَأَصْلَحُوا فَإِنَّ اللَّهَ غَفُورٌ رَّحِيمٌ } (آل عمران: 89)

Except for those that repent (even) after that, and make amends; for verily Allah is Oft-Forgiving, Most Merciful. (The Family of Imran: 89)

Every day Balal, who is in the ninth grade, returned home from school, went into his room and locked the door. He spent all his time in his room and didn't allow his mother to enter. He said the room was clean and he would tidy it himself. His mother began to suspect that something was wrong. She decided to pay a surprise visit to his school and find out how he behaves there and who his friends are. "Today Balal didn't come to school and recently he has often been absent, "said his teacher. The mother was alarmed. She told the teacher that Balal had changed recently and was behaving strangely. The teacher agreed and said that, when the boy did come to school, he was irritable and fought with the other boys. After being cautioned, Balal had promised to improve but there had been no change.

Balal's parents began to watch him and discovered that he was going around with a group of high school boys who were stealing gold and silver articles from homes in the village and selling them. They had obtained keys of all kinds and tools for breaking in. When the parents went into Balal's room while he was out, they found the tools and stolen property. They debated whether to inform the police. The father called Balal for a talk and recited the verse: **"Except for those that repent (even) after that, and make amends; for verily Allah is Oft-Forgiving, Most Merciful."** There was no need to say anything more because Balal burst into tears and admitted everything.

Explanation: "Better late than never," according to the folk saying. Balal's parents were rather late in beginning to worry about him. There were probably early indications that he was not studying, was playing truant from school, making friends with undesirable boys, spending time alone in his room and perhaps even going out at night. The closer the ties between parents and children, the less the chance that such things will occur. It is important that parents maintain close contact with their child, his friends and his teachers. This does not mean that the connection should be critical and repressive but it should be based on sincere interest in the life of the child and the desire to help him or her. The father did well to utilize the Quran verse and not to launch into a shouting match and impose punishments. Balal sensed his father's pain and disappointment. The important Quran verse gave Balal hope that if he changed his ways, he would be forgiven.

3. What can we say to someone who is impressed by evildoing?

﴿ قُل لَّا يَسْتَوِي الْخَبِيثُ وَالطَّيِّبُ وَلَوْ أَعْجَبَكَ كَثْرَةُ الْخَبِيثِ فَاتَّقُوا اللَّهَ يَا أُولِي الْأَلْبَابِ لَعَلَّكُمْ تُفْلِحُونَ ﴾ (المائدة: 100)

Say: "Not equal are things that are bad and things that are good, even though the abundance of the bad may dazzle thee; so fear Allah, O ye that understand; that (so) ye may prosper. (The Table: 100)

Sixteen-year-old Yusef goes out every evening with his friends. They roam the streets, smoke and do other unacceptable things. For some time, he has abandoned his best friend and no longer sees him. His parents asked him why he no longer sees his friend and has joined a new gang. Yusef replied that most of his classmates go out in groups, roam the streets, smoke, laugh and return home late. He added that his best friend refused to behave like that and stayed home, prepared his homework and sometimes went to see a movie. "The truth is that I go out with my new friends although I'm not attracted by what they do. But if I stay at home with my friend, they laugh at me," he told his parents.

Yusef's parents talked to the educational counselor who explained that their son was now an adolescent and at that time in their lives boys and girls are very much influenced by their friends. He equipped them with a Quran verse and asked them to explain to their son that even if most of the class behaved like that, this did not mean that it was the right path.

Explanation: the counselor was right to say that in adolescence there is great peer pressure on the individual, and boys and girls may be influenced to their detriment. The Quran verse which reminds us that often evil may dazzle us is highly appropriate for this situation. The boys smoke and possibly make inappropriate remarks to girls or do other forbidden things, feeling that the bad endows them with power. But the Quran adjures them not to be impressed by the power of the bad.

Deep within himself, Yusef knew the truth, and if he conducts himself in future according to the Quran, he will be acting wisely and will flourish.

4. What can we say to a boy who joins a gang of miscreants?

{ خُذِ الْعَفْوَ وَأْمُرْ بِالْعُرْفِ وَأَعْرِضْ عَنِ الْجَاهِلِينَ } (الأعراف: 199)

Hold to forgiveness; command what is right; but turn away from the ignorant. (The Elevations: 199)

One day the father of Yusef, an eighth-grader, contacted the counselor and said he must talk to her urgently about his son. He told her how worried he was about him. Although Yusef was a good student, he said, he had recently joined up with a group of boys who did not study, hung around in the village and looked for ways of doing damage. "The whole village asks me why he is going about with that gang because it is not fitting for him. I've tried to talk to him, to guide him in the proper path but recently he won't listen. He says he has a good time with those friends and he doesn't think they are bad boys. What irritates me is that we have a neighbor, a classmate of Yusef, who is an outstanding student. He has been trying to make friends with Yusef for some time but Yusef doesn't want his company because he comes from a poor family."

The counselor called Yusef to her office and told him about his father's complaint. Then she opened the Quran at Surah 7, Verse 199 and read out: **"Hold to forgiveness; command what is right; but turn away from the ignorant".**

"What did you understand from that?" she asked. Yusef said that the Quran commanded him to keep his distance from his bad friends. "But the Quran commands you something else that you have forgotten," she said. "To act mercifully towards your neighbor, who is trying to be your friend and not to hold aloof from him because he comes from a poor family."

Explanation: The Quran preaches mercy and forgiveness. The command to forgive and have mercy on the other is reiterated again and again. But it also advises Yusef to turn away from his bad friends. These two pieces of advice can pave Yusef's way in life. This verse can help many parents whose sons or daughters make undesirable friends. They can show their children how, on the one hand, they have not turned away from the "ignorant" and, on the other, do not forgive good friends. Forgiveness is one of the most noble emotions in collective Arab society and enables the individual almost to enter into the skin of the other and to feel what he feels. In modern Western society, people are not so willing to forgive. They are ready to understand the other (to empathize but not to identify as is customary in traditional societies.

5. What can we say to someone who spreads false rumors?

{ لِيُحِقَّ الْحَقَّ وَيُبْطِلَ الْبَاطِلَ وَلَوْ كَرِهَ الْمُجْرِمُونَ } (الأنفال: 8)

That He might establish the Truth and nullify Falsehood, distasteful though it be to those in guilt. (The Spoils: 8)

Hanin, who is in the ninth grade, noticed that all her friends were keeping away from her and her classmates were casting suspicious glances at her and whispering behind her back. She tried to understand what was going on and why they were treating her like that. She asked her best friend who told her that there was a rumor in school that she had stolen a gold chain from one of the girls. Hanin burst into tears and did not know what to do and how to act. In the end she turned to her teacher, told her about the rumors and claimed that someone wanted to slander her and she did not know why. The teacher asked Hanin to calm down and restrain herself until the matter was clarified and the truth revealed. If she was sure she had done nothing wrong, she should ignore the rumors.

The teacher summoned the girl who claimed that Hanin had stolen from her, and the girl told her that during a sports lesson she had suddenly discovered that the chain was missing from her bag. The teacher asked her where the bag had been left and she replied that it had been in the school courtyard under the pomegranate tree. The teacher asked her to accompany her on a search under the tree but the girl objected and said she had looked there and found nothing. She again accused Hanin. Now the teacher began to suspect that something was wrong. She questioned the girl thoroughly and several of her girlfriends as well and soon discovered the truth: the accuser was infatuated with one of the boys in the class who was Hanin's boyfriend, and she was jealous. She wanted to take revenge on Hanin and persuade everyone, including the boy, to keep away from her, by spreading rumors.

The teacher reprimanded the girl, summoned Hanin and told her that the truth had been revealed and that she was innocent. She told the two girls that when there is faith in Allah, the truth will always emerge, as the Quran writes: **"That He might establish the Truth and nullify Falsehood, distasteful though it be to those in guilt".**

Explanation: false rumors are often spread and one should exercise caution with regard to them. People who wish to harm someone can spread rumors and half-truths. There have been cases of girls murdered because of claims that they violated family honor although it later transpired that the stories were false. The Quran commands us again and again to adhere to the truth, not to spread lies and not to believe stories without firm factual foundations. The spreaders of rumors deserve severe punishment. The teacher was right to investigate the case until she uncovered the truth, because Hanin, who suffered so much, deserves to be acknowledged as innocent.

The truth is that spreading rumors damages a society. It makes people believe falsehoods and weakens the social fabric. Everyone is liable to be afraid of being the victim of untruths, there is no justice and people are hostages to the evil intentions of others. The Quran warns us to adhere to the sacred value, truth.

6. What can we say to someone who steals from a charity box?

{ إِنَّمَا الصَّدَقَاتُ لِلْفُقَرَاءِ وَالْمَسَاكِينِ وَالْعَامِلِينَ عَلَيْهَا وَالْمُؤَلَّفَةِ قُلُوبُهُمْ وَفِي الرِّقَابِ
وَالْغَارِمِينَ وَفِي سَبِيلِ اللَّهِ وَابْنِ السَّبِيلِ فَرِيضَةً مِّنَ اللَّهِ وَاللَّهُ عَلِيمٌ حَكِيمٌ }
(التوبة: 60)

Alms are for the poor and the needy, and those employed to administer the (funds); for those whose hearts have been

(recently) reconciled (to the truth); for those in bondage and in debt; in the cause of Allah; and for the wayfarer: (thus is it) ordained by Allah, and Allah is full of knowledge and wisdom. (The Repentance: 60)

Ahmed is one of the leading teachers in the school when it comes to educational initiatives. Recently he launched the collection of funds to help families whose children could not afford notebooks and textbooks. He explained the importance of the project to the pupils and let them share in collecting the funds. They responded enthusiastically, visited all the families in the village and people gave as much as they could afford.

Asi, who is a hard-working boy, was not idle for a moment and collected a large sum. He boasted to his friends about his achievement. Fadi told his older brother, who asked for more details. That evening Fadi's brother tried to persuade Fadi to steal the money from Asi, and promised him his old cell phone as a reward. In the recess, Fadi tried to filch the money from Asi's school bag but he was seen and the incident was reported to the teacher. He summoned Fadi and his brother and explained the gravity of their actions. "To attempt to steal money from a friend is not only betrayal of the friend," he said. "What is worse: this money was earmarked for people who need it, including orphans who have no parents to buy them a cell phone like yours." He concluded by reading them Verse 60 of Surah 9: **"Alms are for the poor and the needy, and those employed to administer the (funds); for those whose hearts have been (recently) reconciled (to the truth); for those in bondage and in debt; in the cause of Allah; and for the wayfarer: (thus is it) ordained by Allah, and Allah is full of knowledge and wisdom".**

Fadi and his brother were deeply ashamed.

Explanation: The Quran has no equals in reinforcing the sense of mutual responsibility. Fund-raising is aimed at all the needy members of the community, including the traveler who passes through. That is the spirit of the Quran – concern for the other and the weak even if they are not relatives. The teacher, Ahmed, was acting in this spirit when he organized fund-raising for needy pupils, and his pupils cooperated with him in the same spirit. The teacher scolded Fadi and his brother not only for stealing but, what is worse – for undermining the spirit of mutual responsibility and concern for the weak. He quoted the appropriate verse from the Quran to illustrate that they were acting in violation of the commands of the Quran. Perhaps he would have done well to allot them an educational task involving concern for the weak, for example to coach weaker pupils or to collect money for some other project.

7. How can we reform a boy who has stolen?

{ أَلَمْ يَعْلَمُوا أَنَّ اللَّهَ هُوَ يَقْبَلُ التَّوْبَةَ عَنْ عِبَادِهِ وَيَأْخُذُ الصَّدَقَاتِ وَأَنَّ اللَّهَ هُوَ التَّوَّابُ الرَّحِيمُ } (التوبة: 104)

Know they not that Allah Is He who accepts repentance from His slaves and receives their gifts of charity, and that Allah is verily He, the Oft-Returning, Most Merciful? (The Repentance: 104)

The mother of Amer, an eighth-grader, noted that his conduct had changed in the past week. She went to his teacher and asked him to check if something was bothering Amer in school. She said that her son was behaving strangely. For example, in bed he covered his head with a blanket as if hiding, he refused to go alone to his grandmother's house etc.

The class teacher called Amer for a talk and realized that Amer had taken part in the theft of money collected for the annual class trip from the bag of the pupil who had collected the money. At their next session, Amer admitted that his partner in the theft was insisting that he keep quiet or else he would beat him. Amer was trembling as he spoke. He was afraid that the principal would expel him and Allah would never forgive him because the parents of his classmates had worked hard to raise the money for the trip. The teacher explained to him the error of his ways and ordered him to carry out various tasks for the general good in class in order to atone for his actions. He added that if someone errs and repents, Allah forgives him, and read him the verse: **"Know they not that Allah Is He who accepts repentance from His slaves and receives their gifts of charity, and that Allah is verily He, the Oft-Returning, Most Merciful?"**

Amer understood how wrong his actions had been, but felt relief at gaining forgiveness.

Explanation: the issue of punishment and forgiveness requires equilibrium. We want Amer to understand the gravity of his actions but if he is very frightened, we will not achieve our objective. Amer needs to refrain from stealing not because of fear but because he has realized that thereby he is wronging someone else. If he stops stealing merely because he is afraid, he may revert to doing so when he is convinced that nobody can see him. Fear is not a good teacher. The difference between a child who refrains from stealing because of fear and one who refrains because he is not willing to harm someone else is very great. The former is motivated by an outside factor and the other is inner-motivated. We prefer internalized education because it accompanies the child wherever he goes and is not dependent on time and place. Since Amer has already stolen, he deserves punishment but the reaction should fit the deed: example, work on behalf of the community in order to repair the damage he has done to the community or financial compensation for the victim. It is important that there be a clear connection between the action and the punishment so that it will be easy for Amer to internalize new rules of conduct. It is no less important to allow Amer some hope, in other words forgiveness, which will enable him to mend his ways. Without forgiveness he will have no reason to improve his behavior. And here we see the greatness of the Quran.

8. What should a boy do when he has been incriminated?

{ إِنَّ اللَّهَ يَأْمُرُكُمْ أَن تُؤدُّواْ الأَمَانَاتِ إِلَى أَهْلِهَا وَإِذَا حَكَمْتُم بَيْنَ النَّاسِ أَن تَحْكُمُواْ بِالْعَدْلِ إِنَّ اللَّهَ نِعِمَّا يَعِظُكُم بِهِ إِنَّ اللَّهَ كَانَ سَمِيعًا بَصِيرًا } (النساء: 58)

Allah doth command you to render back your Trusts to those to whom they are due; And when ye judge between man and man, that ye judge with justice: Verily how excellent is the teaching which He giveth you! For Allah is He Who heareth and seeth all things. (Women: 58)

For the past two weeks Ali, a sixth-grader, has been behaving strangely at home and at school. He has almost stopped talking and every morning he complains of stomach pains and says he doesn't want to go to school. When he is forced to go, he cries. He also complains that he can't get out of bed or stand up. When his mother allows him to stay at home, he gets up an hour later and moves around as if nothing is wrong with him. When she tries to go out, he clings to her, asks her not to leave him alone, and never goes out to play with his friends. When he does attend school, he complains of stomach pains after the third lesson and then his mother is summoned to take him home. He looks frightened, says his teacher. Last night, his mother told the teacher, he woke up crying and trembling, soaked in sweat. He clung to his mother and wanted her to sleep beside him.

The teacher decided to talk to Ali to discover what had caused the drastic change in his behavior. She assured him she had his interests at heart and that he had no reason to be afraid because everyone wanted to help him. Then Ali told her that his friends were stealing from other pupils and hiding their loot in his school bag. When they left school at the end of the day, they recovered the objects from his bag. They had threatened him that if he reported them, they would take revenge on him.

The teacher looked at Ali, who sat there terrified and said: "First, you are a brave boy for having told me the truth. Good for you! Now I want to read you an important verse from the Quran." The opened Surah 4, Verse 58:

"Allah doth command you to render back your Trusts to those to whom they are due; And when ye judge between man and man, that ye judge with justice." "If a trust must be returned, what do you think, Ali, about theft?" she asked. "Next time I won't be afraid," Ali said. "I won't let them put anything into my bag and if they do, I will give it back to the owner, just as the Quran says." "Good, Ali," the teacher replied. "The Quran often says that those who tell the truth are protected by Allah and have no need to fear."

Then the teacher sent for Ali's friends……

Explanation: many children live in fear of strong and violent classmates. It is very important for teachers to protect them because schools do not exist so that the violent can exploit the weak. Children go to school to study and when one is afraid, one cannot learn. It is also very important that teachers should not yield to fear because if they give in to violence in any way and grant excessive privileges to the more violent students, they will never be able to teach the class that violence does not pay. The children will learn that the rules of the jungle prevail and the stronger will always win. So, whenever a teacher senses that there is some threat in the class, he or she must act immediately to neutralize it. In extreme cases, when the teacher feels that he cannot control the situation himself, he may contact the police or some other outside authority able to settle the situation. One thing is forbidden: to ignore violence and pretend we have seen nothing.

9. How can we rehabilitate someone without harming him?

{ وَيَا قَوْمِ أَوْفُواْ الْمِكْيَالَ وَالْمِيزَانَ بِالْقِسْطِ وَلاَ تَبْخَسُواْ النَّاسَ أَشْيَاءهُمْ وَلاَ تَعْثَوْاْ فِي الأَرْضِ مُفْسِدِينَ } (هود: 85)

And O my people! give just measure and weight, nor withhold from the people the things that are their due: commit not evil in the land with intent to do mischief. (Hud: 85)

Ali owns the only grocery store in the village and everyone buys from him. The villagers began to notice that Ali did not weigh the goods honestly. In other stores they received more for their money. So, they appealed to the village sheikh who explained that it is forbidden to judge a man without clear proof that he is cheating. He promised to check the facts.

One day the sheikh went into the grocery store, bought several articles, and started a casual conversation with Ali about the fact that it is forbidden to cheat on weight because Islam and all other religions forbid such actions. "Those who cheat," said the sheikh, "eventually lose everything." He spoke in general terms and did not refer to Ali himself and then he quoted from the Quran: **"And O my people! give just measure and weight, nor withhold from the people the things that are their due: commit not evil in the land with intent to do mischief".**

Two days later, Ali came to the sheikh and confessed that he had been cheating on weight. "What you said touched my conscience," he told the sheikh. "Please tell me what I can do to atone?" he said and thanked the sheikh for not taking action although he had known what Ali had done.

Explanation: The sheikh's wisdom is impressive. If he had come to Ali and told him what people were saying or caught him red-handed, Ali would have felt the need to defend himself and would have found it difficult to confess. He would have raised all kinds of excuses. But the sheikh hinted that he knew the truth without offending Ali, thereby giving him the opportunity to confess on his own initiative and to ask for forgiveness. No school can teach such wisdom except the school of life. Both Ali and the sheikh know the truth – that Ali has been stealing by cheating on weight. But only Ali can say so explicitly. And thus, the Quran teacher us to pursue justice and honor it, and the sheikh, in his wisdom, knew how to convey this important message.

10. What can we say to someone who believes rumors without trusting himself?

{ وَكَذَلِكَ أَنزَلْنَاهُ حُكْماً عَرَبِيّاً وَلَئِنِ اتَّبَعْتَ أَهْوَاءهُم بَعْدَ مَا جَاءكَ مِنَ الْعِلْمِ مَا لَكَ مِنَ اللّهِ مِن وَلِيٍّ وَلاَ وَاقٍ } (الرعد: 37)

Thus have We revealed it to be a judgment of authority in Arabic. Wert thou to follow their (vain) desires after the knowledge which hath reached thee, then wouldst thou find neither protector nor defender against Allah. (The Thunder: 37)

One of the teachers has succeeded in inciting the principal against another teacher. He concocted various stories against that teacher and the principal began to persecute that teacher, who was a dedicated and hardworking professional. With time the harassment increased and he made the teacher's life a misery. When the good teacher could no longer tolerate this attitude, he came to the principal and asked him why he was treating him like that. The principal repeated all the stories he had heard from the troublemaker. The good teacher replied: "Sir, you are a learned man of high standing. How could you be influenced by such stories although you have never seen me behaving badly?" The principal was adamant and continued to believe the stories. Then the good teacher told him that Allah knows the truth and expected him not to be influenced by slander: **"Thus have We revealed it to be a judgment of authority in Arabic. Wert thou to follow their (vain) desires after the knowledge which hath reached thee, then wouldst thou find neither protector nor defender against Allah".**

Explanation: People are often influenced by various stories and do not try to clarify the truth. Even more often people spread false tales about others in order to harm them. Those who spread false stories deserve severe punishment because they can cause harm or even murder (for example, by spreading the rumor that a girl is violating the family honor). But those who believe the stories without examining the facts also deserve punishment because they are collaborating in a crime and will themselves probably continue to disseminate the story. The teacher did well to remind the principal that the Quran commands us not to listen to false rumors, because Allah has given us wisdom and we must use it. This command is vital for the maintenance of a healthy society.

5 | The Parent as a Model

1. Could the source of the child's aggressiveness lie in the home?

{ وَإِذْ أَخَذْنَا مِيثَاقَ بَنِي إِسْرَائِيلَ لاَ تَعْبُدُونَ إِلاَّ اللّهَ وَبِالْوَالِدَيْنِ إِحْسَاناً وَذِي الْقُرْبَى
وَالْيَتَامَى وَالْمَسَاكِينِ وَقُولُواْ لِلنَّاسِ حُسْناً وَأَقِيمُواْ الصَّلاَةَ وَآتُواْ الزَّكَاةَ ثُمَّ تَوَلَّيْتُمْ إِلاَّ
قَلِيلاً مِّنكُمْ وَأَنتُم مِّعْرِضُونَ } (البقرة: 83)

And remember We took a Covenant from the Children of Israel (to this effect): worship none but Allah; treat with kindness your parents and kindred, and orphans and those in need; **speak fair to the people;** be steadfast in prayer; And practice regular charity. Then did ye turn back, except a few among you, and ye backslide (even now).(The Cow: 83)

A tidy school, a clean environment, trees in the courtyard. It is hard to believe how quiet a place can be, even though it is filled with pupils. It was the lunch recess; the teachers were roaming the courtyard and corridor and several of them were in the teachers' lounge, chatting and exchanging opinions, while the principal sat in his office. Suddenly loud shouting broke the silence. The father of one of the pupils burst in through the door, shouting, threatening and cursing one of the teachers.

The teacher invited the parent to sit down and discuss things quietly. His invitation seemed to infuriate the man even further. The pupils watched, the teachers stood surprised and the principal could not believe his eyes and invited the two of them into his room: "Come in so that we can understand what the problem is and examine what we can do to help you," he said. In the principal's office, the father explained that his son had failed a math's test although he was a clever and diligent student. "The teacher is to blame. He deliberately failed him because of discipline problems," he fumed. The teacher replied that the boy was indeed a bright boy but he had many behavioral problems connected to his classmates. He was not focused in class and so his grades were dropping. "Recently he has become particularly aggressive," the teacher added, "but he received the grade he deserves according to his work and knowledge and not his conduct."

The father asked the teacher's pardon and explained that his son had described the situation entirely differently. "I should have asked you before shouting," he added. Then the principal talked to the father about the change for the worse in his son's behavior. He added that he knew what the root of the problem was and that only the father could help his son. The father looked at him and asked how he could help his son to be more pleasant and calm and less aggressive and undisciplined.

The principal explained that many children are the reflection of their parents. "He is imitating your behavior. If you treat him aggressively, he will be aggressive towards his surroundings. I think that your attitude, the way you came into the school, is likely to be adopted by your son. It is very important to be courteous to others, as the Quran says in Surah 2, Verse 83: **"Speak fair to the people".**

Explanation: the principal was right. It is likely that the father behaves similarly towards his family although outwardly he appears to be defending his son. In any event, the son sees his father's behavior and takes it as a model so that it is not surprising that he treats his friends in the same way. It is not always easy to practice restraint, certainly not when we are frustrated and angry. Thanks to the moderate and restrained reactions of the teacher and the principal, the father was able to calm down. If they had responded aggressively to his aggression, the situation would have deteriorated even further. The angry father encountered the calm and even sad eyes of the teacher and the principal. They were sad that he, the father, felt like that. In moments of stormy emotion, the Quran exhortation: **"Speak fair to the people"**, can appease and the entire situation for the better. Then it is possible to discuss the child and his difficulties and to decide how to help him. When anger reigns, discussion is impossible.

2. Is it permissible for a father to be miserly towards his family?

{ لاَّ جُنَاحَ عَلَيْكُمْ إِن طَلَّقْتُمُ النِّسَاء مَا لَمْ تَمَسُّوهُنَّ أَوْ تَفْرِضُواْ لَهُنَّ فَرِيضَةً وَمَتِّعُوهُنَّ عَلَى الْمُوسِعِ قَدَرُهُ وَعَلَى الْمُقْتِرِ قَدْرُهُ مَتَاعًا بِالْمَعْرُوفِ حَقًّا عَلَى الْمُحْسِنِينَ }

(البقرة: 236)

There is no blame on you if ye divorce women before consummation or the fixation of their dower; **but bestow on them (a suitable gift), the wealthy according to his means, and the poor according to his means; a gift of a reasonable amount is due from those who wish to do the right thing.** (The Cow: 236)

Rima has three children and is devoted to them and tends them as mothers do and spares no effort on behalf of them and her husband and home. Towards the end of the school year, her son Samir, who is in the first grade, asked her to accompany him on the school's annual trip. It is customary for parents and children to go together but Rima refused. It was the first time she had disappointed her son on such an important matter. She invented all kinds of excuses and promised that next year she would go on the trip with him. Samir told his teacher that his mother could not come but said he did not know the reason. The teacher asked the mother to come for a talk but the mother did not come to the scheduled meeting. When the teacher telephoned Rima to ask why she was not coming, Rima gave various excuses, she was busy, she had other important things to do that day etc. The teacher was not convinced and asked to visit her at home for a tete a tete. When she entered the house, she immediately understood Rima's situation. The house lacked such basic items as a refrigerator and a table. Rima told her that she did not have the money for the trip, not to mention money for clothes and shoes so that she could look like the other mothers. She said she was embarrassed because of her shabby appearance. The teacher realized that the problem was not lack of money; the family was not poor. Her husband was simply a miser and kept all his money for himself.

The teacher approached the psychological service for aid in solving the problem. One of the solutions proposed was that she talk to the father and explain to him that financial support for his family was his personal responsibility. Every individual has rights and obligations and a man has the obligation to support his family and in particular his wife, as is written in Verse 236 of Surah 2: **"Bestow on them (women) a suitable gift, the wealthy according to his means, and the poor according to his means; a gift of a reasonable amount is due from those who wish to do the right thing".**

The teacher was now confident enough to talk to the father, knowing she had something of value to say to him.

3. Is it permissible to judge a child according to her father's actions?

{ لَّيْسَ عَلَيْكَ هُدَاهُمْ وَلَكِنَّ اللّهَ يَهْدِي مَن يَشَاء وَمَا تُنفِقُواْ مِنْ خَيْرٍ فَلأنفُسِكُمْ وَمَا تُنفِقُونَ إِلاَّ ابْتِغَاء وَجْهِ اللّهِ وَمَا تُنفِقُواْ مِنْ خَيْرٍ يُوَفَّ إِلَيْكُمْ وَأَنتُمْ لاَ تُظْلَمُونَ }
(البقرة: 272)

It is not required of thee (O Messenger), to set them on the right path, but Allah sets on the right path whom He pleaseth.

Whatever of good ye give benefits your own souls, and ye shall only do so seeking the "Face" of Allah. Whatever good ye give, shall be rendered back to you, and ye shall not be dealt with unjustly. (The Cow: 272)

Yusra is in the ninth grade, a quiet, polite girl who does not have many friends. Her school work is average. Recently her grades have dropped and she tends to draw away from her friends. She appears lonely and depressed and has begun to neglect her appearance. Her father is in prison and this is apparently why she has lost her self-confidence and begun to suffer from a sense of inferiority and to feel different from her classmates. She feels rejected. Her friends have not given up on her and keep trying to encourage her, with the exception of one good friend who is keeping her distance at her mother's urging.

The teacher decides to summon Yusra's friends for a discussion of her condition so that they can think together how to help her. She starts the discussion by quoting Verse 272: **"Whatever of good ye give benefits your own souls, and ye shall only do so seeking the "Face" of Allah. Whatever good ye give, shall be rendered back to you, and ye shall not be dealt with unjustly".**

She explains to the girls that by helping Yusra they would be helping themselves. Several of the girls do not understand her meaning so she talks about the positive feelings they would have after helping their friend and of the reward they would receive from Allah. Nobody can foresee the future and know who will have need of help, she adds. The friend whose mother insisted that she keep away from Yusra sits in silence. Then she says: "Now I know what to say to my mother. I'll read that verse to her and it will convince her to let me go on seeing Yusra."

The teacher praises her and says that what she herself thinks is much more important that what others say and how good she will feel after helping her friend.

The next day the principal hears about the teacher's initiative, summons to his office, takes his copy of the Quran and reads out the same verse to her. "You too deserve this compliment," he said.

Explanation: life is not easy for a young girl whose father is in prison. Society often takes a poor view of the entire family and people say that the daughter is probably like her father. Such an attitude is liable to drive the daughter to engage in criminal behavior because her milieu has abandoned her. She may see this as a way of taking revenge on those who rejected her. It is not true that a daughter will inevitably end up like her father. In many cases the reverse is true. Some children of criminals act blamelessly and contribute to society. Hence generalizations of this kind are unfair and harmful. Moreover, Yusra should be encouraged not to be ashamed of her father's actions. They are his and not hers and elsewhere in the Quran there are verses which clearly emphasize the fact that every individual is responsible for his or her actions. In this case the teacher has stressed a very important fact, namely that when we do good to another, we are actually benefiting ourselves. We are making peace with our own weakness in the understanding that we too need help. When we give to others, we are giving to ourselves and accepting the fact that we are not perfect. This is a highly significant psychological process which the Quran clarifies in this verse.

4. Is the orphan entitled to study?

﴿ وَآتُواْ الْيَتَامَى أَمْوَالَهُمْ وَلاَ تَتَبَدَّلُواْ الْخَبِيثَ بِالطَّيِّبِ وَلاَ تَأْكُلُواْ أَمْوَالَهُمْ إِلَى أَمْوَالِكُمْ
إِنَّهُ كَانَ حُوبًا كَبِيرًا ﴾ (النساء: ة2)

To orphans restore their property (when they reach their age), nor substitute (your) worthless things for (their) good

ones; and devour not their substance (by mixing it up) with your own. For this is indeed a great sin. (Women: 2)

Rim, who is in the twelfth grade, is an orphan. When she was ten her mother died and her father remarried. The second wife is an unkind woman who nags her husband for loving and pampering his daughter. Since the remarriage, Rim has changed. From a happy lively girl, she has become melancholy and withdrawn. Her teacher, on coming into the classroom one day, found her shouting and crying: "Why did Mummy leave me? Why? Why do I deserve it? Why me?" She tried to calm the girl but without success. Then she sent her to the school counselor.

Counselor: Rim, what brings you to me?

Rim: My teacher sent me. I didn't want to come.

Counselor: Why? What happened?

Rim: I'm very angry and I don't feel like talking. I shouted in class so my teacher sent me to you (angrily).

Counselor: You don't have to tell me if you don't want to but I'm here to help you. You can trust me that anything you tell me will be kept secret and will never reach the ears of anyone who shouldn't know.

Rim: (painfully): I'm an orphan. I miss my mother. My father used to be good to me but since he married everything has changed. My stepmother rules the household and he does what she says. I feel alone, lost without my mother (crying).

Counselor: Has anything happened recently to make you feel so bad?

Rim: I asked for money for a preparatory course for the university entrance exams but my father refused to give it.

Counselor: Perhaps he has no money?

Rim: My father is quite rich because he received a lot of money from my mother. She came from a well-to-do family and she gave my father all her money. Now he buys his new wife expensive clothes and jewelry. But it's my money and he gives me nothing.

Counselor: Rim, have you spoken to your father directly and asked him for money?

Rim: Yes, I talked to him and asked but he said he didn't have the money.

Counselor: Rim, I want to visit your home when your father is there with his wife and I'll try to talk to him indirectly.

Rim agreed and the counselor scheduled a meeting.

Counselor: I've come because we try to visit the twelfth-grade pupils' homes to talk to the parents and encourage them to enroll their children at university for further studies.

Rim: I'm waiting for my father to pay for the preparatory course.

Counselor: When do you intend to enroll her?

The father is silent and looks at his wife who is surprised and flushes.

Counselor: There is a Quran verse which has always impressed me: **"To orphans restore their property (when they reach their age), nor substitute (your) worthless things for (their) good ones; and devour not their substance (by mixing it up) with your own. For this is indeed a great sin".**

Really, it is very good of you to encourage Rim to continue her studies and to give her the opportunity to learn. Well done! (Turning to Rim). Do you want to go to university?

Rim: Yes, I'm dying to study. I want to be an engineer. It's what my mother and I always wanted for me. But first I must register for the preparatory course.

Counselor: Then hurry because there is not much time left.

Explanation: the counselor chose this way of persuading the parents to send Rim to university without hurting their feelings. She thinks it is very important for girls to study and make progress because she believes that children need a clever mother and not one who knows nothing about the world and never leaves the home. "A strong mother produces strong children," she always says to parents. She could of course have invited the father for a separate talk and explained to him that it was important for his talented daughter to continue her studies. But it was also important to preserve his dignity in order to achieve the aim – Rim's university studies. The counselor made wise use of the Quran, where many verses relate to the need to protect the weak. After hearing this verse, what was left for the father to say? In future talks the counselor can discuss with Rim her pain at being an orphan, and try to ease her suffering.

5. Is the authority figure all-knowing?

{ قُل لاّ أَقُولُ لَكُمْ عِندِي خَزَآئِنُ اللّهِ وَلا أَعْلَمُ الْغَيْبَ وَلا أَقُولُ لَكُمْ إِنِّي مَلَكٌ إِنْ
أَتَّبِعُ إِلاَّ مَا يُوحَى إِلَيَّ قُلْ هَلْ يَسْتَوِي الأَعْمَى وَالْبَصِيرُ أَفَلاَ تَتَفَكَّرُونَ { (الأنعام: 50)

Say: "I tell you not that with me are the Treasures of Allah, nor do I know what is hidden, nor do I tell you I am an angel. I but follow what is revealed to me." Say: "Can the blind be held equal to the seeing?" Will ye then consider not? (The Livestock: 50)

Thirteen-year-old Sulaf came to the counselor and told her that lately she her relations with her parents had become very tense. "All the time they dictate to me how to behave, what to wear, how to talk and when to go out. They have something to say about everything I do and it really depresses me. Do you have a solution for me so that I can do whatever I want without annoying my parents?" The counselor realized that Sulaf wanted her approval for her actions and to be told that she and not her parents was right. "You want something that I can't give you," she replied.: **"I tell you not that with me are the Treasures of Allah, nor do I know what is hidden"**, she said, quoting the Prophet to help Sulaf take responsibility for her actions instead of expecting a magic formula. **"Nor do I tell you I am an angel"**, she added, in order to remind Sulaf that she, the counselor, would not be able to protect her if she behaved badly and was punished. **"Can the blind be held equal to the seeing? Will ye then consider not?"** she concluded, in order to explain to Sulaf that she, Sulaf, was not blind and knew what the right path was, the golden path where both she and her parents could live together contentedly and peacefully.

Explanation: children often seek from their parents or teachers or counselors answers or promises which those figures of authority cannot give. Sulaf wants the counselor to organize her life so that she can do whatever she wants and have her parents' consent. In other cases, for example, children want to extract a promise that if they study well, they will succeed in their exams. This usually happens but it cannot be guaranteed. Some children simply want a promise from a parent or teacher that everything will go well and adults cannot promise this. In these situations, and others, the figure of authority must act with humility, encouraging the child to take responsibility for himself or herself. In other words, Sulaf understands that she is responsible for her actions and that the counselor cannot substitute for her. She alone will be judged by her actions. Here the words of the Prophet come to the aid of the counselor and of every parent who wants to convey to his children the important message that he, the parent, does not know everything.

6. Should a father support his child so that he can study?

{ قَدْ خَسِرَ الَّذِينَ قَتَلُواْ أَوْلاَدَهُمْ سَفَهاً بِغَيْرِ عِلْمٍ وَحَرَّمُواْ مَا رَزَقَهُمُ اللّهُ افْتِرَاء عَلَى اللّهِ قَدْ ضَلُّواْ وَمَا كَانُواْ مُهْتَدِينَ } (الأنعام: 140)

Lost are those who slay their children, from folly, without knowledge, and forbid food which Allah hath provided for them, inventing (lies) against Allah. They have indeed gone astray and heeded no guidance. (The Livestock: 140)

Samir is in the tenth grade and his grades are a little higher than average. His teachers think he has a good chance of succeeding in the matriculation examinations. In the previous summer vacation, he worked on a building site and told his friends how hard the work was. He said it made him appreciate his studies and understand how important it is to advance in life. He dreamt of being a scholar, he said, so that in the future he could live comfortably and not have to exhaust himself with hard physical labor.

A week later Samir told his friends that his father had decided to kill him. His shocked friends asked for an explanation. "He passed a death sentence on me when he decided to kill my dream. He told me that one can't buy food through studies, and found me a permanent job on a building site belonging to a friend of his. He said it was my future and that it's not worth my while to waste years of my life at school. He also said he has no money for me and I must look out for myself because I'm a pampered boy who doesn't work and doesn't bring money home, just wastes time and enjoys himself."

Samir told his friends he was depressed and in despair. He had tried to persuade his father in every possible way to let him complete his studies – but in vain. There was no longer any meaning to his life and he intended to end it.

Samir's friends were very worried about him and came to his aid. They explained to him how precious his life was and urged him to preserve it and they promised to talk to his father. They invited Samir's father to one of their homes without telling Samir. He told them how hard it was for him to support his large family and said that Samir, as the oldest, must help. "He must sacrifice himself for his little brothers and sisters," he stressed.

The friends did not give up. They explained to the father that Samir too was his son and deserved part of his father's income. "He deserves for you to make sacrifices for him," they said, and told him that Samir was depressed and that his father's conduct was killing him. The father was stunned and replied" What are you saying? No father kills his son. I want what is best for him." Then they told him that his son was threatening suicide. Samir's father was alarmed and did not know whether to believe them but they calmed him and promised that they would not let Samir do anything foolish. "I never knew my son was so serious about his studies and I didn't realize how important they are to him. I've been blind," the father said. He looked anxious and tense and expressed his regret. Then one of the friends quoted: **"Lost are those who slay their children, from folly, without knowledge, and forbid food which Allah hath provided for them, inventing (lies) against Allah. They have indeed gone astray and heeded no guidance".** This time the father listened in silence.

He went home and knocked on the door of Samir's room.

Samir: Who is it?
Father: Your father.
Samir: You can come in.
Father: How are you?
Samir: All right…no, not really…
Father: My son, I want you to feel good all the time.
Samir: (surprised): Really, Father?
Father: Yes, Today I understood what is important to you, my son. You can continue your studies. I agree. I

	will always support you and what Allah gives me is intended for the whole family and for you too…
Samir:	(cannot believe his ears. Embraces his father and his father sheds a tear). Are you crying, Father?
Father:	They are tears of joy, my son.

Explanation: Samir's family situation is common in many societies, particularly among low-income groups. It is no disgrace to be poor, but it is hard. The parent faces a test. What to do with the limited funds at his disposal> Will he really deal with the important matters at the expense of the less important ones? Will he be ready to work hard for the sake of his children's future so that they can escape the vicious circle of poverty through education? The father is required to sacrifice himself for the sake of his children. This is not easy and not self-evident. If Samir works on a building site, his family's economic plight will be eased. Perhaps he can study and work at the same time. But here the Quran intervenes with its full moral force and tells the father not to deny his children what he can give them, because it is his sacred duty as a father to help his children to advance in life and succeed. Moreover, it is the father's duty to aspire to a situation where his children succeed more than he did. Regrettably, in many families this is not self-evident and some parents do not want their children to surpass them.

7. Is it a father's duty to respect his children and nurture them?

{ قُلْ تَعَالَوْاْ أَتْلُ مَا حَرَّمَ رَبُّكُمْ عَلَيْكُمْ أَلاَّ تُشْرِكُواْ بِهِ شَيْئاً وَبِالْوَالِدَيْنِ إِحْسَاناً وَلاَ
تَقْتُلُواْ أَوْلاَدَكُم مِّنْ إمْلاَقٍ نَّحْنُ نَرْزُقُكُمْ وَإِيَّاهُمْ وَلاَ تَقْرَبُواْ الْفَوَاحِشَ مَا ظَهَرَ مِنْهَا
وَمَا بَطَنَ وَلاَ تَقْتُلُواْ النَّفْسَ الَّتِي حَرَّمَ اللّهُ إِلاَّ بِالْحَقِّ ذَلِكُمْ وَصَّاكُمْ بِهِ لَعَلَّكُمْ تَعْقِلُونَ
(الأنعام: 151) }

Say: "Come, I will rehearse what Allah hath (really) prohibited you from": join not anything as equal with Him; be good to your parents; **kill not your children on a plea of want - We provide sustenance for you and for them** - come not nigh to shameful deeds, whether open or secret; take not life, which Allah hath made sacred, except by way of justice and law: thus doth He command you, that ye may learn wisdom. (Livestock: 151)

Maryam is in the tenth grade and her teacher asked the guidance counselor to intervene. He told her that recently Maryam had become a loner, staying apart from all the other children and no longer participating in lessons. "She has never acted like that in the past and I think she has a problem," he said. The counselor called Maryam into her office that same day and told her what the teacher had said. Maryam agreed that she had changed. "It's nothing to do with school and there's no reason to talk about it at all," she said. The counselor explained to her that it was her task to help pupils outside school as well and promised to help her. "My problem is with my parents. I'm in the tenth grade, a teenager, but I feel that my parents don't respect me and don't take an interest in me. They don't care what I think or feel. When I talk, they don't listen even if I have important things to say. It depresses me and makes me feel that I'm worthless and I have no place at home. And they don't let me buy anything. When I ask for something little, something personal, they always say: 'We give you everything and you lack for nothing.' I'm tired of that life; they don't respect me and don't give me even the most basic things. My friends' parents behave very differently."

The counselor reassured Maryam and promised to deal with the problem.

The next day she invited Maryam's parents for a talk and told them about their daughter's complaints and how this was affected her emotionally and interfering with her studies. "I want to read you an important verse from the Quran," she said, and read them Verse 151 from Surah 6. **"Kill not your children on a plea of want - We provide sustenance for you and for them."**

"Does Allah provide sustenance for you?" she asked the parents and they assented. "But what Allah gives you is intended for all your children. Why should Maryam suffer the fear of poverty?!" She needed to add nothing more. The parents understood the message.

Explanation: we do not know why Maryam's parents behave like that. Perhaps they treat all their children in the same way. Perhaps they, like many parents, discriminate against her when compared to their sons. Now that she is a teenager, they feel that they need to suppress her even more so that she will not forget her role as a woman. They are simply uninterested in her and do not even buy her little personal items. Sometimes we hear from gynecologists who perform ultrasound scans on pregnant women that in some cases the sex of the fetus is more important to the parents than its health. These parents regard a female fetus as flawed and of no advantage to the family. Needless to say, this attitude does not stem from the Quran. The counselor was right to find the appropriate Quran verse which commands parents to nurture and respect their children, not only to provide all their needs but also to ensure that they feel wanted and do not suffer privation.

8. Is it permissible to discriminate against children, to give boys preferential treatment?

{ وَلاَ تَقْرَبُواْ مَالَ الْيَتِيمِ إِلاَّ بِالَّتِي هِيَ أَحْسَنُ حَتَّى يَبْلُغَ أَشُدَّهُ وَأَوْفُواْ الْكَيْلَ وَالْمِيزَانَ بِالْقِسْطِ لاَ نُكَلِّفُ نَفْساً إِلاَّ وُسْعَهَا وَإِذَا قُلْتُمْ فَاعْدِلُواْ وَلَوْ كَانَ ذَا قُرْبَى وَبِعَهْدِ اللّهِ أَوْفُواْ ذَلِكُمْ وَصَّاكُم بِهِ لَعَلَّكُمْ تَذَكَّرُونَ } (الأنعام: 152)

And come not nigh to the orphan's property, except to improve it, until he attains the age of full strength; give measure and weight with (full) justice; no burden do We place on any soul, but that which it can bear, **whenever ye speak, speak justly, even if a near relative is concerned;** and fulfill the Covenant of Allah: thus doth He command you, that ye may remember (Livestock: 152)

The Karim family has five children. The parents naturally love them all but Samar always feels that they discriminate against her. Her father contacts her oldest brother every day, asks him how he is and if he needs anything. He does the same with the oldest girl, asks how her examinations are proceeding and if she needs anything. He plays all kinds of games with her two younger brothers. But he is not interested in Samar. She tries to be a good girl and performs all the hard chores at home. But when her brothers make a mistake, their father forgives them easily and when she errs, he is angry and punishes her. Recently her brothers have begun treating Samar as her father does and she is very miserable. She told her class teacher how she feels and the teacher asked her father to come and see her to talk about Samar and how his conduct is hurtful for her. Then she opened the Quran and showed him Surah 6, Verse 152: **"Whenever ye speak, speak justly, even if a near relative is concerned."** "Are you treating Samar justly?" she asked him. He admitted that he was depriving his daughter. The teacher explained that the verse also refers to just treatment among children, and how important it is for a parent to treat children equally without discrimination between the sexes. "And perhaps because Samar is a girl," she added, "you must be sevenfold careful not to deprive her."

Explanation: This important Quran verse encourages us all to be more objective with regard to our families. Parents must not discriminate against their daughters and favor their sons in any way. In many families the boys receive preferential treatment. But it was with good reason that the Quran commands us to act with justice and equality. A daughter like Samar who grows up with a sense of deprivation will find it hard in the future to function as a good mother. In her maternal role, she needs to feel secure and to transmit this security to her children. A mother who is weak and has internalized a sense of inferiority will raise children who are also weak and feel inferior. Children imbibe from their mothers not only milk but also a sense of security. Moreover, such a mother will find it hard to make a contribution to the society in which she lives, to initiate and to take responsibility. She will always prefer the passive stance and allow her husband to undertake all the difficult tasks because she has never been encouraged or trusted or told how wonderful she is. She will be dependent on her husband but will not be a helpmate for him and assist him, her family and her society.

9. Are parents who neglect their children harming themselves?

{ وَقَطَّعْنَاهُمُ اثْنَتَيْ عَشْرَةَ أَسْبَاطاً أُمَماً وَأَوْحَيْنَا إِلَى مُوسَى إِذِ اسْتَسْقَاهُ قَوْمُهُ أَنِ
اضْرِب بِّعَصَاكَ الْحَجَرَ فَانبَجَسَتْ مِنْهُ اثْنَتَا عَشْرَةَ عَيْناً قَدْ عَلِمَ كُلُّ أُنَاسٍ مَّشْرَبَهُمْ
وَظَلَّلْنَا عَلَيْهِمُ الْغَمَامَ وَأَنزَلْنَا عَلَيْهِمُ الْمَنَّ وَالسَّلْوَى كُلُواْ مِن طَيِّبَاتِ مَا رَزَقْنَاكُمْ وَمَا
ظَلَمُونَا وَلَكِن كَانُواْ أَنفُسَهُمْ يَظْلِمُونَ (الأعراف: 160)

We divided them into twelve Tribes or nations. We directed Musa by inspiration, when his (thirsty) people asked him for water: "Strike the rock with thy staff": out of it there gushed forth twelve springs: each group knew its own place for water. We gave them the shade of clouds, and sent down to them manna and quails, (saying): "Eat of the good things We have provided for you": (but they rebelled. **To Us they did no harm, but they harmed their own souls.** (The Elevations: 160)

Yusuf, who is in the fourth grade, is a wild boy with many disciplinary problems. He has been prescribed Ritalin to calm him and enable him to concentrate and listen. His parents do not check that he takes his medication regularly before going to school. This means that when he tires, at about noontime, he begins to behave wildly and hit out at his classmates. His class teacher is new to the school and has no experience of dealing with children with his problem. She sends him to the library where he continues to act violently and disturbs the other children. The librarian has asked the teacher not to send him again.

Facing with a dilemma, the teacher talked to the counselor, who summoned Yusuf's parents for a talk. She detailed her plan to improve Yusuf's conduct and help him find his place in the class. "But first, you must take responsibility for your child," she said. "If you don't, nobody will do so for you." In order to emphasize her message, she read them the verse: **"To Us they did no harm, but they harmed their own souls"** and added, "By not taking responsibility for Yusuf's conduct you are harming yourselves first and foremost because he is your child. The school also suffers, but above all you are the sufferers." The parents promised, in the first instance, to ensure that their son took his medication regularly, and then to collaborate with the counselor in a plan to help their son.

Explanation: Many parents tend to blame the school and the teachers for their children's problems rather than themselves. It is naturally harder to take responsibility than to blame others, but it is more effective. Until the parents understand that it is their responsibility to care for their son and in this case to make sure that he takes his medication, he will not improve and they, and he too of course, will pay the price. Some parents bring their child to kindergarten or school in the hope that he or she will be reformed there and receive everything his parents do not provide. Yusuf's parents must collaborate fully with the teacher and the counselor and take an interest in what happens to their son as school. It is not feasible for parents not to know what happens to a child at school. The problems begin at home and the parents, with the aid of the school team, can help the child. Hence, a good and non-recriminatory relationship between the school and the parent is very important. The counselor was right to remind the parents that, first and foremost, they were causing harm to themselves and to their son and needed to cooperate with the school.

10. What can we say to an abusive parent?

{ أَلَمْ يَعْلَمُواْ أَنَّ اللّهَ هُوَ يَقْبَلُ التَّوْبَةَ عَنْ عِبَادِهِ وَيَأْخُذُ الصَّدَقَاتِ وَأَنَّ اللّهَ هُوَ التَّوَّابُ الرَّحِيمُ} (التوبة: 104)

Know they not that Allah doth accept repentance from His votaries and receives their gifts of charity, and that Allah is verily He, the Oft-Returning, Most Merciful? (The Repentance: 104)

Sami is a quiet boy, who always sits at the back of the class and during recess stands in a corner. Recently his grades have dropped, he doesn't prepare his homework and does not participate in lessons. Today the teacher noticed that Sami is wearing a long-sleeved shirt even though it is a hot, dry day. She called him during recess and asked him to sit beside her. He looked frightened, sat down quietly and did not raise his glance.

Teacher: Aren't you hot?
Sami (glancing at himself): No.
Teacher: What's the matter?
Sami: Nothing.
Teacher: Nothing? Something is troubling you.
Sami: No, no, no (looks scared).

Teacher: Sami, I'm your teacher. I can see that something is troubling you. I only want to help you and see you smile, play and have fun with your friends.

Sami: I'm OK.

Teacher: The why don't you play with them?

Teacher: I don't feel like it.

Teacher: Every day you don't feel like it.

Sami: Yes, it's better like that… (starts crying). Why do you care about me? I'm not worth it. Nobody asks about me, I'm worth nothing, nobody loves me…

Teacher: I like you. You are a good, quiet pupil and I care about you.

Sami: But I'm not worth anything…My father always says so…

Teacher: (understands the secret of Sami's solitude, and why he is wearing a long-sleeved shirt). Can you roll up your sleeves a little?

Quietly Sami rolls up his sleeve as his tears fall. The teacher straightens the sleeves and is deeply upset. He runs out to the courtyard and she goes to the counselor's office.

The next day Sami's father is invited to the counselor's office.

Counselor: I just want you to look out the window. I want to show you something lost. (The father looks out and sees children running and playing happily). Do you see all the smiles outside?

Father: Yes, but why did you want to see me?

Counselor: Tell me first where your son's smile is?

Father: (looking out). I can't see him…

Counselor: You can't see him because he isn't there.

Father: But my son came to school today. He isn't absent.

Counselor: I'm referring to his smile, he didn't bring it.

Father: (looking at her quietly…) But where is he?

Counselor: Look in the corner at the end of the courtyard. He is a long way away which is why you can't see him.

Father: (looks at Sami and sees him sitting quietly alone). What's wrong with him? Why did you call me?

Counselor: He's lost his smile.

Father: What do you mean?

Counselor: Your child is suffering; he is alone because of your abuse. Because of the blows and the hurt you are inflicting on him – physical and mental. Because of you he is lost. Look at his classmates living their childhood and how you've thrown his childhood into the garbage can. I want to read you a verse from the Quran and please think about it: **"Know they not that Allah doth accept repentance from His votaries and receives their gifts of charity, and that Allah is verily He, the Oft-Returning, Most Merciful?"** "It is never too late to mend your ways," she told him. "You can repent and give your son back his smile. You can compensate him for the suffering you caused him."

Father: (sunk in thought): Thank you. You have enlightened me. You have given me back that child's father.

The father hastens out. The counselor looks out of the window and sees him going over to the corner where his son sits alone, but now she sees not the pain of a solitary child but the joy of a father and son who are reunited. The corner of pain has become a corner of renewed joy and the lost smile has been found.

Explanation: There are numerous cases in this world of battered children who lose all joy in life and childhood pleasures and live in a state of constant mourning and suffering. A child should be allowed to be a child, to enjoy his childhood, play and blossom. Childhood begins with birth. From the first a father must treat his son and daughter properly and not only when they are older. The parent should place the child at the center and view the world through his eyes, because the Quran commands him to nurture the child and respect him. Only a child who is given love by both parents can grow into an adult able to bestow love on his own family and surroundings and become a partner n a healthy society. Sami is a battered child. His father apparently beats him frequently and makes him feel that he has no value and is unworthy. That is the fate of battered children. The counselor was right not to reprimand the father or threaten him because to punish him as he punishes his child would not apparently prove effective. She did the reverse, told him that Allah loves those who repent. She addressed him with warmth and love and served as a model of how to treat others. Now we can only hope that Sami's father will learn from the counselor's generous conduct and give his son respect and meaningfulness. However, today the law requires the counselor or anyone who uncovers abuse of children to report it to the police, because the state authorities hold that it is their duty to protect children. In such cases the father could be punished severely.

6 | On Flattery, Boastfulness and Other Negative Qualities

1. What can we say to someone who is dazzled by false appearances?

{ وَمِنَ النَّاسِ مَن يُعْجِبُكَ قَوْلُهُ فِي الْحَيَاةِ الدُّنْيَا وَيُشْهِدُ اللّهَ عَلَى مَا فِي قَلْبِهِ وَهُوَ أَلَدُّ الْخِصَامِ * وَإِذَا تَوَلَّى سَعَى فِي الأَرْضِ لِيُفْسِدَ فِيِهَا وَيُهْلِكَ الْحَرْثَ وَالنَّسْلَ وَاللّهُ لاَ يُحِبُّ الفَسَادَ } (البقرة: 204-205)

There is the type of man whose speech about this world's life may dazzle thee, and he calls Allah to witness about what is in his heart; yet is he the most contentious of enemies. When he turns his back, his aim everywhere is to spread mischief through the earth and destroy crops and cattle. But Allah loveth not mischief. (The Cow: 204-205)

One day the guidance counselor came into the principal's office and asked him if he could devote fifteen minutes to her because she wanted to talk to him. "Yes, of course, please come in and let me hear what you have to say", he replied. The counselor said that this time she did not want to talk about the problems of pupils or general school issues. "I've come to talk about something to do with you", she said. The principal was surprised. "With me?" he asked. "Don't be alarmed, I want to talk to you about the chemistry teacher. I can see that she impresses you, but I want to tell you that a number of teachers and pupils have complained to me about her and her teaching methods. They say she is arrogant, that she does nothing at all but tries to impress you. So, every time she sees you, she starts working busily and tidying up, but when you are not around, she sits in the teachers' lounge and drinks coffee". The counselor added: "I'm telling you this because I want to warm you against people who make too good an impression so that you can know which of the teachers really works and which one doesn't". To make her meaning clear, the counselor read him Verses 204-205 from Surah 2: **"There is the type of man whose speech about this world's life may dazzle thee, and he calls Allah to witness about what is in his heart; yet is he the most contentious of enemies. When he turns his back, his aim everywhere is to spread mischief through the earth and destroy crops and cattle. But Allah loveth not mischief".**

Explanation: each of us may be dazzled from time to time by people who create a false impression. At such times it is difficult to exercise caution. For example, we all enjoy being complimented but the compliment may be insincere. Sometimes an individual can charm us by his appearance, his personality or his eloquence. This may be the case with the chemistry teacher and the principal. She knows what he wants to see and is, but behind his back she acts differently. In this case the counselor reminded the principal that the Quran too cautions us against such people and God does not love their conduct. Thus, it teaches us to rely on ourselves and not to be deceived by false impressions.

2. How can we overcome envy?

{ وَلاَ تَتَمَنَّوْاْ مَا فَضَّلَ اللّهُ بِهِ بَعْضَكُمْ عَلَى بَعْضٍ لِّلرِّجَالِ نَصِيبٌ مِّمَّا اكْتَسَبُواْ وَلِلنِّسَاء نَصِيبٌ مِّمَّا اكْتَسَبْنَ وَاسْأَلُواْ اللّهَ مِن فَضْلِهِ إِنَّ اللّهَ كَانَ بِكُلِّ شَيْءٍ عَلِيمًا} (النساء: 32)

And in no wise covet those things in which Allah hath bestowed His gifts more freely on some of you than on others: to men is allotted what they earn, and to women what they earn:

but ask Allah of His bounty. For Allah hath full knowledge of all things. (Women: 32)

Sali, who is in the third grade, is always asking her parents why this friend has nicer clothes than she does, why that friend has more toys, why a third friend was taken out by her parents and she wasn't. What began as envy became a habit, and in this way Sali wheedles her parents into giving her gifts.

Sali's parents want to help their daughter to overcome her obsessive envy which is troubling to her and to everyone around her. At first, they explained that there would always be some boys and girls who had something she didn't have and that she was not being deprived. But Sali continued to pester them. Eventually they talked to the school counselor who called Sali to her office and read her a verse: **"And in no wise covet those things in which Allah hath bestowed His gifts more freely on some of you than on others".** "Yes, Sali," said the counselor. "Some people have more than you but God has exhorted us not to be envious of those who have more, because there is no end to envy. There will always be those who have more than you and those who have less", she added. Sali listened and mumbled the verse to herself as if trying to absorb the message.

Explanation: envy is a fierce and destructive emotion not only among children, but also among adults. How often do we envy someone who has more than we do? This emotion is natural but we must learn to overcome it. Sali, however, is incapable of overcoming her envy. She looks at her friends and feels deprived. Children who feel more confident at home are less envious while children who lack basic confidence tend to be more envious. We must remember that a child who is very envious is telling us, in his own way, that he wants us to give him more attention because he feels that something is lacking. The Quran deals with this issue and commands us not to be envious of those who have more because that is the will of God. And this being so, Sali can only accept this and remember that it is also the will of God that she should have more than some of her friends.

3. What does God think about braggarts?

﴿ وَاعْبُدُواْ اللّهَ وَلاَ تُشْرِكُواْ بِهِ شَيْئًا وَبِالْوَالِدَيْنِ إِحْسَانًا وَبِذِي الْقُرْبَى وَالْيَتَامَى وَالْمَسَاكِينِ وَالْجَارِ ذِي الْقُرْبَى وَالْجَارِ الْجُنُبِ وَالصَّاحِبِ بِالجَنبِ وَابْنِ السَّبِيلِ وَمَا مَلَكَتْ أَيْمَانُكُمْ إِنَّ اللّهَ لاَ يُحِبُّ مَن كَانَ مُخْتَالاً فَخُورًا ﴾ (النساء: 36)

Serve Allah, and join not any partners with Him; and do good to parents, kinsfolk, orphans, those in need, neighbours who are near neighbours who are strangers, the companion by your side, the way-farer (ye meet) and what your right hands possess: **for Allah loveth not the arrogant, the vainglorious.** (Women: 36)

Jamila, who is in the ninth grade, is a beautiful girl. Her teachers and classmates say that she has a special kind of beauty. Her father is a teacher at the school. One of her classmates is Sukheina, a fat, unkempt girl who is both clever and well-mannered. One day the sports teachers asked the girls to split up into two groups to compete in a ball game. When Sukheina tried to join Jamila's group, Jamila said: "Go to the other group. With you we can only lose the game. You're fat and you're not in shape". Sukheina replied without hesitation: "Who do you think you are?" Jamila replied: "I'm better looking than you and my father is a teacher here. Be careful!"

Sukheina left the lesson in tears and went to her class teacher. The teacher talked to Sukheina about her beautiful qualities and her winning personality and told her not to be upset by Jamila or to be afraid of her. Then she invited Jamila to join in the conversation. She opened the Quran and read out: **"for**

Allah loveth not the arrogant, the vainglorious". "What do you understand from this verse?" she asked Jamila, who replied submissively that Allah wants us to respect others and be humble.

Explanation: Many adults enjoy boasting and so do some children. When someone boasts and tells everyone how wonderful he is, he is actually telling them that they are not as good as he, and hence he may hurt their feelings. It is said that those who are really outstanding do not need to boast because this fact is generally known. Bragging often attests to lack of self-confidence, since otherwise, why boast? The Quran is saying to Jamila: "You received your beauty as a gift from Allah but Allah can also give others gifts and take away your gift", and it is recommending that she be humbler and avoid offending her classmates. The Quran has no equal in teaching modesty and consideration for others and often quotation of a single verse can suffice to help a child to exercise self-control and act more humbly.

4. **What can we say to a boy who does not take study seriously and fails his exams?**

{ إِنَّ اللّهَ لاَ يَظْلِمُ النَّاسَ شَيْئاً وَلَـكِنَّ النَّاسَ أَنفُسَهُمْ يَظْلِمُونَ } (يونس: 44)

Verily Allah will not deal unjustly with man in aught: It is man that wrongs his own soul. (Jonah: 44)

Nadi, who is in the eighth grade, claimed that the study material was easy and did not require effort. When his mother urged him to study for an exam, he told her he could make good grades without working. Towards the end of the year, Nadi made a wager with his friend Muhammed that he could achieve a grade of more than 90 without studying at all. Muhammed warned him that he was taking a risk, but Nadi replied: "Forget it, who needs to study!"

Nadi took the exam without having prepared. When the teacher returned the exam papers, Nadi was shocked. "Something's wrong, I think there must be a mistake", he said. He went up to the teacher and said angrily: What happened? I don't deserve to fail". The teacher replied that he had received the grade he deserved. "You've done almost no work this year", he added.

Nadi was depressed. Am I really so worthless, he asked himself. He went to the counselor and told her that God did not love him. She realized that she needed to work with him and to persuade him to accept responsibility for his actions instead of blaming God. She opened the Quran at Surah 10, Verse 44 and read out to him: **"Verily Allah will not deal unjustly with man in aught: It is man that wrongs his own soul".** "What do you think of that verse?" she asked him. Nadi pondered and replied: "Yes, I'm to blame and not God. Perhaps God loves me and wants me to invest more in my studies".

Explanation: It is interesting to see the rapid change in Nadi from contempt for study and feelings of superiority to a sense that he is worthless. Such transitions frequently occur in children who inflate their importance and then the bubble bursts; they fly high and then they crash. Nadi, who failed, is initially angry at the teacher, then at God. The main thing is not to take responsibility himself. And here the Quran restores his sense of responsibility which is the sole way of persuading him to improve. It tells us again and again not to cast responsibility on others because nothing good will come of it. It is not easy to take responsibility and it may even be difficult and painful but there is no other way. Only those who accept responsibility will try to improve matters; others do not try and do not make progress.

5. How should one accept success and failure?

{ إِلاَّ الَّذِينَ صَبَرُواْ وَعَمِلُواْ الصَّالِحَاتِ أُوْلَئِكَ لَهُم مَّغْفِرَةٌ وَأَجْرٌ كَبِيرٌ } (هود: 11)

But if We give him a taste of (Our) favours after adversity hath touched him, he is sure to say, "All evil has departed from me:" Behold! he falls into exultation and pride. Not so do those who show patience and constancy, and work righteousness; for them is forgiveness (of sins) and a great reward. (Hud: 11).

Muhammed decided to improve his grades when he entered the seventh grade. Before every examination in mathematics he studied hard and his grades were on the rise: 75, 80, 89, 92. Muhammed was very satisfied and persuaded himself that he knew the material well and no longer needed to work so hard. Towards the end of the year, the teacher scheduled a summarizing test and explained that this time they would need work hard to succeed. But Muhammed was convinced that he knew the material inside out and that he would have no problems.

When the exams were returned, Muhammed was stunned. He had failed. "It's not fair, I really studied hard", he claimed, and asked the teacher for a second chance. The teacher agreed to give Muhammed and several other pupils a repeat exam. This time he studied hard, but when the exams were returned, he discovered that he had failed again. He was depressed and said: "God is taking revenge on me. What have I done to Him?"

Muhammed lost his newly-gained. He thought he would have to study all the material again from the beginning and didn't know how to do it. He appealed to the school counselor who decided to restore his self-confidence but not to an excessive degree. She encouraged him to continue practicing mathematics and explained that not every exam is a precise reflection of the effort invested. "It happens", she said. "Sometimes we study for an exam but we don't succeed. But if we don't study at all, we are certain to fail. In your case, Muhammed, there is an appropriate verse which says: **"But if We give him a taste of (Our) favours after adversity hath touched him, he is sure to say, "All evil has departed from me:" Behold! he falls into exultation and pride. Not so do those who show patience and constancy, and work righteousness; for them is forgiveness (of sins) and a great reward".** "No, no", Muhammed replied. "I've learned something from this and from now on, even when I succeed, I won't boast or think that there's no need to study any more. I've learned something important in life. From now on, I will be one of those who show patience and constancy".

Explanation: it is only human nature. When we succeed time and time again, we may become arrogant and over-confidence and forget the taste of previous failures. This is true in various spheres and people who have reached high positions often are incapable of understanding the difficulties of others (for example, a parent who doesn't understand his children or a teacher who does not understand his pupils' problems). These people are actually not connected to themselves and are liable to encounter crushing failure one day. They are distancing themselves from the less confident elements that each individual contains within himself, denying their existence and are liable to fall. This is Muhammed's story. It is the counselor's task to restore his self-confidence but in balanced fashion. He needs to be aware that in order to succeed he needs to work hard, that he should not be afraid of failure. On the other hand, he should not fall into the trap of boastfulness when he succeeds, and should maintain the balance between success and failure and be aware that both linger at his doorstep. The Quran teaches us that human beings display two kinds of attitudes to success - disproportionate and balanced. Let us hope that Muhammed will belong to the second category.

6. What can we say to someone who helped his friend and was not thanked?

{ وَاصْبِرْ فَإِنَّ اللّهَ لاَ يُضِيعُ أَجْرَ الْمُحْسِنِينَ } (هود: 115)

And be steadfast in patience; for verily Allah will not suffer the reward of the righteous to perish. (Hud: 115)

Aisha is in the fifth grade in the Shalom school. She is an outstanding pupil because, as everyone knows, her sister Amira sits with her for two hours every day and coaches her. The family are relatively poor.

One day the teacher asked Aisha: "How come you are such a good student despite the difficulties in your home?" Aisha replied that it was all thanks to her own efforts, because she worked very hard. The teacher knew Amira because she had taught her as well. Because of the family's financial straits, Amira had dropped out of school and begun to work to help her parents raise her siblings. One day, Amira visited Aisha at school and met the teacher. Amira asked her about her sister and told the teacher what she thought everyone knew, that she spent two hours every day helping Aisha. The teacher replied: "Yes…yes, certainly, she succeeds because of your help". Amira asked if anyone had said something different and the teacher said that Aisha had told her how Amira helped her.

The teacher decided to summon Aisha for a talk. She started out by saying that she wanted her to give her sister, Amira as a gift a verse from the Quran: "**And be steadfast in patience; for verily Allah will not suffer the reward of the righteous to perish.**" Aisha realized that the teacher had talked to Amira, and now she apologized for having tried to deprive her sister of her due. Then the teacher suggested that she thank her sister for all her help over the years.

Explanation: life is full of examples of situations where someone helps another and is not thanked. Not everyone is capable of saying thank you. Acknowledgement of help demands a degree of maturity and renunciation of the illusion that one has achieved everything alone. Aisha wants to persuade everyone that she is an outstanding pupil because of her own talents and that her sister has no part in her success. Is this a form of boastfulness? Perhaps. But the Quran commands us to behave humbly and to tell the truth, particularly in light of the fact that Aisha's sister gave up her studies in order to help her siblings. Aisha has succeeded thanks to the sacrifice made by her sister on behalf of the family.

7. What can we say to a girl who is ashamed of her father?

{ وَقَضَى رَبُّكَ أَلاَّ تَعْبُدُواْ إِلاَّ إِيَّاهُ وَبِالْوَالِدَيْنِ إِحْسَاناً إِمَّا يَبْلُغَنَّ عِندَكَ الْكِبَرَ أَحَدُهُمَا أَوْ كِلاَهُمَا فَلاَ تَقُل لَّهُمَا أُفٍّ وَلاَ تَنْهَرْهُمَا وَقُل لَّهُمَا قَوْلاً كَرِيماً * وَاخْفِضْ لَهُمَا جَنَاحَ الذُّلِّ مِنَ الرَّحْمَةِ وَقُل رَّبِّ ارْحَمْهُمَا كَمَا رَبَّيَانِي صَغِيراً } (الإسراء:24-23)

Thy Lord hath decreed that ye worship none but Him, and that ye be kind to parents. Whether one or both of them attain old age in thy life, say not to them a word of contempt, nor repel them, but address them in terms of honour. And, out of kindness, lower to them the wing of humility, and say: "My Lord! bestow on them thy Mercy even as they cherished me in childhood. (The Night Journey: 23-24)

Maryam is in the fifth grade and her father is the school janitor. Whenever she sees him at school, she is ashamed and says: "Ach….it bothers me that you're my father!" Her father feels humiliated because she is shaming him before the whole school and so he tries not to encounter her at school. One day her friend Yasmin was present when Maryam met her father. She was very surprised and said to Maryam: "Apparently you haven't heard what God commanded us in Surah 17, Verses 23-24: **"Thy Lord hath decreed that ye worship none but Him, and that ye be kind to parents. Whether one or both of them attain old age in thy life, say not to them a word of contempt, nor repel them, but address them in terms of honour. And, out of kindness, lower to them the wing of humility, and say: "My Lord! bestow on them thy Mercy even as they cherished me in childhood."**

"Maryam", her friend added, in this life "it is very important to be clever, but it is more important to respect one's parents. You know, I have only one parent, my mother and I envy you and the others who have two parents. Ask yourself, why does your father work all day from morning to night? For whose sake? You must do something for your father before it is too late".

Explanation: many children of various ages are ashamed of their parents. Sometimes they are the children of emigrants whose parents are unfamiliar with the country's culture while the children speak the language fluently; sometimes the parents are uneducated and their children have more education; sometimes the parents' occupations are not considered prestigious and so forth. There is no shortage of reasons why children feel ashamed of their parents. But a child must remember that he would not have reached his present status, a place where he feels superior to his parent, without that parent's help. Moreover, causing pain to a parent can be compared to cutting off the branch on which you are perched. Your parent is your connection with your own self and your family and without a past there can be no future. Thus, the command to respect parents exists in every culture and has profound psychological reasons. This does not mean that a parent is always right, or that a child must obey blindly at every age and on every matter. But the Quran exhorts him always to treat a parent with respect.

8. What can we say to someone who feels self-important?

{ وَلاَ تَمْشِ فِي الأَرْضِ مَرَحاً إِنَّكَ لَن تَخْرِقَ الأَرْضَ وَلَن تَبْلُغَ الْجِبَالَ طُولاً * كُلُّ ذَلِكَ كَانَ سَيِّئُهُ عِنْدَ رَبِّكَ مَكْرُوهاً } (الإسراء: 37-38)

Nor walk on the earth with insolence: for thou canst not rend the earth asunder, nor reach the mountains in height. Of all such things the evil is hateful in the sight of thy Lord. (The Night Journey: 37-38)

Yasmin, who is in the seventh grade, failed several times to do her mathematics homework. The teacher sent a message to her parents and briefed them and also explained that her failure could affect her achievements in that subject.

The next day, during recess, her father drove to the school, parked his car opposite the school gate, descended and stalked in. He passed the school guard without looking at him and without greeting him. The guard heard a loud voice ask: "Where is the principal's room?" The guard directed him and he mumbled thanks without glancing in the guard's direction.

Then he strode in, straight to the principal's room and flung the door open without knocking. "Why did you send me a letter about my daughter? She is an outstanding pupil and lacks for nothing. How does that teacher dare to judge her? I can transfer my daughter to a prestigious school, I've no shortage of money and I can do it. This is my daughter you are dealing with!" Then he boasted the principal about his business affairs and how successful he was.

The principal explained to him that the teacher's intentions had been good, namely to enable him to share in his daughter's schooling and to help. There was no intention to suggest that his daughter lacked anything or was not worthy. "But even if we are the most powerful people in the world", the principal continued, "there are things to which we are committed and they include a pleasant attitude towards others and good education". He opened the Quran and read out to the father: **"Nor walk on the earth with insolence: for thou canst not rend the earth asunder, nor reach the mountains in height. Of all such things the evil is hateful in the sight of thy Lord".** "You must treat the teacher well and other people too", he explained politely, "because they are doing their job well and have the pupils' interests at heart".

Explanation: there are some people who consider it demeaning to be like everyone else. Yasmin's father demands a special status for himself and for his daughter. He refuses to permit his daughter to be treated like any other pupil who doesn't prepare homework. His arrogant attitude towards others is liable to offend them. He also attributes nefarious intentions to the teacher although her intentions are good. The principal was right not to take him seriously and not to be offended. The Quran commands us not to be insolent, to act with humility, however strong we are. Thus, it promotes equality, this time in the emotional sphere.

9. What can we say to someone who is afraid to report for fear of revenge?

{ ذَلِكَ وَمَنْ عَاقَبَ بِمِثْلِ مَا عُوقِبَ بِهِ ثُمَّ بُغِيَ عَلَيْهِ لَيَنصُرَنَّهُ اللَّهُ إِنَّ اللَّهَ لَعَفُوٌّ غَفُورٌ}
(الحج: 60)

That (is so). **And if one has retaliated to no greater extent than the injury he received, and is again set upon inordinately, Allah will help him:** for Allah is One that blots out (sins) and forgives (again and again). (The Pilgrimage: 60)

Nuara, who is in the fifth grade, is the best pupil in her class. In the past year, the girls in her class have been boycotting her. The story began when Samah asked her if she could copy from her in the arithmetic exam and Nuara was afraid to consent.

After the exam, Samah went over to her and told her that she was a liar and that she had refused not because she was afraid but because she wanted to be the only one who passed the exam. The incident was repeated after the science exam. Nuara explained to Samah that she was afraid she would be caught and Samah replied that she was lying and would regret it.

The incident was repeated with other girls and they all began to boycott her until she was left alone and friendless in class. When she tried to approach them, they spurned her. Then they tore up some of her notebooks, trampled on her book-bag as if by accident, and broke her pencil, again as if unintentionally. Nuara contemplated telling the teacher but knew that then she would be accused of telling tales and the revenge would be even harsher. She began to suffer from dizzy spells and headaches. She had not lied to them, she told herself; she was really afraid of letting them copy and she would not mind if there were other outstanding pupils in the class apart from her.

Nuara decided to confide in her mother and told her about the harassment and the mockery and asked her mother to transfer her to another school. Her mother hugged her and said that to move to another school was no solution; it would be evading the problem. They would talk to the teacher, she said, and if that didn't help, they would talk to the principal. "But the girls will take revenge on me", said Nuara. "**And if one has retaliated to no greater extent than the injury he received, and is again set upon inordinately, Allah will help him**", her mother quoted to her from the Quran. "Do you know that verse?" she asked. Nuara, who was an excellent pupil, replied without hesitation that it was Verse 60 from Surah 22. "If we talk to the teacher, we will be retaliating", her mother continued, "and if the girls harass you again, Allah will help you".

Nuara and her mother talked to the teacher who devoted an entire lesson to a class discussion about the unjust boycott. Instead of admiring her for her achievements, her friends were envious and had been trying to exploit her. The teacher again quoted the verse: "**And if one has retaliated to no greater extent than the injury he received, and is again set upon inordinately, Allah will help him**" in order to explain to the girls that Nuara had not told tales against them by confiding in her mother but had been retaliating and so they should all apologize to her. The teacher added that she would have been even happier if Nuara had refused to allow them to copy not for fear of being caught but because she was honest and knew that it was wrong. After the lesson, the girls went over to Nuara one by one and apologized.

Explanation: Nuara did not retaliate and did not try to injure them out of envy and a desire for revenge, as they did to her. She simply wanted to defend herself. The Quran encourages people to retaliate and tells us that if someone retaliates against another who then tries again to injure him, Allah will help him. This is logical because it is permissible to defend oneself. Why should Nuara become a victim? Her mother did well to reassure her by quoting this verse and the teacher did well in explaining to the girls what Nuara's rights were, again by means of that same verse. But the Quran teaches us another important message: Nuara should not be afraid to retaliate, or be afraid of the girls and she did well to report to her mother, her teacher and anyone who could help. Because if they tried to injure her, Allah would help her.

10. What can we say to an arrogant boy?

﴿ وَكَمْ أَهْلَكْنَا مِن قَرْيَةٍ بَطِرَتْ مَعِيشَتَهَا فَتِلْكَ مَسَاكِنُهُمْ لَمْ تُسْكَن مِّن بَعْدِهِمْ إِلَّا قَلِيلاً وَكُنَّا نَحْنُ الْوَارِثِينَ ﴾ (القصص: 58)

And how many populations We destroyed, which exulted in their life (of ease and plenty)! now those habitations of

theirs, after them, are deserted,- All but a (miserable) few! and We are their heirs! (The Stories: 58)

Ahmed, who is in the fourth grade, brags regularly to his classmates that his father buys him all kinds of expensive items. "My father is rich", he tells them and shows them his new clothes and his shiny new shoes. "We have an amazing house, not like yours", he adds. Recently he has begun saying that he can do whatever he likes in class and that he is better than all the other pupils. One day the teacher heard him mocking one of the other boys whose father was a physical laborer and saying: "Look at my father; he has a luxurious office and he gives me one hundred shekel a week to buy whatever I like. Why isn't your father like mine?" She summoned Ahmed for a talk, opened the Quran and read him the verse: **"And how many populations We destroyed, which exulted in their life (of ease and plenty)! now those habitations of theirs, after them, are deserted,- All but a (miserable) few! and We are their heirs!"** She explained to Ahmed that he too "exulted in a life of ease and plenty" and that if Allah chose, He could take it all away and give it to his friend. When Ahmed heard that, he was very alarmed and began to cry. The teacher soothed him and explained that since he had acted unknowingly, Allah would forgive him. But now he must change his behavior. From that day on Ahmed stopped boasting to his friends and began wearing simpler clothes to school.

Explanation: everyone likes to boast sometimes. Both children and adults like to attract attention and to feel that they are better than others. That is human nature. But the Quran teaches us again and again that we must avoid arrogance and conceit, and all conduct which is intended to convey to those around us that we are better than they. Such conduct is offensive and hence it is sinful. The Quran also tells us that life is a circle and those who have everything may lose it when Allah gives it to others. It would seem that no therapeutic intervention and no explanation can compare to the power of the verse which the teacher quoted.

7 | Truth, Promises and Personal Responsibility

1. Is a promise also a promise to yourself?

﴿ لَّيْسَ الْبِرَّ أَن تُوَلُّواْ وُجُوهَكُمْ قِبَلَ الْمَشْرِقِ وَالْمَغْرِبِ وَلَكِنَّ الْبِرَّ مَنْ آمَنَ بِاللّهِ وَالْيَوْمِ الآخِرِ وَالْمَلآئِكَةِ وَالْكِتَابِ وَالنَّبِيِّينَ وَآتَى الْمَالَ عَلَى حُبِّهِ ذَوِي الْقُرْبَى وَالْيَتَامَى وَالْمَسَاكِينَ وَابْنَ السَّبِيلِ وَالسَّآئِلِينَ وَفِي الرِّقَابِ وَأَقَامَ الصَّلاةَ وَآتَى الزَّكَاةَ وَالْمُوفُونَ بِعَهْدِهِمْ إِذَا عَاهَدُواْ وَالصَّابِرِينَ فِي الْبَأْسَاء والضَّرَّاء وَحِينَ الْبَأْسِ أُولَئِكَ الَّذِينَ صَدَقُوا وَأُولَئِكَ هُمُ الْمُتَّقُونَ ﴾ (البقرة: 177)

It is not righteousness that ye turn your faces Towards east or West; but it is righteousness- to believe in Allah and the Last Day, and the Angels, and the Book, and the Messengers; to spend of your substance, out of love for Him, for your kin, for orphans, for the needy, for the wayfarer, for those who ask, and for the ransom of slaves; to be steadfast in prayer, and practice regular charity; **to fulfil the contracts which ye have made;** and to be firm and patient, in pain (or suffering) and adversity, and throughout all periods of panic. **Such are the people of truth, the Allah-fearing.** (The Cow: 177)

Every morning the teacher starts the first lesson with stories. Sometimes she reads to the children and sometimes she asks them to read aloud or to tell their classmates a brief story.

Omer is a shy boy and always tries to avoid reading. When the teacher asks him, he refuses. Recently she has talked to him several times in order to encourage him and help him overcome his shyness. They have agreed that on Tuesday Omer will read a story to the class, and he has announced that this time he will keep his word.

But as the moment approaches Omer keeps wondering what to do and how to revoke his commitment. Perhaps he can say that he has an appointment with the doctor, or perhaps, simply, he will stay home that day – in the end he goes to his mother and asks her: "What will happen if I don't keep my promise to the teacher?" His mother replies: "Listen, my son, you promised. As the Quran says: **'Fulfil the contracts which ye have made… Such are the people of truth, the Allah-fearing'.**"

Explanation: it is easier to make a promise than to keep it, as we all know. Adults sign contracts and appeal to the courts when one of the parties goes back on his promise. But it is not always possible to sign a contract, certainly not where children are concerned. We want to teach our children to keep their promises because a society in which words are of no value and nobody can be trusted is anarchic. The demand that the individual keep promises ensures that he will be reliable in his own eyes and not a liar. He will understand how important it is not to delude others and not to arouse expectations which will not be fulfilled. He will understand that when pressure is exerted on him to make a commitment, he should reject the pressure and think twice if he is willing and able to keep his promise. It is better to say 'No' and face the consequences now than to promise and fail to deliver in the future. Once an individual has promised, he must make every effort to keep his word. The Quran urges people to honor their commitments.

2. Is it a friend's duty to tell the truth even if it is painful?

{ قُلْنَا اهْبِطُواْ مِنْهَا جَمِيعاً فَإِمَّا يَأْتِيَنَّكُم مِّنِّي هُدًى فَمَن تَبِعَ هُدَايَ فَلاَ خَوْفٌ عَلَيْهِمْ وَلاَ هُمْ يَحْزَنُونَ } (البقرة: 38)

We said: "Get ye down all from here; and if, as is sure, there comes to you Guidance from me, **whosoever follows My guidance, on them shall be no fear, nor shall they grieve.** (The Cow: 38)

Ahmed and Sami are related and are very good friends who do everything together. They prepared for the annual school trip together. Ahmed prepared everything – clothes, sun-glasses, penknife, candies etc., and Sami checked the list to see if he had forgotten anything. Later Sami telephoned Ahmed to make doubly sure.

On the first day of the trip, everything went according to plan and the pupils and teachers enjoyed themselves. On the second night, Ahmed suggested to Sami that they should slip away to the nearest pub without asking permission. When they entered the pub, Sami sat quietly but Ahmed handed some money to an older girl with whom he struck up acquaintance and asked her to buy him alcoholic drinks. He even gave her a tip for helping him. Sami refused to drink and wanted to go back to the group. Ahmed insisted on staying and stopped Sami from leaving. He drank till he was intoxicated and then broke bottles and created such an uproar in the pub that he was thrown out. Only then did he agree to return to the group. The pub owner decided to seek him out and searched until he finally located the teachers who were in charge of the schoolchildren. The teachers made all the pupils stand in a row and the pub owner immediately identified Ahmed and Sami. Ahmed denied the whole incident. The teacher turned to Sami and said: "Sami, tell the truth, were you in the pub?" Sami was silent, struggling with himself, and the teacher asked again: "Sami, tell the truth!" Then Sami said:

"Yes, I was with Ahmed and he drank alcohol and raised a riot. I love him but I'll tell the truth".

Ahmed shouted at him: "I'll get you for this, Sami. You'll be sorry". Sami was frightened. He knew that Ahmed's older brother could beat him up.

Then the teacher read Sami Verse 38 of Surah 2 in order to reassure him and restore his confidence. **"Whosoever follows My guidance, on them shall be no fear, nor shall they grieve".**

Explanation: we all know how difficult it is sometimes, and not only for children, to tell the truth. For example, someone who witnesses a crime may refrain from reporting it for fear that the criminals will take revenge and nobody will protect him. In many cases, people avoid reporting out of fear and society as a whole is the loser. We need to encourage children and adults to tell the truth without fear and we must do our utmost to guarantee them maximum protection. In this particular case, if Sami does not tell the truth about Ahmed because he is afraid of Ahmed's family, he will remain dependent on Ahmed and will be his "slave". We want people to be dependent on the truth and not on others, and the verse which the teacher read to Sami can help promote this objective.

3. Should we judge an individual according to his own conduct or by his family's conduct?

{قُلْ أَتُحَاجُّونَنَا فِي اللهِ وَهُوَ رَبُّنَا وَرَبُّكُمْ وَلَنَا أَعْمَالُنَا وَلَكُمْ أَعْمَالُكُمْ وَنَحْنُ لَهُ مُخْلِصُونَ}
(البقرة: 139)

Say: Will ye dispute with us about Allah, seeing that He is our Lord and your Lord; **that we are responsible for our doings and ye for yours;** and that We are sincere (in our faith) in Him? (The Cow: 139)

Amina is in the sixth grade. She is gifted and well-mannered, is generally liked and likes everyone. Recently her uncle was sentenced to a long prison term for drug trading. Since then the entire village has turned its back on the family and nobody wants contact with them. The children have begun snubbing Amina. They jeer at her and refuse to invite her to their homes. In her distress, Amina appealed to the school counselor and described the situation. "I didn't choose him as my uncle", she said to the counselor. "It's God's choice and I accept His will. But let them at least treat me like a human being because I have feelings as well". At the next education hour, the counselor came into the class and talked about accepting that which is different in all kinds of areas – religious, social, cultural etc. She also emphasized how important it is to judge individuals only on the basis of their own actions and not those of their relatives, because each of us is responsible for his actions and not those of others. She asked the pupils how they would feel if someone in their family had committed a crime and they were being judged because of it. One of the pupils said that he knew why the counselor had chosen this subject for discussion – it was because of Amina. She confirmed it, took out the Quran and asked the pupil to read out Verse 139 of Surah 2: **"that we are responsible for our doings and ye for yours".**

After the lesson many of the pupils went over to Amina and asked her pardon. Several of them invited her to their homes.

Explanation: we often tend to judge an individual according to his or her family. For example, when parents seek to arrange a marriage for a son or daughter, they sometimes make great effort to uncover details about the family of the future bride or groom. It is customary to think that if someone is from a good family, there is a greater chance that he will be a good person than if he comes from a dubious family. But both the Quran and plain logic caution us against generalization which may be doing an injustice. One should try to judge an individual on the basis of his own actions and not those of his relatives. Thus, we may gain the impression that someone is a positive human being although several of his relatives are known for wrongdoing. This is the case with Amina and children like her who suffer because someone in their family has committed a crime. If we judge the individual on the basis of his own actions, we will be encouraging him to feel that he is responsible for his fate. If my good name depends on my family why should I make an effort? I have already been labeled as bad, been told that I resembled my relatives and I will have no alternative but to be like them. But if I alone am responsible for my reputation and my fate, it is worth my while to behave well. In this way the Quran encourages the individual to take responsibility for his actions, and to judge others solely according to their actions.

4. Does keeping promises enhance one's self-esteem?

{ بَلَى مَنْ أَوْفَى بِعَهْدِهِ وَاتَّقَى فَإِنَّ اللّهَ يُحِبُّ الْمُتَّقِينَ } (آل عمران: 76)

Nay - **Those that keep their plighted faith and act aright,- verily Allah loves those who act aright.** (The Family of Imran: 76)

Adnan is in the sixth grade. This year his parents are particularly concerned about his grades because next year, in the seventh grade, the pupils are classified into various study level groups in the basic subjects. His parents keep reminding him about this but he says: "Don't worry, everything will be fine". After the first few months, his grades were low. His parents were furious but he reassured them: "I'm going to start studying harder and you will be pleasantly surprised at the end of the semester". But he did not seem to be working hard. His parents constantly reminded him but he kept insisting that they had no reason to worry.

At the end of the semester there was no improvement in Adnan's grades and in mathematics they had even deteriorated. His parents informed him that from now on – no friends, no computer games and no hobbies. Adnan pleaded and assured them that he had understood the message and would be serious about his studies. His parents told him they were giving him one last chance.

In the first week of the second semester, Adnan worked really hard and his parents were persuaded that he was taking the work seriously. But after about two weeks he reverted to his old habits. He prepared his homework late at night and only after he had finished playing with his friends. At the end of the year his grades were very disappointing in all subjects.

Adnan was afraid that he would be punished. He knew he would not be given another opportunity and began to defend himself and to find excuses. "I tried", he said, "but the exams were hard. I promise to work seriously next year. Please give me another chance". And then his father replied: **"Those that keep their plighted faith and act aright,-verily Allah loves those who act aright".** "We have given you enough chances", he said. "You promised and didn't keep your word so how can we give you another chance?"

Explanation: the ability to keep one's word is of inestimable importance not only for society, which expects the individual to keep his promises to others, but also to the individual himself. A person who makes a promise is addressing himself as well. If he doesn't keep his word, in future it will be difficult for him to trust himself and his own abilities. Adnan did not keep his word but feels that if he had wanted to, he could have done so. Keeping his promise would have endowed him with the sense of power and ability which is so important for us in so many areas, from solving a mathematical exercise to coping with life's problems. We want to teach Adnan not to be afraid of investing effort. Perhaps not all the responsibility lies with Adnan; perhaps his parents are partly responsible. His success is a joint family objective. Perhaps his parents can make life easier for him by helping him with his studies, helping him to define smaller and more manageable tasks than success in all his studies, because success invites success. For example, Adnan could start by focusing on one subject and succeeding in it. Thereby he could develop an awareness that he is capable of keeping promises. The role of parents is not to stand aside and award their children grades like teachers, but to help them to succeed. They should be warm and empathetic, encourage them along the way instead of merely waiting for results. Such an attitude would make it easier for Adnan to act in accordance with that important Quran verse.

5. What can we say to someone who swears a false oath?

{ وَلَا تَجْعَلُوا۟ اللَّهَ عُرْضَةً لِّأَيْمَانِكُمْ أَن تَبَرُّوا۟ وَتَتَّقُوا۟ وَتُصْلِحُوا۟ بَيْنَ النَّاسِ وَاللَّهُ سَمِيعٌ عَلِيمٌ } (البقرة: 224)

And make not Allah's (name) an excuse in your oaths against doing good, or acting rightly, or making peace between persons; for Allah is One Who heareth and knoweth all things. (The Cow: 224)

Fifteen-year-old Abed, who is in the tenth grade, often stayed out till late at night. Both his parents are career-oriented and spend many hours away from home. His father is a doctor and his mother an elementary school principal in the village. They return home very late, eat a hasty family meal with Abed and his little sister, Zinab, and then each return to his occupations: the father goes back to the hospital or takes the opportunity to go to bed early and the mother shuts herself in her study and busies herself with paperwork. It seems that they do not know where he goes and when he goes to bed.

One evening, when they happened to eat supper together, the mother mentioned how difficult it was to rouse Abed in the morning. She suggested taking him to the local clinic for a blood test to discover why he was so tired in the mornings. Then Zinab intervened and said that perhaps Abed found it difficult to get up because he often came home late at night. Now both parents turned to Abed and asked together: "Is that true?" Abed swore by Allah that it was not true and that he went to bed early every night.

Later that same day, Zinab came running to her mother, crying, and told her that Abed had hit her and said she was a tattletale. Again, Abed swore by Allah that his sister was inventing the story. His mother decided it was time to intervene. She took him aside for a talk, asked about his evening activities and criticized his tendency to swear solemn oath on every occasion even when he was not telling the truth. She explained to him that God was everywhere and watches our actions, sees and hears everything. To bear out her explanation, she quoted him the verse: **"And make not Allah's (name) an excuse in your oaths against doing good, or acting rightly, or making peace between persons; for Allah is One Who heareth and knoweth all things".** When Abed heard the verse, he promised his mother that he would never again swear in the name of Allah and would stop going out late at night. His mother noted that this was the first time he had made a promise without swearing an oath.

Explanation: Abed was taking the name of God in vain because he had learned that when he swore, people tended to believe him. But the Quran, which teaches people to tell the truth, tells us that those who take the name of Allah in vain as an excuse may not necessarily be telling the truth. Otherwise, why would they need to swear so often. An oath in the name of God is of special value. In court Muslims take an oath by laying their hand on the Quran and other religions take oaths on their holy books. We simply want to teach children to tell the truth without needing to swear an oath; a lie damages do not only damage the society in which the individual is a partner, but often when someone lies to another, he is also lying to himself. Then the damage is twofold. For example, if Abed denies that he goes to bed late he is also lying to himself and therefore will not mend his ways. This is also true about his attack on his sister.

6. Is the individual alone responsible for his actions?

{ ذَلِكَ بِمَا قَدَّمَتْ أَيْدِيكُمْ وَأَنَّ اللَّهَ لَيْسَ بِظَلاَّمٍ لِّلْعَبِيدِ } (آل عمران: 182)

This is because of the (unrighteous deeds) which your hands sent on before ye: For Allah never harms those who serve Him. (The Family of Imran: 182)

The father of Fadi, a fifth-grader, was invited to school by the principal. The summons he received said that Fadi had been cursing his friends, and not for the first time, and so the principal wanted to talk to his parents. Present at the talk were the principal, Fadi and his father.

Principal: I've invited you here because Fadi has been cursing his classmates.

Father: At home Fadi causes no trouble. He's a quiet boy, well-mannered, I'm very surprised.

Principal: But at school he curses. That's why I've invited you and Fadi to discuss the problem.

Father: Fadi, is it true that you curse your classmates?

Fadi: It only happened once, and perhaps one other time a month ago.

Principal: I want to know the reason for your conduct. Do you know what it is, Fadi?

Fadi: At home Mother always curses me and talks to me roughly.

Father: I'm at work all day and you've never told me this, Fadi. You've never complained about your mother. And I know that you are the apple of her eye. Perhaps you've been pestering her? I don't know.

Fadi: I don't like helping her and she doesn't understand that. She destroys me when she curses me. Then I feel tense and I want to let out the anger.

Principal: Fadi, even if your mother curses you, you mustn't curse other children. I'm sure you know Verse 182 of Surah 3, which talks about personal responsibility. (He opens the Quran and reads out): **"This is because of the (unrighteous deeds) which your hands sent on before ye: For Allah never harms those who serve Him".** What do you understand from that verse, Fadi?

Fadi: (silent for a moment): The verse is saying that I'm the one who creates the problems and not my mother and my mistakes return to me.

Principal: Very good, Fadi. And if you have problems with your mother you can discuss them with her or with your father. Problems at home or with friends are solved by discussion where you explain what you find hurtful, and not by cursing.

Explanation: it seems that Fadi is really the apple of his mother's eye. She pampers him but he doesn't feel obliged to help her with the housework. He is angry at her for even asking. Then she loses control and curses him. She seems to have difficulties in her relationship with him. She should be capable of demanding that he helps her and of insisting firmly but not aggressively. She may be a weak character. On the one hand, she is very close to Fadi and on the other, treats him aggressively. In any event, the principal's message was the correct one. Fadi can't absolve himself of all responsibility even if his mother treats him like that. The message of the Quran, which is reiterated in many verses like this one, is uniform and it is very meaningful from the educational viewpoint: each individual holds personal responsibility for his actions and nobody should cast responsibility for his actions on to others.

7. What can we say to a boy who lies constantly?

{ وَلَا تَكُونُوا كَالَّتِي نَقَضَتْ غَزْلَهَا مِن بَعْدِ قُوَّةٍ أَنكَاثًا تَتَّخِذُونَ أَيْمَانَكُمْ دَخَلًا بَيْنَكُمْ أَن تَكُونَ أُمَّةٌ هِيَ أَرْبَىٰ مِنْ أُمَّةٍ إِنَّمَا يَبْلُوكُمُ اللَّهُ بِهِ وَلَيُبَيِّنَنَّ لَكُمْ يَوْمَ الْقِيَامَةِ مَا كُنتُمْ فِيهِ تَخْتَلِفُونَ } (النحل: 92)

And be not like a woman who breaks into untwisted strands the yarn which she has spun, after it has become strong. Nor take your oaths to practise deception between yourselves, lest one party should be more numerous than another: for Allah will test you by this; and on the Day of Judgment He will certainly make clear to you (the truth of) that wherein ye disagree. (The Bees: 92)

Ali, who is in the twelfth grade, makes many promises to his parents which he does not keep. He asks for the car and promises to return it in time but then returns two hours late. His parents are very worried. Sometimes he asks permission from his parents to go somewhere and then goes elsewhere. When he is caught, he promises that this is the last time he will break a promise or the last time he will lie but he keeps his word only till the next promise. His parents have tried everything from serious talks and explanations to threats and punishment. Nothing helped. Ali continued to lie and to break his promises. In their predicament, his parents consulted the school counselor. She opened the Quran which lay on the desk and asked Ali to read out verse 92 of Surah 16: **"And be not like a woman who breaks into untwisted strands the yarn which she has spun, after it**

has become strong. Nor take your oaths to practise deception between yourselves, lest one party should be more numerous than another: for Allah will test you by this; and on the Day of Judgment He will certainly make clear to you (the truth of) that wherein ye disagree". When Ali finished reading the verse, he was flooded with a sense of heavy responsibility. "No, I won't use promises and oaths in order to cheat", he said. "I didn't know that the Quran was talking about me and referring to me". And from that day on, Ali tried hard not to make promises but when he did promise, he usually kept his word.

Explanation: truth is a very important value. When someone promises and does not keep his word or when he takes a false oath, he is actually deceiving the other and perhaps himself as well. These deceptions destroy a society, because they create a society in which it is impossible to believe anyone and a word is worth nothing. In such a society, you cannot know what will happen tomorrow and uncertainty reigns. It is not easy to adhere to the truth but it is a vital condition required if we are not to exist in a living hell. Hence, children must be taught first and foremost to be loyal to their inner truth. When they do not tell the truth, they should feel uncomfortable, since they have betrayed themselves and others. In such a society there are many difficult moments. One man will tell another that he does not agree with him, instead of nodding his head and deluding the other into believing that he agrees in order to maintain the illusion of good relations. He will argue and confront the other because the truth is important and not the illusion. When an illusion is shattered, because at the decisive moment, truth will out, the disappointment is great. The Quran has no equal in conveying the vast important of telling the truth.

8. What can we say to someone who spreads falsehoods?

﴿ وَلَا تَلْبِسُوا۟ الْحَقَّ بِالْبَاطِلِ وَتَكْتُمُوا۟ الْحَقَّ وَأَنتُمْ تَعْلَمُونَ ﴾ (البقرة: 42)

And cover not Truth with falsehood, nor conceal the Truth when ye know (what it is). (The Cow: 42)

Nur is in the tenth grade; she is pretty, hard-working, well-behaved and serious. She is interested in nothing but studies and invests great effort in succeeding. Her girlfriends are busy with romantic matters but she tries to ignore them and refuses to discuss them.

Yusuf is a pupil at her school, who is proud and arrogant, and likes chatting to the girls. He believes that there is not a single girl who will refuse to talk to him. One day Nur passed by while he was laughing with his friends. One of the friends said something to her and Nur responded politely which surprised them. Yusuf too was surprised because he knew she was a serious girl who never talked to boys. He whispered to his friends that he was going to show them how to behave with her. He called out something impolite to her and to his surprise she responded rudely, in a manner which insulted him before his friends, something which had not happened to him before. He promised his friends that he would not leave her alone until he had humiliated her and forced her to apologize.

Yusuf tried to slander Nur and began to spread rumors at school that she was in love with him and wanted him as a boyfriend. He made sure that the rumor reached everyone, particularly her older brother. Nur's brother was very angry with her and without checking the story, he shouted at her and slapped her. "There's no smoke without fire", he said Yusuf's friends added to the story by confirming that Nur was infatuated with Yusuf, thus helping Yusuf to take his revenge. Yusuf tried to force her to talk to him and she tried to explain the truth to her brother and family but nobody would believe her.

Eventually Nur went to the counselor and told her what had happened. The counselor checked the story with Nur's friends and Yusuf's mates and finally invited all of them for a discussion. She explained to Yusuf's friends who had given false witness against her that their conduct was inappropriate both socially and religiously and could cause conflict in Nur's family. She also reprimanded Yusuf for his conduct, namely spreading rumors and lies. Finally, she took out her Quran and asked Yusuf to read Surah 2, Verse 42: **"And cover not Truth with falsehood, nor conceal the Truth when ye know (what it is)"**. There was no need to say anything more.

Explanation: spreading rumors is a dangerous act and there have been cases where girls were murdered because of the unfounded rumor that they had violated family honor. Fortunately, Nur was strong enough not to yield, to adhere to the truth although nobody believed her, and to ask for aid from the counselor. Weaker girls than Nur are liable to admit to deeds they have not committed, to feel unjustifiably guilty or to succumb to blackmail. The Quran has a great deal to say about Yusuf's conduct, and his excessive pride. On this occasion the counselor quoted the Quran verse which emphasizes how important it is to adhere to the truth. It was wrong for Yusuf to spread rumors and it would have been wrong for Nur to yield and renounce her own truth. Moreover, they should all have upheld the truth and not concealed it as they did, whether for fear of Yusuf or for other considerations. It is dangerous to live in a society where people do not respect the truth.

9. What can we say to a parent who blames a child for a death in the family?

{ كُلُّ نَفْسٍ ذَائِقَةُ الْمَوْتِ وَإِنَّمَا تُوَفَّوْنَ أُجُورَكُمْ يَوْمَ الْقِيَامَةِ فَمَن زُحْزِحَ عَنِ النَّارِ
وَأُدْخِلَ الْجَنَّةَ فَقَدْ فَازَ وَمَا الْحَيَاةُ الدُّنْيَا إِلاَّ مَتَاعُ الْغُرُورِ } (آل عمران: 185)

Every soul shall have a taste of death: And only on the Day of Judgment shall you be paid your full recompense. Only he who is saved far from the Fire and admitted to the Garden will have attained the object (of Life): For the life of this world is but goods and chattels of deception. (The Family of Imran: 185)

Maher, who is in the fifth grade, is a hard-working boy who takes his studies seriously, but he also likes dangerous games. Recently he hit his friend for refusing to play a game which is considered dangerous. The principal heard about the incident and ordered Maher to bring his father to school next day. She thought that his dangerous games and his violent conduct required the authoritative intervention of his father. Next day Maher arrived at school with his mother.

Principal: Maher, I asked you to bring your father. Why did you bring your mother?

Mother: Maher's father is very strict with him. What happens at home is enough. If we tell him about what happened at school, it will not go well.

Principal: What do you say, Maher?

Maher: I'm afraid of my father. Mother knows that. I feel very small and weak when I face him. He always beats me and I can't stand him.

Mother: My husband is very harsh. I've talked to him many times but it didn't help. There is nothing I can do. It comes from Allah.

Maher: The whole village knows that I was born on the day my father's father died. My father always reminds me of that and punishes me. He thinks that the day of my birth was a bad day, so he punishes me for everything I do, big or little. Am I a bad boy, Mother?

Mother: You are a very good boy, Maher. We have to suffer and hope that time will have some effect.

Principal: Now I understand why you hit other children. It's because your father hits you. And I think I understand why you love dangerous games. It's as if you don't care about your life and you think that it's worth nothing. I want to talk to your father. Will he agree to come?

Mother: I think so. He respects you.

The principal contacted the father and invited him to come. The next day he arrived alone, without knowing what she wanted.

Principal: Why don't you ever come to school and take an interest in your son's studies and behavior.

Father: I'm busy, there's no time. If there are problems, just tell me…

Principal: Maher is a good boy, but you should listen to him and talk to him.

Father: It's hard for me to sit and talk to him. I love him but there is a wound inside me because he was born on the day my father died. It's hard for me to accept him.

Principal: I want to read you Verse 185 of Surah 3, which says that death is from God. It is God who determines a man's end and we cannot change that time. (She takes out the Quran and reads slowly and with emphasis: **"Every soul shall have a taste of death: And only on the Day of Judgment shall you be paid your full recompense".** If you want a reward from God, you must give your son the attention he

> needs. I sense that he misses you very much and wants you and all you have to do is open your heart to him. Begin and you will see.

Explanation: the principal's psychological analysis of Maher's behaves behavior is apparently correct. He is playing with his life and his fate because he does not feel that his father values him. This is also why he is violent. It is good that the principal insisted on talking to the father, because in families where the father is authoritative and the mother is weak, it is often the case that unless the matter is discussed with him, nothing will change. Luckily for Maher, his father respected the principal. Often it is difficult for a female principal to invite a man for a talk and to treat him authoritatively and professionally. This can be even more difficult if he is not from her village. But if a principal or a teacher or a counselor wants to do their job properly, they should not be afraid to invite a father even if he appears contemptuous. They are the professionals and the welfare of the child takes priority over every other consideration. On some other occasion, it is worth talking to the father and explaining to him that the entire family will gain if he allows the mother some authority and power. Maher needs a strong mother who is able to help him and influence him, and not a weak mother who suggests, as did his mother, that they wait passively for better times to arrive.

10. Is a promise to God also a promise to oneself?

{ وَلَا تَشْتَرُوا۟ بِعَهْدِ ٱللَّهِ ثَمَنًا قَلِيلًا إِنَّمَا عِندَ ٱللَّهِ هُوَ خَيْرٌ لَّكُمْ إِن كُنتُمْ تَعْلَمُونَ }
(النحل: 95)

Nor sell the covenant of Allah for a miserable price: for with Allah is (a prize) far better for you, if ye only knew. (The Bees: 95)

When Maali came into the house, she heard her father talking on the telephone to a woman, saying flattering things to her and suggesting that they meet in a hotel. Maali was stunned. She rushed out, furious at her father. He was known to be a religious man, who prayed observantly. The relations between her parents had been good till six months previously, when he began to stay away from home at night. Her mother had protested but he explained that his work demanded absences.

Now Maali ran to her aunt, her father's sister, and told her the story. The aunt approached her brother and talked to him. "What is going on with that woman?" she asked. "How can you leave everything, your family, your wife who is a good woman, your children; you are a religious man! Have you forgotten that Allah sees everything? Why are you abandoning everything for a woman who can't be worth it if she treats you like that?! I want to read you a verse from the Quran: **"Nor sell the covenant of Allah for a miserable price: for with Allah is (a prize) far better for you, if ye only knew".** And do not forget that a man's commitment to God to be faithful to his wife is also a commitment to himself. You must honor God and yourself and break off this relationship at once!"

Explanation: the aunt was right in saying that a commitment to God is a commitment to oneself because God is within each of us. When Maali's father promised at his wedding to be faithful to his wife, he was promising God and also himself. When he lies to God, he is also lying to himself. For children, God is external rather than within them and they tend to tell the truth because they fear the wrath of God. But when an individual matures and becomes an adult, the divine experience becomes a part of himself. If he lies to his wife, he is in conflict not only with God but also with himself, and feels guilty for having injured her. He is liable to regret what he has done. When the external conflict between him and his God becomes an internal conflict, wages with himself, it is a sign of maturity. If Maali's father has a conscience, it will punish him and make him aware that he has betrayed his wife and has not been a good husband. And if he lacks a conscience, the wrath of God will hover over him because of his action. Thus, his sister did well to quote a verse from the Quran to remind him of his commitment to God and to himself.

8 | Patience, Humility and the Need to Acknowledge Limitations

1. What should a child do when a parent or teacher doesn't appreciate him?

{ أَيَّامًا مَّعْدُودَاتٍ فَمَن كَانَ مِنكُم مَّرِيضًا أَوْ عَلَىٰ سَفَرٍ فَعِدَّةٌ مِّنْ أَيَّامٍ أُخَرَ وَعَلَى الَّذِينَ يُطِيقُونَهُ فِدْيَةٌ طَعَامُ مِسْكِينٍ فَمَن تَطَوَّعَ خَيْرًا فَهُوَ خَيْرٌ لَّهُ وَأَن تَصُومُوا خَيْرٌ لَّكُمْ إِن كُنتُمْ تَعْلَمُونَ } (البقرة: 184)

(Fasting) for a fixed number of days; but if any of you is ill, or on a journey, the prescribed number (Should be made up) from days later. For those who can do it (With hardship), is a ransom, the feeding of one that is indigent. **But he that will give more, of his own free will,- it is better for him.** And it is better for you that ye fast, if ye only knew. (The Cow: 184)

Ahmed, who is in the tenth grade, always helps his teachers. He tidies the classroom and cleans the blackboard, brings in chalks etc. He helps his classmates with their studies. He is the kind of boy who never refuses a request. But again, and again he is surprised when the class teacher praises another pupil and not him. Feeling hurt, he went to the counselor one day and told him everything. He added that he had decided that from now on he would not do favors for anyone and would worry about himself alone. The counselor listened to Ahmed as he gave rein to his feelings and then suggested that he goes to the teacher and share the feelings with him. Ahmed refused and said that he expected the teacher to understand for himself how hurt he was. Then the counselor read him the Quran verse: **"But he that will**

give more, of his own free will,- it is better for him". He added that he had no doubt that in the end the teacher would notice Ahmed and give him the praise he deserved.

Explanation: A teacher who has a large class finds it difficult to pay attention to all his pupils however hard he tries. Often a pupil can feel neglected. The same is true of a large family. It is hard for parents to give attention to all their children all the time. Often one of the children can feel slighted. Thus, the counselor is right to advise Ahmed to go to the teacher and tell him how he feels. Sometimes, if we fail to tell the other how we feel, he simply does not notice. But Ahmed may be right in thinking that the teacher will interpret his remarks as an accusation that he is discriminating against the boy. It is hard to ascertain the truth. We don't know Ahmed or the teacher well enough. The counselor acted wisely. He examined with Ahmed what suited him and found that a verse from the Quran would equip the boy with the strength to continue acting generously and wait patiently until the teacher and the classmates eventually acknowledged his conduct.

2. **What can we say to someone who is ashamed to accept psychological therapy?**

{ يَا أَيُّهَا الَّذِينَ آمَنُوا كُونُوا قَوَّامِينَ بِالْقِسْطِ شُهَدَاءَ لِلَّهِ وَلَوْ عَلَىٰ أَنفُسِكُمْ أَوِ الْوَالِدَيْنِ
وَالْأَقْرَبِينَ إِن يَكُنْ غَنِيًّا أَوْ فَقِيرًا فَاللَّهُ أَوْلَىٰ بِهِمَا فَلَا تَتَّبِعُوا الْهَوَىٰ أَن تَعْدِلُوا وَإِن
تَلْوُوا أَوْ تُعْرِضُوا فَإِنَّ اللَّهَ كَانَ بِمَا تَعْمَلُونَ خَبِيرًا } (النساء: 135)

O ye who believe! stand out firmly for justice, as witnesses to Allah, even as against yourselves, or your parents, or your kin, and whether it be (against) rich or poor: for Allah can best protect both. Follow not the lusts (of your hearts), lest ye swerve, and if ye distort (justice) or decline to do justice, verily Allah is well- acquainted with all that ye do. (Women: 135)

Salem's wife made an appointment with a marriage counselor and asked him to help her solve her marital problems because of her tense relationship with her husband. If the situation continued, she said, there could be serious repercussions. She told him about problems connected to the children and to her as well as serious problems outside the home. The counselor listened and then asked her to come to a therapeutic session with her husband. He recommended that they attend several sessions of therapy as a couple. He also explained that it was often worth solving problems between a husband and wife within the framework of family therapy and not individual therapy.

Salem's wife asked her husband to come but he refused. "That's the last thing I need", he said and added, "I want you to know that what you are doing is wrong and unacceptable". He accused her of involving outsiders in their relationship. When the counselor heard this, he told Salem's wife to quote Verse 135 of Surah 4 to him: **"O ye who believe! stand out firmly for justice, as witnesses to Allah, even as against yourselves, or your parents, or your kin".** "This verse enables us to accept responsibility and to criticize ourselves or our relatives", the counselor explained to her. "We should not despair", he added. "We must persist and pressure your husband in various directions until he agrees to come for therapy and improves the atmosphere at home".

Explanation: it is no disgrace to accept counseling or therapeutic help from a professional (psychologist, educational counselor, social worker etc.). We all have problems of different types and the ability to admit to difficulties and be willing to treat them generally attests to emotional maturity. Denial of difficulties often attests to weakness. As in the case of physical disease, various emotional problems require treatment and should not be neglected. But people are frequently ashamed to ask for emotional aid. They say: "I'm not crazy. Why should I need psychological treatment?" However, the reverse is usually true. People who ask for psychological help are often healthier than those who are afraid to seek aid. Thus, the act of approaching a mental health counselor can attest to maturity and emotional strength.

Now the counselor has a tricky task: to explain all this to Salem, who does not want to begin therapy. He has equipped Salen's wife with a Quran verse which refers to the importance of the individual's personal responsibility 1 towards himself. By accepting therapy, we are bearing witness against ourselves and examining ourselves and others. We are accepting responsibility instead of considering some other person to be responsible. This verse can encourage the husband to take responsibility and enter therapy.

3. Is explanation preferable to punishment?

﴿ وَالَّذِينَ كَذَّبُوا بِآيَاتِنَا سَنَسْتَدْرِجُهُم مِّنْ حَيْثُ لَا يَعْلَمُونَ ﴾ (الأعراف: 182)

Those who reject Our signs, We shall gradually visit with punishment, in ways they perceive not. (The Elevations: 182)

Abed, who is in the eleventh grade, is a diligent student. One day, when he returned from school after a long day, his mother smelled smoke on his clothes. She discovered that he was in the habit of smoking cigarettes with his friends after school. Distressed, she went to see the class teacher who told her that she was aware that a group of her pupils smoked. Abed's mother demanded that the teacher expose the smokers and punish them, but the teacher said she had other plans. She was preparing a short video about smoking and its risks. "First through a video, then through lecturers, stage by stage, we'll get them away from smoking", she explained to the mother. "For example, these children like sports and I've also made a short video on the damage that smoking causes to athletes". Abed's mother was still not persuaded by the teacher's non-punitive method until the teacher said: **"Those who reject Our signs, We shall gradually visit with punishment, in ways they perceive not".** "This is what the Quran teaches us", she said and the mother was convinced.

Explanation: indeed, imposing punishment is generally the less successful alternative and it is usually preferable to employ explanation. The reason is simple. A punishment contains an element of revenge and is liable to generate frustration and resistance. Punishment can evoke fear in the child and we want him to understand the importance of good behavior and not merely to behave properly out of fear of punishment. An explanation is internalized, makes the child think and enables him to internalize and adopt the principles of the authority figure (parent, teacher) not out of fear but out of admiration and love. While punishment may lead him to change his conduct out of fear, this change will not be long-lasting because, when the threat is removed, the child will revert to the bad behavior.

Hence, the counselor did well in deciding that, instead of punishing the pupils, she would explain the facts of life to them and what is known today about smoking and its risks. She even found support in the Quran for the need to be patient and not to expect immediate change.

4. What can we say to a child who has been hurt but told not to retaliate?

{ وَالّذِينَ صَبَرُواْ ابْتِغَاءَ وَجْهِ رَبّهِمْ وَأَقَامُواْ الصّلاَةَ وَأنفَقُواْ مِمّا رَزَقْنَاهُمْ سِرّاً وَعَلاَنِيَةً وَيَدْرَؤُونَ بِالْحَسَنَةِ السّيّئَةَ أُوْلَئِكَ لَهُمْ عُقْبَى الدّارِ } (الرعد: 22)

Those who patiently persevere, seeking the countenance of their Lord; Establish regular prayers; spend, out of (the gifts) We have bestowed for their sustenance, secretly and

openly; and turn off Evil with good: for such there is the final attainment of the (eternal) home. (The Thunder: 22)

Shifa told her mother that one of her classmates, Amal, had hit her. Her mother advised her not to hit back and to wait and see if the girl did it again. If she did it again, Shifa should talk to the teacher. A few days later, Amal asked Shifa to help her with her homework. Again, Shifa asked her mother whether to help a girl who had hit her. The mother opened the Quran at Surah 13, Verse 22 and read out: **"Those who patiently persevere, seeking the countenance of their Lord; Establish regular prayers; spend, out of (the gifts) We have bestowed for their sustenance, secretly and openly; and turn off Evil with good: for such there is the final attainment of the (eternal) home".** "I'm referring mainly to the Quran recommendation to turn off evil with good", she explained to her daughter. Shifa decided to explain the homework to her friend and they became good friends and forget the incident. "It's all thanks to the Quran", Shifa told her mother some time later.

Explanation: parents should remember that children quarrel and then make peace. Adults often have a "long memory" which is not appropriate for their children. They keep reminding them that another child treated them badly and that they should take revenge by refusing help. But the Quran exhorts us, in many cases, not to bear a grudge and recommends that we 'turn off evil with good'. There is a great deal of wisdom in this advice, because if the individual overcomes the urge for revenge, there is a good prospect of developing new and good relations. Revenge, on the other hand, is a vicious circle. The injured individual will want to take his revenge and there will be no end to the story. Therefore, repaying evil with good can break the vicious circle in many cases.

5. How can we restore hope to an abused child?

{ وَلاَ تَحْسَبَنَّ اللهَ غَافِلاً عَمَّا يَعْمَلُ الظَّالِمُونَ إِنَّمَا يُؤَخِّرُهُمْ لِيَوْمٍ تَشْخَصُ فِيهِ الأَبْصَارُ}
(إبراهيم: 42)

Think not that Allah doth not heed the deeds of those who do wrong. He but giveth them respite against a Day when the eyes will fixedly stare in horror. (Abraham: 42)

Shirin, an eleventh-grader, asked for a meeting with the school counselor on a very personal matter.

Counselor: I'm here to help you. You can ask anything; I will do whatever I can.

Shirin: It's a big problem and I don't know where to start. I've never talked to anyone about it…I don't want anyone to know…

Counselor: I can't promise not to tell anyone because sometimes in order to help I have to confide in the education team on certain matters. But I promise to let you know about every step I take and to consult you first. I'm glad you've decided to come to me.

Shirin: The truth is that I have a big problem at home. I don't know what to say, I'm living in sheer hell and I don't know what to do… (starts crying. The counselor gives her a glass of water and Shirin takes a deep breath and continues). My mother died four years ago. I spent a year alone with my father. It was hard for him to take care of me and run the household and work. A year ago, he decided to marry…He met a girl and chose her as his wife and as a mother for me. He brought her home to meet me. She was so nice to me, hugged me…and I felt that there would be love again in the house and I'd have a mother again…but it didn't happen. My happiness was short-lived. It flew out of the window

> and followed my mother…Several days after the wedding I found out that we had brought a witch into the house. When my father is home, she is very sweet to me. When he is out, all I get are shouting and scolding…she is always angry at me…I do everything I can to maintain a quiet atmosphere at home. I help her, tidy my room, but it seems to irritate her more. I don't want to involve my father because I can see he's happy with her and she treats him well. Several times I've thought about leaving home but I thought about my father and couldn't do that to him. I appealed to her and said that I want good relations with her and for us to be friends. She said that I pester her and don't let her live freely and in peace …Now I lock myself in my room or go out with my girlfriends and I spend days at a time in my grandmother's house so as to give her freedom. But none of it helps and when I come home, she shows me how hard and cruel she can be.

The counselor suggested that Shirin talk to her father but the girl insisted that she didn't want to talk to him or other relatives. "There's no solution and nothing will change that woman", she said. "I just want my father at least to be happy and have a quiet life, even at my expense".

The counselor felt that she had no solution to offer Shirin except to try and talk to her father and step-mother. So, she told Shirin that she was a big girl and would soon be leaving home for a life of her own. Then she could decide with whom to live and could run her life as she saw fit. "You must be patient", she explained, "until the time comes when you will be happy and live peacefully. As for that woman, the day will come when your father will discover who she is and she will receive her punishment, which she brought on herself". The counselor opened the Quran which was lying on her desk and read out:

"Think not that Allah doth not heed the deeds of those who do wrong. He but giveth them respite against a Day when the eyes will fixedly stare in horror".

Explanation: many children whose parents or relatives or friends abuse them have only one hope in their hearts: to grow up fast and get away from the authority of those who are torturing them. Rarely, in extreme cases, does the state decide to remove a child from his parents' care and transfer him or her to another family or a children's home. In most cases, children suffer in silence through a long, harsh childhood and yearn to leave home. What can a teacher or counselor say to someone like Shirin? They cannot alter her destiny and, in many cases, cannot persuade the parents to change their attitude. It is of course desirable to talk to the abusive person and it is essential to make the effort. It is a pity that the counselor gave in so fast. It would have been preferable for her to summon the father and step-mother for a talk. In cases of physical or sexual abuse it is obligatory to involve the police. But in most cases the impact of a talk on parents will be minor and they will persist in their attitude. Here the Quran comes to our aid and instills hope in the victim, giving him or her the strength to withstand the suffering till they can leave home.

6. How can we encourage restraint?

{ وَلَقَدْ نَعْلَمُ أَنَّكَ يَضِيقُ صَدْرُكَ بِمَا يَقُولُونَ * فَسَبِّحْ بِحَمْدِ رَبِّكَ وَكُن مِّنَ السَّاجِدِينَ}
(الحجر: 98-97)

We do indeed know how thy heart is distressed at what they say. But celebrate the praises of thy Lord, and be of those who prostrate themselves in adoration. (The Rock: 97-98)

Samir, a high-school mathematics teacher, is known to be a teacher who does everything possible for his pupils and always makes sure that they all understand the lessons. One day, when he came into the classroom after a matriculation exam, a riot began. The pupils claimed that the exam had been too difficult and that he was to blame. Samir became angry and asked them all to sit down. Then one of the pupils started shouting and using unacceptable language. Samir was angry but because he loved his pupils, he said nothing and merely said to that pupil: "Thank you for your attitude", and walked out of the classroom. His other pupils, who worshipped him, followed him and apologized for what their comrade had said. Samir did not respond.

Then Ahmed, a well-behaved boy, who always read the Quran, said to Samir: "It's true that someone talked to you in a way that made you angry. But I want to tell you something and please remember it, because God knows that you give your heart and soul. There will always be people who say inappropriate things. But at such times remember the verse: **"We do indeed know how thy heart is distressed at what they say. But celebrate the praises of thy Lord, and be of those who prostrate themselves in adoration".** Then Samir embraced Ahmed and said: "Ahmed, you are truly a wise boy".

Explanation: it happens to all of us at some time that somebody says hurtful and untrue things to us. This was what happened to Samir. He is not responsible for the examinations administered by the Ministry of Education. The pupils apologized to him but it was hard for him to forget. What helped him to accept the apology and overcome his anger was the Quran verse which relates that the Prophet too was once in a similar situation and Allah commanded him to exercise restraint and continue along the path of righteousness. To practice self-control is not easy and is not self-evident, but it is very important. Otherwise, anything or anyone can infuriate us and cause us to do things which we will regret. Ahmed restored Samir's independence and he again became his own master. The Quran encourages independence, restraint and self-control.

7. Is participation in a process more important than the final grade?

﴿ وَمَا أَهْلَكْنَا مِن قَرْيَةٍ إِلَّا لَهَا مُنذِرُونَ ﴾ (الشعراء: 208)

Never did We destroy a population, but had its warners. (The Poets: 208)

Salem, a tenth-grader, came into the counselor's office angry and full of complaints against the teachers. The counselor calmed him and asked him to tell her what had happened. "They don't warn the pupils. They wait till we make a mistake and fail and then they warn us", he said. The counselor asked what had happened to him personally. He told her that one of his classes on "Life Skills" was taught as a workshop. He had not taken an active part and preferred to listen to others. "At the end of the year, the teacher told me that I would not get a good grade because I had scarcely taken part. I asked her why she hadn't warned me during the year and she said that now she couldn't help me". The counselor promised to talk to the teacher.

She told the teacher what Salem had said. Then she opened the Quran and read her the verse: "**Never did We destroy a population, but had its warners".** "You should have cautioned Salem so that he could improve", she said. The teacher thanked her for having taught her something important.

Explanation: the counselor's comment is very important for every parent and teacher. There is good reason why schools hold parent-teacher meetings several times a year to report to parents on their child's progress. This feedback is vital so that a child can understand his situation and improve and not receive unpleasant surprises at the end of the year. A parent or teacher who does not provide feedback from time to time is not fulfilling his or her mission properly. The process of growth which we want to encourage is not based on a single result at the year's end in the form of a grade but is a continuous process of growth in which a constant dialog exists between the child and the authority figure. As parents and teachers, we must be present in the child's world not only as judges and critics but mainly as providers of support and encouragement every day and every hour. The counselor did well to convey this important message through the Quran verse.

8. What can we say to a girl whose teacher insults her?

{ وَوَصَّيْنَا الْإِنسَانَ بِوَالِدَيْهِ حَمَلَتْهُ أُمُّهُ وَهْناً عَلَى وَهْنٍ وَفِصَالُهُ فِي عَامَيْنِ أَنِ اشْكُرْ لِي
وَلِوَالِدَيْكَ إِلَيَّ الْمَصِيرُ * وَإِن جَاهَدَاكَ عَلَى أَن تُشْرِكَ بِي مَا لَيْسَ لَكَ بِهِ عِلْمٌ فَلَا
تُطِعْهُمَا وَصَاحِبْهُمَا فِي الدُّنْيَا مَعْرُوفاً وَاتَّبِعْ سَبِيلَ مَنْ أَنَابَ إِلَيَّ ثُمَّ إِلَيَّ مَرْجِعُكُمْ
فَأُنَبِّئُكُم بِمَا كُنتُمْ تَعْمَلُونَ } (لقمان: 15-14)

And We have enjoined on man (to be good) to his parents: in travail upon travail did his mother bear him, and in years twain was his weaning: (hear the command), "Show gratitude to Me and to thy parents: to Me is (thy final) Goal. But if they strive to make thee join in worship with Me things of which thou hast no knowledge, obey them not; yet bear them company in this life with justice (and consideration), and follow the way of those who turn to me (in love): in the end the return of you all is to Me, and I will tell you the truth (and meaning) of all that ye did. (Luqman: 14-15)

Nahiya hates sports lessons not because she is plump and finds it difficult to perform the exercises but because her teacher, Faten, makes sarcastic comments all the time. "You don't have to jump so hard", she says. "This exercise is not suited for you, don't do it", she comments. But this week she really went too far when she told Nahiya that a certain exercise was not meant for bears.

Nahiya was very offended and began to slander the teacher and to say offensive things about her: "a teacher with a dirty mouth", "a teacher who doesn't do a thing during the lesson", etc. The teacher complained to Nahiya's class teacher who summoned Nahiya and asked her why she was talking like that.

Nahiya: She doesn't talk to me nicely. She insults me.

Teacher: So why don't you go over to her at the end of the lesson and tell her?

Nahiya: I won't tell her. I'll just pay her back.

Teacher: I promise you I'll talk to the sports teacher and tell her she has been insulting you. And I promise that after that, she'll stop.

Nahiya: As soon as she stops, I'll stop too.

Teacher: I want you to stop irrespective of what she does. I'm going to read you a Quran verse which teaches us to treat authority figures with respect even when they are in error. She read out: **"And We have enjoined on man (to be good) to his parents: in travail upon travail did his mother bear him, and in years twain was his weaning: (hear the command), "Show gratitude to Me and to thy parents: to Me is (thy final) Goal. But if they strive to make thee join in worship with Me things of which thou hast no knowledge, obey them not; yet bear them company in this life with justice (and consideration), and follow the way of those who turn to me (in love): in the end the return of you all is to Me, and I will tell you the truth (and meaning) of all that ye did."**

Teacher: These two verses talk about the need to treat parents with respect even when they are wrong but teachers have an educational task like parents and that is why I chose to read you that verse.

Explanation: none of us would want to be in Nahiya's place. Some teachers do indeed insult their pupils and they are not worthy to be teachers. Nahiya was right not to concede to the teacher and to defend herself. If she doesn't do so, nobody will do it for her. But the class teacher is also right in saying that if she talks to the sports teacher and if Nahiya stops retaliating, their relationship will improve. The Quran teaches us a most important lesson: how to treat authority figures who try to take us along the wrong path or who hurt our feelings. We should not emulate them but we should treat them with respect, says the Quran. It is not easy for Nahiya to treat this teacher with respect but the way of the Quran is undoubtedly the right path to desirable results, because Nahiya decided not to behave like the sports teacher and not to pay her back in the same coin.

9. What can we say to someone whose parents do not allow him to study what he wants?

{ يَا حَسْرَةً عَلَى الْعِبَادِ مَا يَأْتِيهِم مِّن رَّسُولٍ إِلاَّ كَانُوا بِهِ يَسْتَهْزِئُونَ } (يس: 30)

Ah! Alas for (My) Servants! There comes not an apostle to them but they mock him! (Ya-Seen: 30)

Muhammed, who is in the tenth grade, is a hard-working student. The school year is about to end and the pupils need to choose study courses for next year. Muhammed's parents are exerting pressure on him and trying to persuade him to take up science and math subjects. Muhammed has outstanding achievements in all subjects but he prefers the humanities. He wants to specialize in languages, and his great loves are drawing and sculpting. His parents keep telling him that these are unimportant subjects and that he should abandon them and think of the promising future awaiting him in medicine or engineering.

The class teacher talked to Muhammed, understood his plight and wanted to help him. He opened the Quran and read him the verse: **"Ah! Alas for (My) Servants! There comes not an apostle to them but they mock him!"** Muhammed immediately understood the implication. "Thank you for your encouragement", he said. "The apostles too suffered greatly when they were mocked", said the teacher. "You must endeavor to persuade your parents as the apostles did. Even if they do not agree, you must not neglect your talents. You must continue to develop them while you are studying medicine or engineering. You must be patient as the apostles were".

Explanation: Muhammed's problem is common to many families. The parents want their son or daughter to study a profession which they consider more suitable or more financially rewarding. The child thinks otherwise and loves a particular subject which his parents do not approve. The choice of a profession resembles the choice of a mate. In modern Western society it is accepted that the boy or girl make their own choices and in collective-traditional societies these decisions are taken by the family because the assumption is that the individual is not independent but part of a family. The class teacher was right to encourage Muhammed to insist by quoting the Quran verse which compared him to the apostles. He gave the boy hope for the future and advised him that if he did not succeed in convincing his parents, he should try to realize his talents in the humanities concomitantly with his science studies.

9 | For giveness and Absolution

1. What can we do about anger?

{ الَّذِينَ يُنفِقُونَ فِي السَّرَّاءِ وَالضَّرَّاءِ وَالْكَاظِمِينَ الْغَيْظَ وَالْعَافِينَ عَنِ النَّاسِ وَاللَّهُ يُحِبُّ الْمُحْسِنِينَ } (آل عمران: 134)

Those who spend (freely), whether in prosperity, or in adversity; **who restrain anger, and pardon (all) men; for Allah loves those who do good.** (The Family of Imran: 134)

Samar, who is in the second grade, is short-tempered, has a high opinion of herself and shouts at anyone who tries to become close to her. She cares for nobody. One morning, as the teacher was coming into the classroom, Samar was shouting at Amir because he had trodden unintentionally on her book-bag. The teacher said: "Thank you Samar, for what you just did". Samar was embarrassed at having been overheard and started crying.

Teacher: Explain to me why you're crying.

Samar: Because I was shouting when you came in.

Teacher: Samar, I want to give you something to think about at home. What would have happened if you had trodden on Amir's bag? Would he have shouted at you?

Samar (hastily): No, he wouldn't.

Teacher: I said it was homework. Bring me your answer tomorrow.

At the end of the day, Amir went over to Samar and said: "Samar, you behaved badly towards me, but I want to help you and give you some advice. At home, open the Quran at Surah 3, Verse 134 and you will find the answer".

Samar ran home, opened the Quran and read the verse: **"who restrain anger, and pardon (all) men;- for Allah loves those who do good".** The next day she brought Amir a little gift and said to him, in front of the entire class: "Please, Amir, take this little gift because you taught me something very important – how to be restrained; please forgive me".

Explanation: Samar is described as being short-tempered and having a high opinion of herself but we see that she is also capable, after the teacher's explanation, of accepting responsibility, crying and admitting that Amir would not have reacted in that fashion. This is to her credit. Amir also deserves credit. He overcame the insult, tried to help Samar and did so very well. Finally, Samar demonstrated her ability to use the Quran verse, to overcome her anger and to ask forgiveness. In essence, all three – Samar, Amir and the teacher – are observing this important Quran verse which reminds us how important it is to control anger and forgive others.

2. Is it always possible to ask forgiveness?

{ وَالَّذِينَ إِذَا فَعَلُواْ فَاحِشَةً أَوْ ظَلَمُواْ أَنْفُسَهُمْ ذَكَرُواْ اللّهَ فَاسْتَغْفَرُواْ لِذُنُوبِهِمْ وَمَن يَغْفِرُ الذُّنُوبَ إِلاَّ اللّهُ وَلَمْ يُصِرُّواْ عَلَى مَا فَعَلُواْ وَهُمْ يَعْلَمُونَ } (آل عمران: 135)

And those who, having done something to be ashamed of, or wronged their own souls, earnestly bring Allah to mind, and ask for forgiveness for their sins,- and who can forgive sins except Allah.- and are never obstinate in persisting knowingly in (the wrong) they have done. (The Family of Imran: 135)

Ahmed, in the eleventh grade, disrupted lessons, insulted teachers and hit his friends. His class teacher was at a loss and sent him to the counselor who invited him for a meeting. While she waited for him to come, the counselor recalled the many teachers' meetings which had discussed Ahmed and his misdeeds without finding a solution. What can she say to him now? Everyone tells him that he is a bad boy and he undoubtedly believes it and continues to behave accordingly. It is not surprising that he wants to take revenge on everyone around him. She picked up the Quran which was lying on her desk, leafed through it and found what she was seeking, Verse 135 of Surah 3. "That's what I shall say to him!" she decided. When Ahmed came into the room, he was convinced that once again the counselor would conduct a long and boring conversation with him. But she said that she had only one sentence to read him: **"And those who, having done something to be ashamed of, or wronged their own souls, earnestly bring Allah to mind, and ask for forgiveness for their sins,- and who can forgive sins except Allah.- and are never obstinate in persisting knowingly in (the wrong) they have done". "Repent, Ahmed", she added. "We will forgive you and God will forgive you".**

Explanation: the counselor apparently identified the vicious circle which needs to be broken. Ahmed is convinced that he is bad because everyone says so. Why, then, should he behave well? He takes his revenge and then people continue to tell him how bad he is. Psychologists would say that he needs a positive experience. He needs to feel that he can also be good and that he is admired because of that. The reprimands and punishment inflicted by his teachers have had no effect and so the counselor refrained from a long tirade accompanied by accusations and threats. On the contrary, she gave him hope by reading him the Quran verse.

3. If God is Merciful and Compassionate, why not human beings?

﴿ فَمَن تَابَ مِن بَعْدِ ظُلْمِهِ وَأَصْلَحَ فَإِنَّ اللَّهَ يَتُوبُ عَلَيْهِ إِنَّ اللَّهَ غَفُورٌ رَّحِيمٌ ﴾ (المائدة: 39)

But if the thief repents after his crime, and amends his conduct, Allah turneth to him in forgiveness; for Allah is Oft-forgiving, Most Merciful. (The Table: 39)

Rania's friendship with Asmahan, is growing steadily stronger and this is what Rania had been hoping for. Her friend Anwar was right – in order to gain what you want, you need to plan ahead and tell lies. "How clever we are. We managed to trick Asmahan and bring her close", Rania and Anwar laughed.

It all began at the end of year trip last year when the school needed a medic to accompany the pupils. Rania proposed her cousin Haled who had graduated from a paramedic's course. Haled was glad of the opportunity to earn some money and joined. During the trip, Rania introduced her handsome cousin to her girlfriends and they all began to dream about him. Asmahan could not take her eyes off him throughout the trip.

Rania knew that this was her opportunity to make friends with Asmahan. She started asking her indirectly what she thought about Haled. Asmahan said that he was very good looking and asked how old he was and what his profession was. Rania told her that he was twenty-three and studying education at college.

One day Rania went over to Asmahan and told her that Haled had sent her his regards and Asmahan was very excited that he had remembered her. Rania added that Haled thought Asmahan was the prettiest girl he had ever seen. Asmahan asked how they had come to be discussing her and Rania invented a reason. From that day on, they had a common subject of conversation and talked about Haled all day.

This year Haled again accompanied the trip. Asmahan waited for him beside the bus but when he arrived, he ignored her. She was very hurt but told herself that perhaps he had not noticed her. She went over to him and greeted him and he replied casually.

Asmahan (offended): I'm Asmahan!
Haled: Who? Do I know you?
Asmahan: Yes, I'm Rania's friend!
Haled: What is it you want? Sorry I must go.

Asmaham was very angry with Rania, shouted at her that she was a liar and said she wanted nothing more to do with her. Rania realized what a mistake she had made by toying with Asmahan's feelings in order to make friends with her. She felt very guilty and confused. How could she repair the damage? She went over to Asmahan who refused to talk to her; she apologized and promised never to do such a thing again. "I just wanted to be your friend", she said and added: **"But if the thief repents after his crime, and amends his conduct, Allah turneth to him in forgiveness; for Allah is Oft-forgiving, Most Merciful".**

This time Asmahan listened.

Explanation: it was not wrong for Rania to want Asmahan's friendship, but the method she chose was wrong. She deceived Asmahan, who may have thought that Rania would help her establish a relationship with Haled. Asmahan was bitterly disappointed. Is that the way to acquire true friends? Of course, not and such lies will eventually blow up in the face of the liar because sooner or later, the truth will emerge. How long did Rania think that she could continue to deceive her friend? She was trying to establish a friendship on a false basis which was unlikely to endure. It is to her credit that when the truth was revealed she asked forgiveness and cited the Quran verse.

4. How can we encourage someone to repay evil with good?

﴿ مَنْ عَمِلَ صَالِحاً فَلِنَفْسِهِ وَمَنْ أَسَاءَ فَعَلَيْهَا وَمَا رَبُّكَ بِظَلَّامٍ لِّلْعَبِيدِ ﴾ (فُصِّلت: 46)

Whoever works righteousness benefits his own soul; whoever works evil, it is against his own soul: nor is thy Lord ever unjust (in the least) to His Servants (Detailed: 46)

Ahmed, a sixth-grader, was referred to the school counselor after behaving violently towards his classmates. His class teacher claimed that he had not behaved like that in the past and said she didn't know what had happened to him. The counselor talked to him and found that he had recently begun to stammer for reasons still unclear, and his classmates had been mocking him and imitating his speech. The teachers had also been impatient and found it hard to wait till he finished a sentence. Ahmed felt hurt and frustrated and consequently was reacting violently.

The counselor explained to Ahmed that even if we are very hurt, we must restrain ourselves and control our actions so as not to resemble the people who are mocking us, who are due for severe punishment from God. She opened the Quran and read out to him: **"Whoever works righteousness benefits his own soul; whoever works evil, it is against his own soul: nor is thy Lord ever unjust (in the least) to His Servants".** "Think about the verse", she requested and sent him back to his classroom.

Ahmed suddenly realized that if he returned good for evil, he would be doing himself good since his mood would improve, but if he retaliated with evil, he would be injuring himself. To a friend who laughed at him in recess, he quoted the verse to make him understand that by laughing at him, he was acting against his own soul.

Explanation: a wonderful and very true verse regarding interpersonal relations. When we are good to others, we are benefiting ourselves because we feel good about ourselves.

When we are evil towards others, we are left with bad feelings instead of transmitting them to the evildoer. One could write a whole tome in psychology based on this verse in the Quran. The verse links one's inner experience with the outer experience and teaches us that there is reciprocity between interior and exterior.

5. What is the borderline between what is enjoyable and what is forbidden?

{ يَا أَيُّهَا الَّذِينَ آمَنُواْ لاَ تُحَرِّمُواْ طَيِّبَاتِ مَا أَحَلَّ اللّهُ لَكُمْ وَلاَ تَعْتَدُواْ إِنَّ اللّهَ لاَ يُحِبُّ الْمُعْتَدِينَ } (المائدة: 87)

O ye who believe! make not unlawful the good things which Allah hath made lawful for you, but commit no excess: for Allah loveth not those given to excess. (The Table: 87)

Ali, Walad and Kamal are friends who live in the same neighborhood. A representative of the neighborhood committee complained to the school counselor that the boys were disturbing the peace. They spent all their time in the street, playing football and other games, even during the afternoon siesta hours and late at night. The counselor summoned the boys to her office. She offered them candies and talked to them about their games. They admitted that they played outside at unacceptable times. Then she opened her copy of the Quran and read out: **"O ye who believe! make not unlawful the good things which Allah hath made lawful for you, but commit no excess: for Allah loveth not those given to excess".** "There is a time for everything", she told them. "There is a time to study and a time to play and we must maintain the proper balance between study and play". The boys were ashamed and promised to stop disturbing the neighbors. They also suggested, on their own initiative, that they go to the representative who had complained and ask him to convey their apologies to the neighbors.

Explanation: in almost everything we do, we need to maintain proportions – not too much and not too little – with regard to food, clothing, friendships etc. The counselor was right to cite this particular verse and to convey to the boys the important message of proper balance. She could have scolded them for disturbing neighbors. She could have ignored the complaints. But she chose the middle road of equilibrium between enjoyable acts and forbidden behavior. She told them that it was permissible to play and even desirable for them to enjoy themselves because games were no less important for their development than studies. These are the good things which God allows the believers and made lawful for them. At the same time, she showed them the border between good and bad, between what is permissible and what is forbidden. It is important for parents in general to remember this important rule. When they tell a child, what is forbidden they should also tell him what is permitted, since otherwise children may feel that everything is forbidden. Many parents treat their children very authoritatively and focus mainly on the "no" and the "mustn't". But the Quran exhorts us not to forget to emphasize what is lawful because God wants us to enjoy good things.

6. How can we arrange reconciliation (Sulha) between families?

{ يَا أَيُّهَا الَّذِينَ آمَنُوا لَا تَقْتُلُوا الصَّيْدَ وَأَنتُمْ حُرُمٌ وَمَن قَتَلَهُ مِنكُم مُّتَعَمِّدًا فَجَزَاءٌ مِّثْلُ مَا قَتَلَ مِنَ النَّعَمِ يَحْكُمُ بِهِ ذَوَا عَدْلٍ مِّنكُمْ هَدْيًا بَالِغَ الْكَعْبَةِ أَوْ كَفَّارَةٌ طَعَامُ مَسَاكِينَ أَوْ عَدْلُ ذَٰلِكَ صِيَامًا لِّيَذُوقَ وَبَالَ أَمْرِهِ عَفَا اللَّهُ عَمَّا سَلَفَ وَمَنْ عَادَ فَيَنتَقِمُ اللَّهُ مِنْهُ وَاللَّهُ عَزِيزٌ ذُو انتِقَامٍ } (المائدة: 95)

O ye who believe! Kill not game while in the sacred precincts or in pilgrim garb. If any of you doth so intentionally, the compensation is an offering, brought to the Ka'ba, of a domestic animal equivalent to the one he killed, as adjudged by two just men among you; or by way of atonement, the feeding of the indigent; or its equivalent in fasts: that he may taste of the penalty of his deed. **Allah forgives what is past: for repetition Allah will exact from him the penalty. For Allah is Exalted, and Lord of Retribution.** (The Table: 95)

Said and Saher are in the same class; there is an age-old dispute between their families. Said refuses to sit beside Saher and often even beats him up. The class teacher has tried to talk to Said about his violent conduct, but Said replied that his parents refuse to allow him to be Saher's friend because he is from an "enemy" family. The hostility between these two pupils has had a bad effect on the entire class and in particular on Saher. His parents report that he is anxious, wakes at night crying, does not sleep well and recently has been referred to the school psychologist who diagnosed anxiety. The counselor decided to take action. She invited the parents of both boys, each family separately, and explained the damage the situation was causing to their children and to the entire class. She suggested that the parents meet to open a new page in relations between the families for the sake of their children and of the generations to come. **"Allah forgives what is past: for repetition Allah will exact from him the penalty. For Allah is Exalted, and Lord of Retribution"**, she quoted to them and added: "If Allah forgives what is past, why can't you too forgive?"

Explanation: Said and Saher feel themselves to be an inseparable part of their families and hence obliged to represent family interests. This is a tragedy because they have no possibility of being friends and getting alone together. In Western society, the counselor could help the parents to distinguish between themselves and their child, and could say that families can quarrel between themselves as much as they choose, but there is no need to involve children who should be allowed to choose their own friends. In traditional societies, where separation between parents and children is not accepted, disputes can easier extend to the next generation. Granting independence to a child can help to resolve the dispute because he may get along harmoniously with the classmate from the "enemy" family. The counselor did well to advise the families to meet and conduct a sulha (peace-making ceremony). She did not suggest that they try to clarify what had happened in the past and why the dispute had begun. She simply utilized the Quran verse which exhorts us to forgives what is past for the sake of a better future.

7. How can we encourage taking responsibility?

{ فَلِذَٰلِكَ فَادْعُ وَاسْتَقِمْ كَمَا أُمِرْتَ وَلَا تَتَّبِعْ أَهْوَاءَهُمْ وَقُلْ آمَنتُ بِمَا أَنزَلَ اللَّهُ مِن
كِتَابٍ وَأُمِرْتُ لِأَعْدِلَ بَيْنَكُمُ اللَّهُ رَبُّنَا وَرَبُّكُمْ لَنَا أَعْمَالُنَا وَلَكُمْ أَعْمَالُكُمْ لَا حُجَّةَ بَيْنَنَا
وَبَيْنَكُمُ اللَّهُ يَجْمَعُ بَيْنَنَا وَإِلَيْهِ الْمَصِيرُ } (الشورى: 15)

Now then, for that (reason), call (them to the Faith), and stand steadfast as thou art commanded, nor follow thou their vain desires; but say: "I believe in the Book which Allah has sent down; and I am commanded to judge justly between you. **Allah is our Lord and your Lord: for us (is the responsibility for) our deeds, and for you for your deeds. There is no contention between us and you.** Allah will bring us together, and to Him is (our) Final Goal. (The Consultation: 15)

Karim, who is in the tenth grade, began to tease Salem because he thought that Salem had too high an opinion of himself. Salem ignored him but Karim continued to pester him. One day Karim waited for Salem and attacked him. They began to fight and Salem, who was stronger, beat him.

Karim decided to take revenge, gathered a group of friends from his hamoula (extended family), the largest in the village, and told them to put Salem in his place. He thought that Salem's standing should be inferior to his because he belonged to a small hamoula. The boys assembled and waited for Salem on the road. When he saw them, he fled to his parents and told them what had happened. His father and other men from their hamoula went to members of Karim's hamoula. They told Karim's father that his son was provoking Salem and attacking him. "Please warn your son. I don't want this dispute to spread to the adults". Abu Karim replied to Abu Salem: "Your son has been provoking my son". And Abu Salem replied: "Stop it. We don't want to continue this dispute or for it to develop into something big. We will not be silent if we are attacked and what will be will be. But I hope that each of us will warn his son, and that each will be responsible for his actions as the Quran says: **"Allah is our Lord and your Lord: for us (is the responsibility for) our deeds, and for you for your deeds. There is no contention between us and you".**

Explanation: It is only natural for a father to support his son and justify him. It is natural for each party to have complaints against the other. But this Quran verse exhorts both sides to take responsibility, each for himself. It is a pity to quarrel, says Salem's father with the aid of the Quran. You, Abu Karim, will be responsible to your son and your hamoula and I, Abu Salem, will be responsible to Salem and my hamoula. Salem's father did not confront Karim's father on the question of who had started the quarrel. He knew that Karim's father could delve into history and cite cases where Salem's hamoula had injured him. He merely said that Allah sees and knows everything and judges each individual according to his actions. Hence, both must take responsibility and prevent the dispute from continuing.

8. Is it one's duty to respect parents even when they anger us?

﴿قُلْ تَعَالَوْاْ أَتْلُ مَا حَرَّمَ رَبُّكُمْ عَلَيْكُمْ أَلاَّ تُشْرِكُواْ بِهِ شَيْئاً وَبِالْوَالِدَيْنِ إِحْسَاناً وَلاَ تَقْتُلُواْ أَوْلاَدَكُم مِّنْ إمْلاَقٍ نَّحْنُ نَرْزُقُكُمْ وَإِيَّاهُمْ وَلاَ تَقْرَبُواْ الْفَوَاحِشَ مَا ظَهَرَ مِنْهَا وَمَا بَطَنَ وَلاَ تَقْتُلُواْ النَّفْسَ الَّتِي حَرَّمَ اللّهُ إِلاَّ بِالْحَقِّ ذَلِكُمْ وَصَّاكُمْ بِهِ لَعَلَّكُمْ تَعْقِلُونَ﴾ (الأنعام: 151)

Say: "Come, I will rehearse what Allah hath (really) prohibited you from": Join not anything as equal with Him; **be good to your parents;** kill not your children on a plea of want;- We provide sustenance for you and for them;- come not nigh to shameful deeds. Whether open or secret; take not life, which Allah hath made sacred, except by way of justice and law: thus doth He command you, that ye may learn wisdom. (The Livestock: 151)

Yasmin, who is in the fifth grade in the Shalom school, is a mediocre student perhaps even less than mediocre, but is endowed with charisma and impressive powers of persuasion. One day her mother came to school to enquire about her daughter's behavior and achievements. She knocked on the door of the classroom and the teacher opened it. When Yasmin saw her mother, she said: "What are you doing here? You didn't tell me you were coming. How could you do that without telling me?" Her mother was taken aback but recovered and said: "I came to enquire about you and to ask if you need anything, my dear daughter". Yasmin replied: "I don't need anything. Go home!" The teacher, stunned by Yasmin's tone, called her in for a talk later in the day.

She explained how important it is to respect parents even if they embarrass us in front of the entire class. To emphasize the message, she quoted to her from Verse 151 of Surah 6: **"Be good to your parents".** Yasmin realized how wrong her conduct had been and promised to ask her mother's pardon and to treat her with respect in the future.

Explanation: Yasmin wants to feel grownup and independent and doesn't want her mother to come to school without telling her in advance. It is likely that many children would feel the same if a parent suddenly appeared in school without their prior knowledge. But none of this justifies offending parents, and in front of the entire class. A child who behaves like that is undermining his own dignity as well as that of the parent. When we respect our parents, we are respecting ourselves. If her mother's conduct embarrasses Yasmin, she can ask her politely at home not to do it again and explain how she feels. In any event, to insult her mother in front of witnesses is unacceptable. The teacher was right to quote the important Quran verse regarding respect towards parents.

9. How can we make peace between two who are quarreling?

{ وَاللَّهُ يَدْعُو إِلَى دَارِ السَّلَامِ وَيَهْدِي مَن يَشَاءُ إِلَى صِرَاطٍ مُّسْتَقِيمٍ } (يونس: 25)

But Allah doth call to the Home of Peace: He doth guide whom He pleaseth to a way that is straight. (Jonah: 25)

After the mid-morning recess, the history teacher came into the eleventh-grade class, which consisted of both fellahin and Bedouin. During the lesson, a dispute broke out between two pupils, one from each group. Quarrels between fellahin and Bedouin are common in the school. The teacher pacified them and continued the lesson. Suddenly the quarrel flared up again and spread to the entire class. The two groups – fellahin and Bedouin – began to curse one another and the curses turned into blows until fighting was raging. The teacher could not control them. Fortunately, the principal heard the noise and came in. He talked to the pupils and pacified them. Then he turned to them and said: "I don't want to suspend a single pupil from school, not even for a day. I want you to conduct a sulha which will hold strong for the future as well". When the pupils heard the word 'sulha' the anger flared up again and neither group was willing to make peace. Then the principal took out the Quran, asked for quiet and read out the verse: **"But Allah doth call to the Home of Peace: He doth guide whom He pleaseth to a way that is straight".** "God commands you to make peace with one another", he explained, "and you are refusing!" This time all the pupils agreed to a sulha. They displayed initiative, decided on a date and what each would bring and invited all the pupils in the school to take part. It was a memorable event.

Explanation: the Quran is the book of peace and those who are not familiar with it should read several verses. Forgiveness, compassion and peace are among its basic elements. When a teacher stands helpless in the face of the fights, what can she say to the pupils? Next time she will probably know. **"Allah doth call to the Home of Peace".** This verse sufficed to calm the quarreling boys. Now they are ready for forgiveness because this is the command of God to his children. The principal could have lectured them for hours and tried to clarify who began and what happened. Would he have achieved a better outcome than did the Quran verse? Perhaps and perhaps not. It is sometimes worthwhile to discover what exactly happened, but the command of God has no equals in bringing hearts together and restoring harmony. No investigation, however thorough, can achieve the same results.

10. How can we persuade warring families to refrain from violence and make peace?

{ وَكَذَلِكَ أَنزَلْنَاهُ حُكْماً عَرَبِيّاً وَلَئِنِ اتَّبَعْتَ أَهْوَاءَهُم بَعْدَ مَا جَاءكَ مِنَ الْعِلْمِ مَا لَكَ مِنَ اللّهِ مِن وَلِيٍّ وَلاَ وَاقٍ } (الرعد: 37)

Thus have We revealed it to be a judgment of authority in Arabic. Wert thou to follow their (vain) desires after the

knowledge which hath reached thee, then wouldst thou find neither protector nor defender against Allah. (The Thunder: 37)

Two friends, Ahmed and Munir, went to the class teacher and told her that they were good friends but that there was a dispute between their families and they didn't want it to affect their friendship. The teacher approached Ahmed's parents and explained that Ahmed was very friendly with Munir and was suffering because of the rivalry between the families. Ahmed's parents were persuaded and agreed to make peace with Munir's family, who refused. They claimed that Ahmed's family were always the ones who started hostilities. The teacher told them that Ahmed's family had already expressed their willingness to make peace and she explained how beneficial this would be for their children. To reinforce her remarks, she quoted from the Quran: **"Thus have We revealed it to be a judgment of authority in Arabic. Wert thou to follow their (vain) desires after the knowledge which hath reached thee, then wouldst thou find neither protector nor defender against Allah".** "You have been endowed with knowledge," she told Munir's parents. "You must not follow your anger and desire for revenge but seek peace". Munir's parents were persuaded to open a new page in relations with Ahmed's family.

Explanation: Generally, in Western societies, parents are less involved in disputes between children, because the children tend to be more independent. In traditional societies, friendship between children or parents often leads to friendship among other relatives, and the relationships are more familial than individual. This can create problems, as in the case of Ahmed and Munir. The teacher was right to recommend a sulha, if not for their own sake then for the sake of their children. She was not only persuading the parents to make peace but also teaching them that sometimes the wishes of the child should be central, particularly when they are positive wishes.

10 | Delinquency and Violence

1. What can we say to a delinquent adolescent?

﴿ كُتِبَ عَلَيْكُمُ الْقِتَالُ وَهُوَ كُرْهٌ لَّكُمْ وَعَسَى أَن تَكْرَهُواْ شَيْئًا وَهُوَ خَيْرٌ لَّكُمْ وَعَسَى أَن تُحِبُّواْ شَيْئًا وَهُوَ شَرٌّ لَّكُمْ وَاللّهُ يَعْلَمُ وَأَنتُمْ لاَ تَعْلَمُونَ ﴾ (البقرة: 216)

Fighting is prescribed for you, and ye dislike it. **But it is possible that ye dislike a thing which is good for you, and that ye love a thing which is bad for you. But Allah knoweth, and ye know not.** (The Cow: 216)

In a certain high school, there is a gang of badly-behaved pupils who respect nobody and try to terrorize younger and weaker children. They hate studying and come to school only in order to pass the time. Recently they have begun to dye their hair, to wear torn jeans and to smoke. The teachers have tried to reason with them but without results. They refuse to acknowledge that their conduct is wrong and unacceptable and appear to be very satisfied with themselves.

After consultations in the Ministry of Education, it was decided to utilize the Quran in order to reform them. The members of the gang were told that if they wanted to remain in school, they must attend several lessons in religion where they would read the Quran and discuss what they read. At the first lesson, the principal chose Verse 216 of Surah 2 in order to begin: **"But it is possible that ye dislike a thing which is good for you, and that ye love a thing which is bad for you. But Allah knoweth, and ye know not".** After he read the verse, there was silence in the room. Then he turned to the pupils and asked them how they understood the verse. It was the first time that they had agreed to attend a lesson and even take part in it. The principal invited their parents and several religious notables to take part in the coming lessons. After six meetings, several teachers reported that the boys' conduct had changed beyond recognition. Their elders, hoping that the change would not be short-lived, decided to continue the religious lessons in order to preserve the achievements.

Explanation: one of the difficult tasks in education is to reform a group of adolescents who treat everyone with contempt and do as they choose. The moment such boys realize that they can rebel and nobody will stop them, they become uncontrollable. In such difficult situations, when adolescents are on the verge of delinquency and are liable to take up drugs and prostitution, there is only one anchor left and that is the Quran. When faced with the authority of the Quran and of God, young boys usually no longer dare to rebel. The Quran should be utilized wisely in order to bring them back into the fold. They should be treated with warmth and love and taught Quran. Reprimands and anger have been proved to be useless. These boys often lack parental warmth and love, and this lack accounts for their conduct. The Quran and religion can provide the warmth they yearn for and can be a vital therapeutic tool.

2. What can we say to adolescents who drink alcohol?

{ يَسْأَلُونَكَ عَنِ الْخَمْرِ وَالْمَيْسِرِ قُلْ فِيهِمَا إِثْمٌ كَبِيرٌ وَمَنَافِعُ لِلنَّاسِ وَإِثْمُهُمَا أَكْبَرُ مِن نَّفْعِهِمَا وَيَسْأَلُونَكَ مَاذَا يُنفِقُونَ قُلِ الْعَفْوَ كَذَلِكَ يُبيِّنُ اللّهُ لَكُمُ الآيَاتِ لَعَلَّكُمْ تَتَفَكَّرُونَ } (البقرة: 219)

They ask thee concerning wine and gambling. Say: "In them is great sin, and some profit, for men; but the sin is greater than the profit." They ask thee how much they are to spend;

Say: "What is beyond your needs." Thus doth Allah Make clear to you His Signs: In order that ye may consider. (The Cow: 219)

During the annual school trip to Eilat, three problematic pupils disappeared for several hours. When they returned to the hotel, they behaved wildly and used insulting language towards the girls. It was clear from their behavior and the strong smell of alcohol that they were drunk. A teacher who came to see what was happening, found the girls on the verge of tears at the boys' crude and disrespectful language. They teachers decided to send the three boys home and to continue the trip without them. When the whole group returned to school after the trip, the principal assembled pupils and teachers and told them what had happened (although they already knew). He asked them what punishment they considered fit for the boys and told them to think about it for several days. He also turned to the culprits themselves and asked them to suggest how he should deal with them. One of them suggested that they read through the Quran and select all the verses relating to their unacceptable conduct. The principal agreed and assigned them this task. After several days, the boys returned with a list of a number of verses dealing not only with the ban on drinking wine but also with the prohibition against insulting others and the need to respect authority. The list commenced with the verse: **"They ask thee concerning wine and gambling. Say: 'In them is great sin, and some profit, for men; but the sin is greater than the profit.'"**

The principal asked the boys to apologize to the girls in front of the entire school. He also informed their parents and finally told them that this time he would forgive them, but would not forgive them if they ever acted like that again.

Explanation: many boys feel the need to experiment with alcohol and drugs. The reason for these dangerous experiments is their urge to feel free of all restraints and inhibitions, and the desire to have new experiences and be drawn into new worlds. They want to detach themselves for a brief time from this world. However, they are facing great risks whether because of the danger of addiction or because, while on drugs, they may harm themselves or others, and sometimes drugs can be fatal. There are many acceptable ways of relieving tension and easing burdens, none of which entail using alcohol or drugs. We can relax at a movie or play, release energy in games, meet with friends etc. Anyone who works with alcoholics or drug addicts knows how difficult and often impossible it is to 'kick the habit'. In this particular case, the Quran comes to our aid and the Divine command and authority can help those who refuse to listen to parents or teachers. The principal was right to use the Quran in order to explain the dangers of alcohol.

3. How can we make peace between quarreling children?

{ وَاعْتَصِمُواْ بِحَبْلِ اللّهِ جَمِيعًا وَلاَ تَفَرَّقُواْ وَاذْكُرُواْ نِعْمَةَ اللّهِ عَلَيْكُمْ إِذْ كُنتُمْ أَعْدَاءً
فَأَلَّفَ بَيْنَ قُلُوبِكُمْ فَأَصْبَحْتُم بِنِعْمَتِهِ إِخْوَانًا وَكُنتُمْ عَلَى شَفَا حُفْرَةٍ مِّنَ النَّارِ فَأَنقَذَكُم
مِّنْهَا كَذَلِكَ يُبَيِّنُ اللّهُ لَكُمْ آيَاتِهِ لَعَلَّكُمْ تَهْتَدُونَ } (آل عمران: 103)

And hold fast, all together, by the rope which Allah (stretches out for you), and be not divided among yourselves; and remember with gratitude Allah's favour on you; for ye were enemies and He joined your hearts in love, so that by His Grace, ye became brethren; and ye were on the brink of the pit of Fire, and He saved you from it. Thus doth Allah make His Signs clear to you: That ye may be guided. (The Family of Imran: 103)

Said and Sami, tenth-graders, were leaders in the classroom, each with his own followers. When a boy from one group squabbled with a boy from the other group, the outcome was violence. Boys who did not belong to either group were forced to join one of them in order to enjoy protection. The atmosphere in the classroom was chaotic and the violence spread to other classes.

The principal summoned all the teachers for an urgent meeting because the situation was intolerable. It was decided to assemble all the tenth graders and to explain new rules to them according to which violence, even verbal violence, would not be tolerated. It was decided to explain to them what was permitted and what was forbidden, to emphasize that anyone who did not observe the rules would not be permitted to remain in the class. The principal also proposed conducting a sulha and telling the pupils that they must live together like brothers since otherwise the situation would deteriorate. He started by reading from the Quran: **"And hold fast, all together, by the rope which Allah (stretches out for you), and be not divided among yourselves; and remember with gratitude Allah's favour on you; for ye were enemies and He joined your hearts in love, so that by His Grace, ye became brethren; and ye were on the brink of the pit of Fire, and He saved you from it. Thus doth Allah make His Signs clear to you: That ye may be guided".**

Explanation: a child must be free of fear in order to focus on learning. The task of the teachers and the principal is to enable each pupil to study without fear. Many pupils are afraid of violence and are reluctant to talk about it. A teacher who ignores violence or grants preferential treatment to a violent pupil will pay a high price. Pupils who are not violent will gain the impression that their teacher fears violence and this will reinforce their own fears. A nervous pupil will find it hard to solve mathematical exercises or to create and the democratic spirit which should prevail in the classroom will vanish and be replaced by the rule of fear. Parents too have an obligation to ensure that their children are free to study and are not ruled by fear. The Quran verse encourages pupils to become friends and foster a warm atmosphere in the classroom.

4. How can we ensure positive rather than negative cooperation between friends?

﴿ وَلْتَكُن مِّنكُمْ أُمَّةٌ يَدْعُونَ إِلَى الْخَيْرِ وَيَأْمُرُونَ بِالْمَعْرُوفِ وَيَنْهَوْنَ عَنِ الْمُنكَرِ وَأُوْلَئِكَ هُمُ الْمُفْلِحُونَ ﴾ (آل عمران: 104)

Let there arise out of you a band of people inviting to all that is good, enjoining what is right, and forbidding what is wrong: They are the ones to attain felicity. (The Family of Imran: 104)

Rami and Rafi are good friends, spend time together between classes at school and in the afternoons and do everything together. When they solved the math's exam together, the mathematics teacher caught them and failed them both. On the last day of school, before the vacation, they decided to take revenge on him. Rafi brought a carton of eggs, called Rami and several other boys and they threw the eggs at the teacher's car. Suddenly their class teacher passed by and saw what they were doing. He called them and reprimanded them for copying during the exam and for vandalism. After explaining that their behavior was unacceptable, he read out to them: **"Let there arise out of you a band of people inviting to all that is good, enjoining what is right, and forbidding what is wrong: They are the ones to attain felicity".**

Explanation: by quoting the Quran verse, the teacher was exhorting his pupils to do what was right and not what was wrong. Mutual responsibility means that each is responsible for his actions and for those of the other. For example, the pupil who asked to copy was wronging his friend and not only himself. The same was true of the act of bringing the eggs to school. Rafi was wronging Rami by urging him to join him, and by failing to dissuade him, Rami was wronging him in turn. The

Quran is referring both to individual and to group responsibility in accordance with circumstances.

5. Should we react to violence with violence?

{ لَئِن بَسَطتَ إِلَيَّ يَدَكَ لِتَقْتُلَنِي مَا أَنَاْ بِبَاسِطٍ يَدِيَ إِلَيْكَ لِأَقْتُلَكَ إِنِّي أَخَافُ اللّهَ رَبَّ الْعَالَمِينَ } (المائدة: 28)

"If thou dost stretch thy hand against me, to slay me, it is not for me to stretch my hand against thee to slay thee: for I do fear Allah, the cherisher of the worlds. (The Table: 28)

Shadi, who is a tenth grader, is friendly with Maali from the ninth grade. They chat on their way home from school and all his classmates known that he likes her.

Two weeks ago, when some of the boys were sitting in the school courtyard, Maali passed by, and one of them commented that she was Shadi's girlfriend. Maali's cousin, who was among them, was very angry and started shouting: "I'll show him". He went looking for Shadi, and when he found him, he attacked him and stabbed him in the forehead with a metal ruler. Shadi's forehead bled profusely; he tried to hit back, but then teachers came running and the other pupils pulled the two fighting boys apart.

The boys were sent to the counselor's office for a talk. The first thing she did was to read then a Quran verse: **"If thou dost stretch thy hand against me, to slay me, it is not for me to stretch my hand against thee to slay thee: for I do fear Allah, the cherisher of the worlds".** Then she went into their classroom and hung a large poster on the wall on which she inscribed the verse. After that she discussed with the pupils the Quran's attitude to violence and illustrated by quoting the verse.

Explanation: This important verse can be quoted in order to combat violent behavior which can spread through a society like wildfire. The verse condemns violence of every kind, even on the part of the victim of an attack. Many parents are uncertain what to tell their child to do when he or she has been attacked by another child. Some say that the child should go and tell a teacher and not retaliate. Others add that if that does not help, they should tell their parents. Many parents, however, feel the need to teach their child to defend himself, because if he does not do it, nobody will do it for him. It is hard to condemn parents who are more concerned for their child's safety than for social morals. We all know how important it is for our children to know how to defend themselves. In extreme cases, parents force their children to retaliate and threaten them with punishment of they do not do so. But the Holy Quran forbids all kinds of violence – not only is it forbidden to attack another, but even if you have been attacked, you must not retaliate. This verse can be utilized to root out all kinds of violence between children and between adults. In other contexts, the Quran encourages the individual to defend himself.

6. What should a juvenile investigator inscribe on his office wall?

{ يَا أَيُّهَا الَّذِينَ آمَنُواْ لاَ تُحِلُّواْ شَعَائِرَ اللهِ وَلاَ الشَّهْرَ الْحَرَامَ وَلاَ الْهَدْيَ وَلاَ الْقَلاَئِدَ
وَلا آمِّينَ الْبَيْتَ الْحَرَامَ يَبْتَغُونَ فَضْلاً مِّن رَّبِّهِمْ وَرِضْوَانًا وَإِذَا حَلَلْتُمْ فَاصْطَادُواْ
وَلاَ يَجْرِمَنَّكُمْ شَنَآنُ قَوْمٍ أَن صَدُّوكُمْ عَنِ الْمَسْجِدِ الْحَرَامِ أَن تَعْتَدُواْ وَتَعَاوَنُواْ عَلَى
الْبرِّ وَالتَّقْوَى وَلاَ تَعَاوَنُواْ عَلَى الإِثْمِ وَالْعُدْوَانِ وَاتَّقُواْ اللهَ إِنَّ اللهَ شَدِيدُ الْعِقَابِ }
(المائدة: 2)

O ye who believe! Violate not the sanctity of the symbols of Allah, nor of the sacred month, nor of the animals brought for sacrifice, nor the garlands that mark out such animals, nor the people resorting to the sacred house, seeking of the bounty and good pleasure of their Lord. But when ye are clear of the sacred precincts and of pilgrim garb, ye may hunt and let not the hatred of some people in (once) shutting you out of the Sacred Mosque lead you to transgression (and hostility on your part). **Help ye one another in righteousness and piety, but help ye not one another in sin and rancour:** fear Allah. for Allah is strict in punishment. (The Table: 2)

Ali, an eighth-grader, is the leader of a gang of boys who vandalize school property, beat up pupils and do as they please. He walks out of lessons and wanders around the school courtyard. Then he calls his friends and they too walk out of their classrooms in the middle of a lesson to join him. They smash windows at school, break faucets and carve on tables and chairs. Every morning Ali's parents fight with him about attending school and he refuses to study seriously.

Last week, Ali quarreled with a teacher who refused to let him leave the classroom. Ali decided to take revenge. He summoned his friends and they damaged the teacher's car, slashing the tires, scratching the body and pouring glue into the locks. When they finished, they fled.

The school investigated with the aid of the police, and discovered that Ali and his gang were responsible. The boys admitted it after a long interrogation, and the police interrogator turned to them and said: **"Help ye one another in righteousness and piety, but help ye not one another in sin and rancour".** He asked them if they knew where the verse appeared and none of them recognized it. They he told them that it was Verse 2 of Surah 5, which he often quoted in his work with delinquent gangs.

Explanation: this wise Quran verse is suited to adolescent or adult gangs of delinquents. The Quran encourages them to work together for righteousness and not for sin. Many children who come from homes where they were abused, deprived and humiliated tend to develop social ties of this type. They often join a gang under the leadership of someone whom they fear and obey. When their fear of the leader is greater than their fear of committing a crime, the path to a criminal career is open. Delinquent youths are often repeating the negative experience they have brought from their families. However, positive cooperation does not require a humiliating and oppressive hierarchy, but rather warm and close group relationships. Those who join groups which help the weak are replicating the good experiences of their childhood. The Quran is very clear as to the type of connection it recommends. It advocates warm and close relations wherein the individual contributes to society. Perhaps the policeman would have done well to hang a poster in his office with this verse inscribed on it.

7. What can we say to someone who is trying to kick a drug habit?

{ وَلَئِنْ أَذَقْنَاهُ نَعْمَاءَ بَعْدَ ضَرّاءَ مَسّتْهُ لَيَقُولَنّ ذَهَبَ السّيّئَاتُ عَنّي إِنّهُ لَفَرِحٌ فَخُورٌ * إِلّا الّذِينَ صَبَرُوا وَعَمِلُوا الصّالِحَاتِ أُولَئِكَ لَهُم مّغْفِرَةٌ وَأَجْرٌ كَبِيرٌ } (هود: 11-10)

But if We give him a taste of (Our) favours after adversity hath touched him, he is sure to say, "All evil has departed from me:" Behold! he falls into exultation and pride. Not so do those who show patience and constancy, and work righteousness; for them is forgiveness (of sins) and a great reward. (Hud: 10-11)

Fuad's father was a drug addict for many years until one day he decided to break the habit. He took control of his life, spent a year in a rehabilitation center and returned clean of drugs. He admitted to his son that it was the hardest year of his life, because the drug had been in his body for many years and he had become totally physically and psychologically dependent on it. He explained to his adolescent children that they were at the dangerous age and that the decisions they took now could have a positive or negative impact on their lives. He had begun to use drugs in his teens.

Today Fuad's father accompanies every step of his children's lives. They tell him about their difficulties and about group pressure to smoke, for example, and he encourages them to be strong and not to give in to pressures. He is grateful to God for being at his side and helping him to turn over a new leaf and be a new man. "I was harming my family and society", he says, "and now I work and I'm a useful member of society. I was re-born thanks to God and I am clean". He also told his son that, during the rehabilitation process, he was warned against the moment when he would decide that he was clean and was tempted to start again. Then he was liable to return to square one. At the rehabilitation center, the former addicts used to recite the verse: **"But if We give him a taste of (Our) favours after adversity hath touched him, he is sure to say, "All evil has departed from me:" Behold! he falls into exultation and pride.Not so do those who show patience and constancy, and work righteousness; for them is forgiveness (of sins) and a great reward".**

Explanation: it is only natural for an individual to believe that his war is over and he can rest on his laurels and do whatever he chooses. But anyone who was once a drug addict knows that his battle is never over and every day he must remind himself of that fact. To lose means to lose his future and perhaps his life as well. Fuad's father teaches his son that what starts with a cigarette can end much more drastically. One must struggle against temptation and be brave enough to withstand group pressure. There is no reason in the world to ruin our health and our bodies which God has given us by smoking. Many children should talk to Fuad's father to understand why it is forbidden to yield to pressure, and to realize that the danger always exists.

God cautions us against complacency based on the belief that it could never happen to us.

8. Should we yield to fear?

{ قَالُواْ أَإِنَّكَ لَأَنتَ يُوسُفُ قَالَ أَنَاْ يُوسُفُ وَهَـذَا أَخِي قَدْ مَنَّ اللّهُ عَلَيْنَا إِنَّهُ مَن يَتَّقِ وَيِصْبِرْ فَإِنَّ اللّهَ لاَ يُضِيعُ أَجْرَ الْمُحْسِنِينَ } (يوسف: 90)

They said: "Art thou indeed Joseph?" He said, "I am Joseph, and this is my brother: Allah has indeed been gracious to us (all): b**ehold, he that is righteous and patient,- never will Allah suffer the reward to be lost, of those who do right."** (Joseph: 90)

In a certain high-school there have recently been numerous incidents of vandalism. Windows were smashed, tables and chairs broken, walls covered in graffiti and equipment was stolen from the computer room. This worried the school administration and the teaching staff as well as the parents, who want to believe that school is a safe environment. The parents asked the administration to discover who was causing the damage and to expel them from school.

One morning, the school counselor heard that Amal, a girl from the tenth grade, knew the identity of the delinquents who had caused the damage; she invited Amal into her office. At first the girl denied everything but later she admitted that she knew who the members of the gang were but that they had threatened that if she told anyone they would beat her and her little sister. The counselor listened and then said: **"behold, he that is righteous and patient,- never will Allah suffer the reward to be lost, of those who do right."** When Amal heard this verse, she plucked up her courage and confessed what she knew.

She said that there was a group of seven girls from the eleventh grade who often broke into school in the afternoon hours and created havoc. The gang were caught and brought before the disciplinary committee, and it was decided to suspend them from school for a week. They returned a week later accompanied by their parents and apologized to the entire school. Their punishment was community service in the form of repair work at the school.

Explanation: Amal was in a difficult situation. The counselor asked her to confess to what she knew, thereby placing her and her family at risk. We can demand such a confession only if it is possible to provide protection for the witness; otherwise it is not a fair demand. The counselor apparently thought that the school administration had the power and authority to protect Amal and her sister. The counselor chose to quote a verse which was very appropriate for Amal. She was terrified and the Quran advised her to be strong because Allah would not suffer her reward to be lost. It is an important lesson – we should not be governed by fear and should overcome it and act righteously. If Amal had succumbed to fear she would have been completely under the thumb of the gang and there would have been no end to the story.

9. What will Satan say on the Day of Judgment to a boy who joined a gang of delinquents?

{ وَقَالَ الشَّيْطَانُ لَمَّا قُضِيَ الأَمْرُ إِنَّ اللّهَ وَعَدَكُمْ وَعْدَ الْحَقِّ وَوَعَدتُّكُمْ فَأَخْلَفْتُكُمْ وَمَا
كَانَ لِيَ عَلَيْكُم مِّن سُلْطَانٍ إِلاَّ أَن دَعَوْتُكُمْ فَاسْتَجَبْتُمْ لِي فَلاَ تَلُومُونِي وَلُومُواْ أَنفُسَكُم
مَّا أَنَاْ بِمُصْرِخِكُمْ وَمَا أَنتُمْ بِمُصْرِخِيَّ إِنِّي كَفَرْتُ بِمَآ أَشْرَكْتُمُونِ مِن قَبْلُ إِنَّ الظَّالِمِينَ
لَهُمْ عَذَابٌ أَلِيمٌ (إبراهيم: 22)

And Satan will say when the matter is decided: "It was Allah Who gave you a promise of Truth: I too promised, but I failed in my promise to you. I had no authority over you except to call you but ye listened to me: then reproach not me, but reproach your own souls. I cannot listen to your cries, nor

can ye listen to mine. I reject your former act in associating me with Allah. For wrong-doers there must be a grievous penalty." (Abraham: 22)

Samar and Inas, who live close to one another and are in the same class, are bosom friends. Recently Samar has noticed that his friend has changed. He has begun to tell lies, disappears for hours at a time, each time with a different excuse. One day he followed Inas to see where he was going and saw him, to his amazement, sitting in the backyard of the school, , smoking and taking some pills with a group of other boys. Samar was shocked, tried to dissuade his friend from using the pills and told him that his behavior was unacceptable. Inas was unimpressed and said he did it for fun. "It's normal and most of the older pupils take those pills. It helps them to concentrate on their studies", he said. He even succeeded in persuading his friend to join him, saying: "If you don't smoke, they'll say you're a coward".

Samar began joining Inas during recess. His brother heard about it and threatened to tell their parents. Samar was frightened and asked Inas to leave him alone and stop persuading him to smoke. But Inas said that what Samar did or didn't do was his own problem. "You must help me because you're the one who got me into this trap", said Samar. They began to quarrel and their teachers and classmates were shocked, because the boys were known to be best friends.

Then Samar's brother called him over and asked him to listen carefully to a certain Quran verse. He read out to him: **"And Satan will say when the matter is decided: "It was Allah Who gave you a promise of Truth: I too promised, but I failed in my promise to you. I had no authority over you except to call you but ye listened to me: then reproach not me, but reproach your own souls. I cannot listen to your cries, nor can ye listen to mine. I reject your former act in associating me with Allah. For wrong-doers there must be a grievous penalty."**

When Samar heard the verse, he began to cry and said: "That's exactly what Inas said. I can't blame him; I can only blame myself. I'm going to take control of my life and keep away from Inas and his gang".

Explanation: at most ages, but certainly during adolescence, the group exerts strong influence on the individual and can entice him into delinquent behavior. The most striking examples are smoking and drug-taking. The individual knows that if he does not respond to pressure, he will be ejected from the gang. Samar is torn between two worlds and has to decide whether to renounce his bosom friend and reject smoking and drugs or remain with Inas and behave like him. To take the courageous decision requires fortitude. Here Samar's brother came to his aid by reading him the verse which echoed what Inas said to him: **"ye listened to me: then reproach not me, but reproach your own souls".**

Samar felt that the Quran understood his dilemma and decided to take control of his life and to reform.

10. Do people sometimes ask us to harm them?

{ وَيَدْعُ الإِنسَانُ بِالشَّرِّ دُعَاءَهُ بِالْخَيْرِ وَكَانَ الإِنسَانُ عَجُولاً } (الإسراء:11)

The prayer that man should make for good, he maketh for evil; for man is given to hasty (deeds). (The Night Journey: 11)

Abed is a very wild boy and the teacher is tired of lecturing him. She has done everything possible to reform him. First, she told him his conduct was inappropriate, then she sent him to the counselor but he refused to cooperate. She has talked to his parents a number of times. This time however he has gone too far, as she told his parents when they met in the principal's office. "Last Tuesday I was away from school and the principal brought in a substitute teacher. Abed was completely uncontrolled that day. He hit Din, cursed Rana, stabbed Rima with a sharp pencil and finally the teacher told him to go to the principal's office. He cursed her in front of the entire class and said: 'I'm not going. What are you going to do about it?". The teacher called the principal to the classroom and only then did Abed agree to go out. The principal was furious, suspended him for two days and told him to write a paper on the subject being studied in the classroom. Abed agreed but sat in the library and did nothing.

When Abed's father heard these stories, he was very angry. "He should be given a more severe punishment", he said. "There is a verse which is appropriate for him: **"The prayer that man should make for good, he maketh for evil; for man is given to hasty (deeds)".** My son must be begging to be punished since otherwise I can't understand his behavior".

Explanation: the Quran tells us that there are children and adults who create the impression that they are begging in some way for punishment. Sometimes we say that they have masochistic tendencies. When in this mood, the individual wants to be punished emotionally and physically and does everything possible to attract this treatment. This behavior is deep-rooted. Sometimes it is a tactic for gaining attention since he knows no other way. It is possible that in childhood this was his way of drawing his parents' attention since otherwise they would ignore him. In such situations, children prefer harsh treatment to indifference. This may be true of Abed. He doesn't even know that he can be treated well as a result of good behavior. In such cases punishment will not always help because it perpetuates the vicious circle. A warm, sympathetic approach, explanation and provision of alternative ways of gaining attention are the solution. Abed's father and his surroundings have been punishing him for some time without result and so a new solution must be tried.

11 | Human Relations

1. How should we treat the orphaned and the weak?

{ وَآتُواْ الْيَتَامَى أَمْوَالَهُمْ وَلاَ تَتَبَدَّلُواْ الْخَبِيثَ بِالطَّيِّبِ وَلاَ تَأْكُلُواْ أَمْوَالَهُمْ إِلَى أَمْوَالِكُمْ إِنَّهُ كَانَ حُوبًا كَبِيرًا } (النساء: 2)

To orphans restore their property (When they reach their age), nor substitute (your) worthless things for (their) good ones; and devour not their substance (by mixing it up) with your own. For this is indeed a great sin. (The Women: 2)

Ranin, who is in the seventh grade, is an orphan and lives with her aunt. She is a quiet, shy girl who never talks unless someone addresses her. Recently she has not been attending school regularly, and when she does come, she asks the teacher to let her out after one or two lessons. The teacher has asked her several times what is going on but she is silent. The last time the teacher asked her, Ranin burst into tears, trembled and then fell silent. Then she told her in a hoarse voice that the girls in her class mock her and hide her belongings, sometimes the book-bag and sometimes the textbooks. Last week they threw one of her books out of the window and when she ran down to pick it up, it had vanished. Ranin told this story to the teacher, choked with tears, and then she stopped, took a deep breath and added: "They steal from me because I'm an orphan and I have nobody to protect me..."

The teacher decided to deal with the matter. She started the next education hour with a Quran verse: **"To orphans restore their property (When they reach their age), nor substitute (your) worthless things for (their) good ones; and devour not**

their substance (by mixing it up) with your own. For this is indeed a great sin". She asked the pupils what the verse meant and then went on to describe Ranin's suffering. She knew that there was no need to conceal the facts because the entire class had taken part. She was not looking for culprits but wanted to bring about a transformation in the class so that Ranin could feel better. She reassured the pupils and promised not to investigate who had done what but made it clear that she was ashamed of all of them. After the lesson, several of the girls went over to Ranin and said that they wanted to be her friends.

Explanation: Children can be very cruel and their conduct often calls for the intervention of an adult. The teacher did well in not seeking culprits. A number of children had taken part in tormenting Ranin and punishment would be ineffective at this stage. Forgiveness and a new start are much more effective. In many classrooms certain children are made scapegoats and are tormented by the rest. The emotional damage can be very great. Often these children are abused at home as well and seem to be inviting their classmates to torment them because this is the treatment, they are familiar with. The tormentors are also unloading their frustrations on their classmate, and they need to have clear borderlines set for them and to be guided. They too are still only children. The important task of the teacher is to prevent such a situation and the Quran verses which call for mutual respect can help in this task.

2. How should we treat other people?

{ وَاعْبُدُوا اللَّهَ وَلَا تُشْرِكُوا بِهِ شَيْئًا وَبِالْوَالِدَيْنِ إِحْسَانًا وَبِذِي الْقُرْبَىٰ وَالْيَتَامَىٰ وَالْمَسَاكِينِ وَالْجَارِ ذِي الْقُرْبَىٰ وَالْجَارِ الْجُنُبِ وَالصَّاحِبِ بِالْجَنبِ وَابْنِ السَّبِيلِ وَمَا مَلَكَتْ أَيْمَانُكُمْ إِنَّ اللَّهَ لَا يُحِبُّ مَن كَانَ مُخْتَالًا فَخُورًا } (النساء: 36)

Serve Allah, and join not any partners with Him; **and do good- to parents, kinsfolk, orphans, those in need, neighbours**

who are near, neighbours who are strangers, the companion by your side, the wayfarer (ye meet), and what your right hands possess: For Allah loveth not the arrogant, the vainglorious; (Women: 36)

Samer, an eighth-grader, is notorious in school. He frequently quarrels with other pupils and after school he continues his quarrels with the children in his neighborhood. He does not allow the teacher to complete a lesson, punches his neighbors in class, vandalizes school property and deliberately turns on faucets. Yesterday he chased another pupil and tried to pour Coca Cola over him, and then he dragged a large garbage container to the middle of the road so that the teachers could not drive past. His class teacher and the principal asked his parents to come to school for a discussion. His mother came alone and told them that she was helpless because Samer cursed her and refused to listen. When his father comes home from work and hears about Samer's conduct, she said, he beats him savagely. But next day Samer reverts to his bad behavior as if he had not been punished.

The principal decided to invite the whole family including Samer for a talk in her office. When they came in, she asked them to sit down and noticed that Samer sat down at a distance from the rest. She asked him to come closer. "I want to read you an important Quran verse", she said. "It is intended for all of us, including me and the teacher and for Samer and his family as well". Then she read out: "and **do good- to parents, kinsfolk, orphans, those in need, neighbours who are near, neighbours who are strangers, the companion by your side, the wayfarer (ye meet)"**. "Do we all observe this verse?" she asked. "I invited you here. Do you feel that I am respecting you?" The parents and even Samer nodded. "Samer, do you abide by this verse?" Samer sat in embarrassed silence. "No, I know that I don't", he finally replied and then his father added: "To tell the truth, I don't always abide by it because I often beat Samer". "There is no more to be said", the principal declared. "From today on, all of us promise one another to abide by the verse and not only to do good to one another but also to those who are strangers to us. And if any of us has a problem we can always talk about it without hurting others".

Explanation: teachers often appeal helplessly to a principal or counselor because of a pupil who disrupts every lesson and is uncontrollable. They have tried everything, talking to parents, punishment and nothing helps. In these severe cases the Quran may help because of the great respect everyone has for the Holy Quran. This verse reflects the spirit of the Quran which exhorts us to do good not only to our families but also to strangers or wayfarers. It is possible to help pupils who behave like Samer within the framework of religious lessons at school. These lessons can introduce order into the lives of children and adolescents with severe behavioral problems and give them a sense of satisfaction and success.

3. Is it permissible to ignore a greeting?

{ وَإِذَا حُيِّيتُم بِتَحِيَّةٍ فَحَيُّوا بِأَحْسَنَ مِنْهَا أَوْ رُدُّوهَا إِنَّ اللَّهَ كَانَ عَلَىٰ كُلِّ شَيْءٍ حَسِيبًا}
(النساء: 86)

When a (courteous) greeting is offered you, meet it with a greeting still more courteous, or (at least) of equal courtesy. Allah takes careful account of all things. (Women: 86)

Because of sanctions by the high-school teachers association, the teachers cancelled the end-of-year party of the ninth graders. The class teacher explained the situation to his pupils and added that this decision affected the entire school and not only them. The pupils were not convinced and decided to punish the teacher. When he entered the classroom for the next lesson and greeted them, they did not. The teacher did not hesitate and quoted to them:

"When a (courteous) greeting is offered you, meet it with a greeting still more courteous, or (at least) of equal courtesy. Allah takes careful account of all things". "Now I will greet you again and we'll see what you do", he said. This time they greeted him in chorus.

Explanation: a greeting is an act of mutual respect which should be nurtured. It is hard to imagine a relationship without greetings, and this custom is of profound importance in interpersonal relations. It is not surprising that the pupils chose to punish their teacher in this manner. On another occasion, a pupil who received a grade he considered unsatisfactory, stopped greeting the teacher. A good teacher takes care to maintain good relations with her pupils. She not only greets them at the beginning of the lesson but also spends the first few minutes asking how they are and if they have any special problems. The Quran emphasizes the need to be generous and to give no less than one receives. So, if someone greets you, says the Quran, your reply should be at least as courteous if not more so. A lesser greeting can be regarded as offensive.

4. Is it better for a child to refrain from forbidden behavior out of fear or out of love for God and for his parents?

﴿ وَاكْتُبْ لَنَا فِي هَذِهِ الدُّنْيَا حَسَنَةً وَفِي الآخِرَةِ إِنَّا هُدْنَـا إِلَيْكَ قَالَ عَذَابِي أُصِيبُ بِهِ مَنْ أَشَاءُ وَرَحْمَتِي وَسِعَتْ كُلَّ شَيْءٍ فَسَأَكْتُبُهَا لِلَّذِينَ يَتَّقُونَ وَيُؤْتُونَ الزَّكَـاةَ وَالَّذِينَ هُم بِآيَاتِنَا يُؤْمِنُونَ ﴾ (الأعراف: 156)

And ordain for us that which is good, in this life and in the Hereafter: for we have turned unto Thee." **He said: "With My punishment I visit whom I will; but My mercy extendeth to all things. That (mercy) I shall ordain for those who do right, and**

practise regular charity, and those who believe in Our signs. (The Elevations: 156)

Rami, a fifth-grader, asked his father for money to buy a toy racing car. His father explained that he had no money at the time and the toy was not a necessity. Rami did not accept this answer. That night he sneaked into his parents' bedroom, opened a drawer and stole two hundred shekels from his father's wallet. A few days later, his mother saw him playing with a new toy car. She asked him where he had got it and he did not reply. Rami's brother told her that Rami had stolen the money from his father. She was furious and when her husband returned from work, she told him about the theft. His parents reprimanded him and told him stories about the punishments God inflicts on thieves. Rami began to cry. He hid in a closet and his conduct changed completely. He began to obey every request of his parents out of fear and anxiety. His parents now regretted having told him frightening stories but did not know how to undo the damage. They appealed to the school counselor.

The counselor tried to dispel Rami's fears of retribution. She told him that his conduct was unacceptable to God, and Rami instantly burst into tears and said: "God will be angry with me just like my mother said". The counselor explained that God can punish but He can also forgive and added that she wanted to read him an important verse: **"He said: "With My punishment I visit whom I will; but My mercy extendeth to all things. That (mercy) I shall ordain for those who do right, and practise regular charity, and those who believe in Our signs".** "Do you understand how forgiving God is?" she asked him. Rami became calmer. He returned home in a better mood and realized that stealing was wrong. He also understood that one may make a mistake and be forgiven by God.

Explanation: many children are afraid of God. Every child, at some time, has committed a forbidden act, in thought if not in deed, and if not in thought then in dreams. In short, many children believe that God is watching them and sees and knows all and are terrified of punishment. It is desirable for authority figures (parents, teachers etc) to explain the true image of God the Merciful and Compassionate and not merely an angry and punitive figure. Fear, particularly if it is exaggerated, is ineffective. We do not want to raise children who are afraid of God; we want them to love God. And we want our children to love us and not fear us. It is important for parents to remember this rule. To frighten a child, as Rami's parents did at first, does not produce the desired results. Forgiveness, on the other hand, enables the child to identify with the soft and accepting aspect of his parents and he will accept their prohibitions with love. Rami will no longer steal, not because he fears God and his parents, but because of love for them and a desire to emulate his parents.

5. What can we say to someone who discriminates against girls?

{ وَإِلَى مَدْيَنَ أَخَاهُمْ شُعَيْباً قَالَ يَا قَوْمِ اعْبُدُواْ اللّهَ مَا لَكُم مِّنْ إِلَـهٍ غَيْرُهُ قَدْ جَاءتْكُم بَيِّنَةٌ مِّن رَّبِّكُمْ فَأَوْفُواْ الْكَيْلَ وَالْمِيزَانَ وَلاَ تَبْخَسُواْ النَّاسَ أَشْيَاءهُمْ وَلاَ تُفْسِدُواْ فِي الأَرْضِ بَعْدَ إِصْلاَحِهَا ذَلِكُمْ خَيْرٌ لَّكُمْ إِن كُنتُم مُّؤْمِنِينَ } (الأعراف: 85)

To the Madyan people We sent Shu'aib, one of their own brethren: he said: "O my people! worship Allah. Ye have no other god but Him. Now hath come unto you a clear (Sign) from your Lord! **Give just measure and weight, nor withhold from the people the things that are their due; and do no mischief on the earth after it has been set in order:** that will be best for you, if ye have Faith. (The Elevations: 85)

Faten is in the eighth grade, a very good pupil who is liked by all the teachers. She is diligent, has initiative and likes to help her classmates. "A positive student who contributes to the atmosphere in school", her teacher wrote in her grade card. But when it comes to sports lessons, she feels uncomfortable. Her teacher, Muhammed, displays a better attitude towards the boys than the girls and in particular Faten, who is considered clever. Every time she proposes a game, he replies that she is a girl and he expects different conduct from her. At every opportunity he emphasizes she is a girl and not a boy. At some lessons he simply makes the girls sit on the sidelines and does not allow them to take part. Faten is afraid to talk to Muhammed about any subject because he immediately replies aggressively and she sometimes thinks twice before turning to him, even on important matters.

Faten decided to talk to the school counselor and told her that she was simply scared of the sports teacher. She asked the counselor not to intervene herself in the problem but to provide her with tools to confront him by herself. They held several discussions and pondered how to answer Muhammed cleverly and without offending him. They did not find a solution.

At one of the sports lessons several days later, Faten plucked up her courage and suggested that a group of the boys play basketball against a team of girls. The teacher shouted at her: "You don't give up, do you, even though you're so clever?" and then Faten turned to him and replied: **"Give just measure and weight, nor withhold from the people the things that are their due; and do no mischief on the earth after it has been set in order:"** "God does not love discrimination between boys and girls", she added. "There is no reason for you to behave like that".

Explanation: many parents and teachers discriminate against girls. We know that not only is this unjust, and the Quran exhorts us not to discriminate or withhold, but that such conduct eventually damages a society and the discriminators themselves.

A parent who discriminates against his daughter is ruining his connection with her. She could have grown to adulthood and developed her talents, succeeded and brought him great honor. A teacher who discriminates against a girl in his class may be preventing her from excelling and fulfilling her potential, and is betraying his mission as a teacher. The standard of the class would increase if the teacher also took into consideration the potential of the girls, and he himself would then be considered a better teacher. Since women constitute half of society, and women are the mothers of our children, any damage to a female's development is a mortal blow to society and to all of us. Faten did well to fight for equality and not to give in, and it is even more laudable that she recruited the Quran to aid her in her search for social justice and equality.

6. What can we say to two who are quarreling?

﴿ يَسْأَلُونَكَ عَنِ الأَنفَالِ قُلِ الأَنفَالُ لِلّهِ وَالرَّسُولِ فَاتَّقُواْ اللّهَ وَأَصْلِحُواْ ذَاتَ بِيْنِكُمْ وَأَطِيعُواْ اللّهَ وَرَسُولَهُ إِن كُنتُم مُّؤْمِنِينَ ﴾ (الأنفال: 1)

They ask thee concerning (things taken as) spoils of war. Say: "(such) spoils are at the disposal of Allah and the Messenger. **So fear Allah, and keep straight the relations between yourselves:** Obey Allah and His Messenger, if ye do believe. (The Spoils: 1)

A bitter quarrel broke out between two good friends, sixth-graders. They stopped talking to one another and sought every possible opportunity to provoke one another. During an education lesson, the teacher asked the pupils to express their opinion on a certain subject. The two boys expressed opposing views, began to argue and in the end quarreled out loud. The teacher summoned them for a talk. He realized that each bore a grudge against the other and was waiting for the moment when he could take revenge. He reminded them that they had once been good friends who spent hours together and asked them to set aside their resentments and make peace. "If you want to succeed in life", he told them, "you must learn to accept other people's opinions even if they make you angry. Do you know the Quran verse which commands people to make peace?" The pupils said they did not know it. He took out the Quran and read to them: **"They ask thee concerning (things taken as) spoils of war. Say: "(such) spoils are at the disposal of Allah and the Messenger. So fear Allah, and keep straight the relations between yourselves: Obey Allah and His Messenger, if ye do believe".** He emphasized the command to 'keep straight relations between yourselves" and added: "God commands you to make peace and to obey the voice of the Prophet and of adults because to make peace is a sign of belief and through belief you can succeed in life. When you are united you have no problem in accepting the opinions of the other". The two boys listened, and then they looked at one another and embraced.

Explanation: it is indeed fear of God, as the verse says, which enables the friends to make peace. Fear of the authority figure in the family, the father, enables children to unite because if he orders them to do so, they will be willing to abandon their anger. The teacher was right to use this verse in order to bring the boys together. One way of resolving a dispute between friends is to sit down with them and begin clarifying what exactly happened and who did what. Such a solution, which opens wounds, can be helpful because it makes it easier to understand why each of them was offended and to draw conclusions for the future. But sometimes it can cause more damage than good. The wounds are reopened and do not heal, the anger surfaces again and there is no resolution. Another way to achieve conciliation is to utilize the authority of the Quran. It reminds them that they are brothers and exhorts them to make peace. Thus, Allah unites his children and does not utilize the "divide and rule" method adopted by certain parents who want their children to squabble in order to reinforce their own authority.

7. What can we say to a child who is mocked?

﴿ أَمْ حَسِبْتُمْ أَن تُتْرَكُواْ وَلَمَّا يَعْلَمِ اللهُ الَّذِينَ جَاهَدُواْ مِنكُمْ وَلَمْ يَتَّخِذُواْ مِن دُونِ اللهِ وَلاَ رَسُولِهِ وَلاَ الْمُؤْمِنِينَ وَلِيجَةً وَاللهُ خَبِيرٌ بِمَا تَعْمَلُونَ ﴾ (التوبة: 16)

Or think ye that ye shall be abandoned, as though Allah did not know those among you who strive with might and main, and take none for friends and protectors except Allah, His Messenger, and the (community of) Believers? But Allah is well- acquainted with (all) that ye do. (The Repentance: 16)

Seif, a third-grader who suffers from a learning disability, complained to the teacher that the pupils in his class mock him and laugh at him because he has difficulty reading and writing. Resentful and helpless, he asked the teacher to permit him to study at home and not come to school at all. She tried to explain the gravity of his request and explained that he would be the one to suffer and not his classmates. "If you stop coming to school", she said, "they will have achieved what they wanted and will be very satisfied". She told him that children with learning disabilities often feel a continual sense of failure which undermines their sense of their own worth. Sometimes they fear authority because things are difficult for them and they err in reading social situations because they interpret everything as directed again them. "That is what happened to you", she added, "and what is occurring is a test from God. He wants to see how you behave in this situation, which is not simple. You must restrain yourself and learn to adapt to a difficult situation and you will slowly acquire tools and skills that will help you to make progress. In the future, you will undoubtedly encounter more problems and you will learn how to overcome them and to adapt to your framework. You must believe in yourself and in God in order to overcome obstacles. I want to give you as a gift a verse from the Quran which relates to another context but is appropriate for you. **"Or think ye that ye shall be abandoned, as though Allah did not know those among you who strive with might and main, and take none for friends and protectors except Allah, His Messenger, and the (community of) Believers? But Allah is well- acquainted with (all) that ye do".**

"That verse really suits me", Seif replied with a smile.

Explanation: how can one fortify a child who is mocked or is the scapegoat for his classmates? If he believes those who humiliate him, he will lose all his self-confidence and self-esteem and nothing good can come of that. He must have faith in himself, in God and perhaps also in a handful of "believers" – in other words, those who still appreciate him. Seif needs to gather strength, ignore those who are harassing him and rely on himself. But who can help him in that task if not God, who knows the truth? Allah Knows that Seif is a good boy who makes a great effort but suffers from a disability, and does not deserve to be treated badly. The teacher did well by linking Seif's need to rely on himself with his faith in God. She added that Allah was testing him and thus set him a goal: to prove that he has faith in himself and in God and not to despair. All this was achieved through the important Quran verse which is appropriate whenever the individual feels weak and alone.

8. How can we foster a spirit of cooperation?

{ لِّلَّذِينَ أَحْسَنُواْ الْحُسْنَى وَزِيَادَةٌ وَلَا يَرْهَقُ وُجُوهَهُمْ قَتَرٌ وَلاَ ذِلَّةٌ أُوْلَـئِكَ أَصْحَابُ الْجَنَّةِ هُمْ فِيهَا خَالِدُونَ } (يونس: 26)

To those who do right is a goodly (reward)- Yea, more (than in measure)! No darkness nor shame shall cover their faces! they are companions of the garden; they will abide therein (for aye)! (Jonah: 26)

The head of the local council decided to hold an 'Environmental Quality Week" in the town. He appealed to all the inhabitants to take part and contribute to the general welfare. He appealed in particular to the school principals and asked them to submit ideas, initiate programs and cooperate with one another.

At a meeting of the principals and teaching staffs, many ideas were raised, including setting aside one day for a clean-up of the town in order to improve its appearance. The principals called on the pupils to volunteer for the task and in order to encourage them to take part in the project, they prepared large posters to be hung in the schools on which they inscribed the verse: **"To those who do right is a goodly (reward)- Yea, more (than in measure)! No darkness nor shame shall cover their faces! they are companions of the garden; they will abide therein (for aye)!"**

The schoolchildren went out into the streets, collected garbage from roads and courtyards, helped old people to look after their gardens, pruned trees, built up broken fences, fixed sidewalks etc. When a local reporter asked one of the pupils the source of all their energy, the pupil replied: **"To those who do right is a goodly (reward)- Yea, more (than in measure)! No darkness nor shame shall cover their faces!"** but admitted that he had forgotten the rest of the verse.

Explanation: the Quran is the best possible source for encouraging people to cooperate for the common good and it promises a goodly reward to those who do right. It is the will of God that brothers should live in peace and help one another and contribute to the common good. The Quran enjoins us on various issues and in various contexts. In modern individualist societies the problem is how to teach people to contribute, because each lives his life for himself and each family is enclosed within its home and world. This is not the case in traditional-collectivist societies, where aid to others and to the community is the highest priority. The principals did well in finding the Quran verse which reflects this spirit and quoting it to their pupils.

9. How can we encourage an outstanding pupil to help a weak pupil?

{ وَالّذينَ صَبَرُواْ ابْتِغَاءَ وَجْهِ رَبّهِمْ وَأَقَامُواْ الصّلاَةَ وَأَنفَقُواْ مِمّا رَزَقْنَاهُمْ سِرّاً وَعَلاَنِيَةً وَيَدْرَؤُونَ بِالْحَسَنَةِ السّيّئَةَ أُوْلَئِكَ لَهُمْ عُقْبَى الدّارِ } (الرعد: 22)

Those who patiently persevere, seeking the countenance of their Lord; Establish regular prayers; spend, out of (the gifts) We have bestowed for their sustenance, secretly and openly; and turn off Evil with good: for such there is the final attainment of the (eternal) home. (The Thunder: 22)

Khaled is a weak student. One day he knocked on the door of the counselor's office and asked for help. His family was in a dire economic condition, he told her, and his parents could not afford private tutoring for him. Since they worked long hours and returned home late, they had no time to sit and help him with his homework. The counselor appealed to a group of the best students in the class and asked them to help Khaled. She explained that by so doing they would be encouraging solidarity in the class and that helping others is an explicit command of the Quran. Then she quoted the Quran verse to them: **"Those who patiently persevere, seeking the countenance of their Lord; Establish regular prayers; spend, out of (the gifts) We have bestowed for their sustenance, secretly and openly; and turn off Evil with good: for such there is the final attainment of the (eternal) home".** The pupils began to take it in turns and each day a different pupil helped Khaled with his homework until, thanks to them, he became one of the best students in the class.

Explanation: sometimes another pupil can explain the study material better than the teacher because it is easier for him to understand where his friend's problem lies. Moreover, there are those who claim that there is no better form of study than to explain the material to someone else, because when a pupil acts as a teacher and his friend asks him questions, he is obliged to think deeply and to comprehend the material in order to answer. Thus, the good students enjoyed a twofold reward, the first for having acted morally and helped a friend, the second for understanding the material even better after explaining it to Khaled. The counselor was right to say that such assistance to a friend creates unity and solidarity in the class and she did well to quote that important verse to the class.

12 | There is Always Hope

1. What can we do when our good deeds encounter ingratitude?

{ أَيَّامًا مَّعْدُودَاتٍ فَمَن كَانَ مِنكُم مَّرِيضًا أَوْ عَلَى سَفَرٍ فَعِدَّةٌ مِّنْ أَيَّامٍ أُخَرَ وَعَلَى الَّذِينَ يُطِيقُونَهُ فِدْيَةٌ طَعَامُ مِسْكِينٍ فَمَن تَطَوَّعَ خَيْرًا فَهُوَ خَيْرٌ لَّهُ وَأَن تَصُومُوا خَيْرٌ لَّكُمْ إِن كُنتُمْ تَعْلَمُونَ } (البقرة: 184)

(Fasting) for a fixed number of days; but if any of you is ill, or on a journey, the prescribed number (Should be made up) from days later. For those who can do it (With hardship), is a ransom, the feeding of one that is indigent. **But he that will give more, of his own free will,- it is better for him.** And it is better for you that ye fast, if ye only knew. (The cow: 184)

Nura is in the eleventh grade; her mother died two years ago and her father has remarried. Nura makes every effort to help her father's new wife with the household chores and care of the children, but her stepmother treats her harshly and never says a good word to her. In fact, she complains all the time that Nura does not perform her chores properly. In her despair, Nura came to the counselor and told her the whole story. The counselor took out a Quran, and leafed through it till she found the appropriate verse which she read out to Nura: **"But he that will give more, of his own free will – it is better for him"**. She reminded Nura that Allah gives the rewards and not human beings and advised her to be patient.

Explanation: it was not easy for the counselor to hear about Nura's predicament. She wondered how she could help the girl and at first could not think of a solution. One possibility was to invite Nura's parents for a talk but she was not sure that they would come. She knew Nura well, and was aware how goodhearted she was and how she helped her classmates, and so she knew the story was true. How could she give her hope? There was no way of changing the circumstances at home. The only solution was to advise her to be patient in the hope that someday things would improve. Perhaps the stepmother would gradually learn to appreciate her, perhaps she would soon be married and leave home for a better life. It was the Quran verse which guided her as to how to help Nura by giving her hope of a better future. And we all know the importance of hope.

2. Does God want us to be strong?

{ يَا أَيُّهَا الَّذِينَ آمَنُواْ اسْتَعِينُواْ بِالصَّبْرِ وَالصَّلاَةِ إِنَّ اللّهَ مَعَ الصَّابِرِينَ } (البقرة: 153)

O ye who believe! seek help with patient perseverance and prayer; for Allah is with those who patiently persevere. (The cow: 153)

Asma is in the ninth grade, a hard-working pupil who likes to help others. Lately her friends have noticed that something is happening to her. She has become quieter, solitary, does not take part in lessons and keeps away from the other girls. The teachers have also noticed the change. Several of her friends have tried to talk to her but she does not cooperate.

One day the teacher found her sitting alone in the classroom. She had not gone to the sports lesson and looked depressed, almost tearful. The teacher went over to her and tried to find out what was troubling her. Asma burst into tears and told the teacher that she was depressed because her parents fought all the time and were about to separate. Her mother was not living at home and had returned to her parents' house in another village. Asma was obliged to care for her little brothers and sisters and was afraid that she would never see her mother again and would be forced to leave school in order to look after her siblings.

The teacher sent her to the counselor who heard the story and tried to reassure her, to restore her hope. She told Asma that God was on her side and would not leave her alone, and added that she must be patient. Then she read her, slowly and with emphasis the Quran verse: **"O ye who believe! seek help with patient perseverance and prayer; for Allah is with those who patiently persevere".** Asma smiled for the first time in months. "God wants me to be strong, and so I will", she said to the counselor.

Explanation: sometimes a situation is complicated and the future is unclear. Nobody can tell if Asma's parents will ever live together again or whether Asma will continue to care alone for her siblings. How can one encourage her in these difficult times? One possibility is to promise that things will improve and her parents will be reconciled. But if her illusions are shattered, her pain will be even greater and she might break down completely when faced with harsh reality. It is not wise to delude people with false promises. The verse the counselor read to her did not delude her and did not promise a happy ending. It merely asked her to trust in Allah and be brave because Allah loves those who persevere. The verse gives her hope and strength rather than illusions.

3. What can we say to a boy who has been crippled?

{يَا أَيُّهَا الَّذِينَ آمَنُواْ اسْتَعِينُواْ بِالصَّبْرِ وَالصَّلاَةِ إِنَّ اللّهَ مَعَ الصَّابِرِينَ} (البقرة: 153)

O ye who believe! seek help with patient perseverance and prayer; for Allah is with those who patiently persevere. (The cow: 153)

Najib, a twelfth-grader, is a hardworking student with high grades. He is an outgoing boy who loves sports and likes to play football in the neighborhood and play rough games. One day, on his way home from school with his friends, he was knocked down by a car being driven at high speed and was seriously injured.

His life was saved in the hospital but he was left in a wheelchair and his doctors told him that he would never again be able to walk. The physical injury affected his emotional state and he sank into a deep depression, as did his entire family. His friends came to visit him in the hospital every day, told him about their examinations and their football games and he was filled with bitterness and pain. He had no future and there was no hope for him, he told the nurse who was tending him. "All my dreams have shattered like glass on a rock and I can't collect the pieces", he said. The nurse took out the Quran from which she often read verses to suffering patients, finding a suitable verse for each. **"O ye who believe! seek help with patient perseverance and prayer; for Allah is with those who patiently persevere"**, she read. Najib felt his strength returning. "God is with those who patiently persevere", he said. "God wants me to be strong and not break down", he added. The nurse looked at him and nodded silently.

Explanation: it is very hard when an adolescent boy experiences a catastrophe, because it is at a time when he is attuned to the future and full of plans. And then, all at once, his future is shattered. What can we say to Najib at this terrible moment? He will learn slowly to adapt his new expectations to his disabilities. He will learn what he is capable of doing and how to develop new expectations and hopes suited to his condition. But the present time is very hard for him, and nothing equals the Quran in providing encouragement. God has said to Najib: be strong and courageous, do not give in and I will be with you. These are the words which can shake Najib out of his passivity and depression and instill new hope in him.

4. How can we encourage children who are going through a difficult time?

{ فَإِنَّ مَعَ الْعُسْرِ يُسْراً * إِنَّ مَعَ الْعُسْرِ يُسْراً } (الشرح: 5-6)

So, verily, with every difficulty, there is relief: Verily, with every difficulty there is relief. (The Soothing: 5-6)

Warod, a pupil in the third grade, is having difficulty with reading and writing. She is a diligent pupil, but suffers from learning disabilities and is trying to keep up with the pace of her classmates. Every afternoon she sits at home, struggling with her homework and does not go out to play until she has completed it. Her teacher has promised her several times that: **"with every difficulty there is relief"**, and that one day she will read and write as well as her classmates. But only when she actually showed Warod the verse, did the girl understand its meaning and realize that these were not just words but the word of God. And, indeed, towards the end of the year, Warod improved to such a degree that she almost caught up with the other children. Now that she is reading and writing quite fluently, she often recalls the verses her teacher quoted and thinks how important it is to repeat them to other children experiencing difficulties.

Explanation: we all know how important it is to offer hope to someone struggling with difficulties. Without hope there is no reason to make an effort to overcome problems. The truth is that in many spheres of life, after the difficulty comes relief, because if we confront the problems and do not give in, we make progress and improve and will probably reach a better place. Sometimes we are dealing with pain which passes with time and sometimes with emotional pain which is also healed by time. But when one is in the midst of the crisis, it is often hard to raise one's head and see the light. The teacher was right not merely to quote the verses but to show them to Warod as they appear in the Quran. The words were an injection of courage and hope for the little girl and the outcome proved how true they were.

5. How can we motivate pupils in a remedial class?

﴿ كُنتُمْ خَيْرَ أُمَّةٍ أُخْرِجَتْ لِلنَّاسِ تَأْمُرُونَ بِالْمَعْرُوفِ وَتَنْهَوْنَ عَنِ الْمُنكَرِ وَتُؤْمِنُونَ بِاللَّهِ وَلَوْ آمَنَ أَهْلُ الْكِتَابِ لَكَانَ خَيْرًا لَّهُم مِّنْهُمُ الْمُؤْمِنُونَ وَأَكْثَرُهُمُ الْفَاسِقُونَ ﴾ (آل عمران: 110)

Ye are the best of peoples, evolved for mankind, enjoining what is right, forbidding what is wrong, and believing in Allah. If only the People of the Book had faith, it were best for them: among them are some who have faith, but most of them are perverted transgressors (The Family of Imran: 110)

The Al-Qamal school has opened a remedial class this year for children who need help in integrating into the school. There are fifteen regular pupils in the class and others join the class for specific subjects. Muhammed recently joined the arithmetic lessons. In the recess he met his friends from his regular class. "How are you, Muhammed? What's new? What's going on? How's your new class?" they asked him. "It's fun. I'm studying better. The teacher sits with me and explains the material and makes sure that I understand it".

"Yes, what fun!" said Suleiman. "Retarded kids. Just like Rami said – all the retards study there". The boys standing around burst out laughing. Muhammed was very embarrassed and tried hard not to cry. From that moment till the end of the day he was sad and withdrawn. The teacher asked him if something had happened but he remained silent.

Next day he stayed in the classroom in recess so as to avoid the classmates from his regular class. He was afraid they would mock him. The remedial teacher noticed and asked him what had happened in the past two days and if something was bothering him. She said that if he didn't tell her, the problem could not be solved and that was a pity because she could help him. Then he said: "It's true, we are a group of retards". The teacher sighed and asked him who had said such nonsense. "The pupils from my class", he said. "I'm going to talk to my parents and tell all my friends to talk to their parents so that we'll all be sent back to our regular classes". The remedial teacher reminded him that at the beginning of the year, the remedial pupils had confessed that they found life difficult in their regular classes. "Yes, but it's better to be in a class you don't like than in a class of retards", he replied. She realized that this was a serious matter and told his regular teacher and together they went to the principal. They told him how the children were suffering from being mocked and what damage was being caused to their self-esteem.

The principal, class teacher and remedial teacher decided to summon the parents of the children in the regular class and the remedial class and to explain the significance of remedial teaching and the need to combat the stigma of a 'class for retards.' At the meeting, the principal explained that the teaching in the remedial class was on an individual basis and adapted to each pupil. The pupils were also given enrichment lessons in art, music etc. The parents were surprised and asked what the curriculum was and some asked if their own children could also participate. In conclusion, the principal turned to the pupils of the remedial class and quoted: **"Ye are the best of peoples, evolved for mankind, enjoining what is right, forbidding what is wrong, and believing in Allah".** From that moment on, the pupils in the remedial class felt proud that both Allah and the school faculty were supporting them.

Explanation: every parent and every teacher know how important a positive self-image is to success in studies. A student who thinks he is retarded will find it hard to succeed. That is why it is so important to express admiration at achievements and to make children feel that everything depends on their own will and determination. A child needs to see a spark of admiration in the eyes of a parent or teacher when he succeeds because such a response allows him to believe in himself and his abilities. The principal did well to invite all the parents so that it would be clear to them that the pupils in the remedial class were as good as those in the regular classes. If a pupil has difficulties in a certain subject that does not mean that he cannot later achieve as much as the other pupils. The verse the principal quoted can reinforce the pride of the pupils in their class.

6. How should a teacher approach a weak pupil?

﴿ وَلاَ تُؤْتُواْ السُّفَهَاء أَمْوَالَكُمُ الَّتِي جَعَلَ اللّهُ لَكُمْ قِيَاماً وَارْزُقُوهُمْ فِيهَا وَاكْسُوهُمْ وَقُولُواْ لَهُمْ قَوْلاً مَّعْرُوفًا ﴾ (النساء: 5)

To those weak of understanding Make not over your property, which Allah hath made a means of support for you, **but feed and clothe them therewith, and speak to them words of kindness and justice.** (Women: 5)

One day Mahmud, a third-grader, went into the counselor's office, and sat down silently. She knew him to be a pupil with serious learning disabilities as well as physiological problems. She said: "Mahmud, you look sad. Has something happened?" and then he told her that the mathematics teacher treated him badly and did not give him as much attention as he gave to other pupils. "He doesn't even look at me during the lesson", he told her, "and I sit separately. He's the only one who makes me feel like that. And in recess he doesn't look after me and doesn't respect me the way other teachers do". The counselor asked Mahmud what he thought the reason was. "It's because I'm weak and different from all the others and that teacher has no sympathy for weak people", he replied. "If you don't talk to him, I'm not going back into his lessons", he added emphatically.

That same day the counselor called the mathematics teacher and read him the verse: **"but feed and clothe them therewith, and speak to them words of kindness and justice".** She asked him if he knew why she had read him that particular verse. He said he didn't know. Then she asked him about Mahmud. The teacher claimed that he treated Mahmud the same way as he treated other pupils but that Mahmud wanted preferential treatment. Then the counselor told him that Mahmud did not feel that way. She explained that it was problematic and wrong to deny the instinctive feelings of a child or, indeed, any person. It was worth the teacher's while, she said, to try and improve his relationship with him, whether Mahmud was right or not. The teacher thanked her for giving him the opportunity to improve relations with Mahmud.

Explanation: The counselor was right in saying that one cannot argue with a feeling. Possibly Mahmud is sensitive and very vulnerable. In that case it is the duty of the teacher, who is responsible for his pupils' good feeling in class, to make an effort to make Mahmud feel better. The Quran verse emphasizes the importance of kindness in approaching the weak. It does not encourage condescendence or disregard for the child's presence and difficulties. The Quran excels in nurturing and encouraging compassion in human society. In Western society, we call this quality empathy, in traditional society compassion or kindness. What is important is that every parent and every teacher remember that only by adopting such an attitude can we raise a child who thinks independently because if a child is humiliated, he will remain dependent. If he is addressed with kindness and justice, he can develop an inner expanse of choice and discretion.

7. Does God want to lighten our burdens?

{ يُرِيدُ اللَّهُ أَن يُخَفِّفَ عَنكُمْ وَخُلِقَ الإِنسَانُ ضَعِيفًا } (النساء: 28)

Allah doth wish to lighten your (difficulties): For man was created Weak (in flesh). (Women: 28)

Thirteen-year-old Abir, who is in the sixth grade, is coping with very heavy burdens. Her mother was killed last summer in a traffic accident, leaving a husband, two daughters and a son. Abir is the eldest; her sister Amal is eleven and Muhammed is eight. Six months after the mother's death, the extended family decided that the widower should choose a girl from the family and marry as soon as possible. The argument was that he needed a wife to help him raise his children. And indeed, within a month the father remarried. However, his new wife made it clear from the very first that she was too young to be "stuck" with children who were not even her own. Abir's father was unable to persuade his young wife and Abir was forced to take responsibility not only for herself but also for her younger siblings.

Abir wakes early every morning, rouses her sister and brother and helps them to prepare for school. She makes breakfast, prepares their sandwiches, accompanies them to school and at the end of the day escorts them home. After they have eaten lunch (the only meal their step-mother prepares for them) she helps them with their homework. In the evening, she again prepares supper, showers then and put them to bed. Only then does she find time to tackle her own homework. One of Abir's teachers referred her to the school counselor because the girl, who had been known for her high motivation and good grades, began to display indifference to her studies. Her grades dropped and it was evident that she was exhausted and irritable.

Abir told her story to the counselor, who pondered what she could say to Abir to encourage her and give her hope. First, she stressed to Abir how important she was, although she was so young, to her siblings and family, who could not manage without her. Then she picked up the Quran and told Abit she wanted to read her a verse: **"Allah doth wish to lighten your (difficulties): For man was created Weak (in flesh)".** "How did you understand this verse?" she asked and Abir replied: "That we are all the same, weak, and Allah will help us in the future". The counselor added that she hoped the verse would accompany Abir in all her tribulations and that she would always see the light at the end of the tunnel because God wanted to lighten her burdens and would do so in the future.

Explanation: it is hard to be an educational counselor or a teacher with a pupil like Abir, because they are anxious to help their pupils but cannot change their circumstances. In situations like Abir's, and this is true of all difficult circumstances which we are powerless to alter, the most effective move is to instill hope. Hope that the future will be better is a powerful force which can help people overcome difficulties and pain. Another method chosen by the counselor was to give meaning to Abir's situation. Abir is a very important figure in her family – for her father and her siblings. They depend on her and what would they do without her? Awareness of her vital contribution to her family can instill new strength and hope in her. And, in addition, her extended family, her fellow villagers and the staff and pupils of her school are all witnesses to her noble conduct. All these facts can bring her comfort, at least partial, and equip her with the strength to continue. The counselor did well to read her the Quran verse which holds out hope.

8. What can we say to someone who is depressed because of sickness or an injury?

{ وَنَبِّئْهُمْ عَن ضَيْفِ إِبْرَاهِيمَ * إِذْ دَخَلُواْ عَلَيْهِ فَقَالُواْ سَلاماً قَالَ إِنَّا مِنكُمْ وَجِلُونَ * قَالُواْ لاَ تَوْجَلْ إِنَّا نُبَشِّرُكَ بِغُلامٍ عَلِيمٍ * قَالَ أَبَشَّرْتُمُونِي عَلَى أَن مَّسَّنِيَ الْكِبَرُ فَبِمَ تُبَشِّرُونَ * قَالُواْ بَشَّرْنَاكَ بِالْحَقِّ فَلاَ تَكُن مِّنَ الْقَانِطِينَ * قَالَ وَمَن يَقْنَطُ مِن رَّحْمَةِ رَبِّهِ إِلاَّ الضَّآلُّونَ } (الحجر: 51-56)

Tell them about the guests of Abraham. When they entered his presence and said, "Peace!" He said, "We feel afraid of you!" They said: "Fear not! We give thee glad tidings of a son endowed with wisdom." He said: "Do ye give me glad tidings that old age has seized me? Of what, then, is your good news?" **They said: "We give thee glad tidings in truth: be not then in despair!" He said: "And who despairs of the mercy of his Lord, but such as go astray?"** (The Rock: 51-56)

Ayad finished school early one day. "What fun! We were let out early. I'll go and rest a little and then I can go for a training session before the big contest", he thought to himself. The day he was awaiting was coming closer. Next week was the bicycle competition, which he had been eagerly waiting because he hoped to win the cup. It had always been his dream but suddenly....

He woke and saw vague figures dressed in white around him. What was going on? Was this a hospital? What was he doing there? How did he get there? Why was he in such terrible pain... his leg and arm were suspended in the air. Suddenly he heard a nurse calling out to a doctor: "Come here, he's awake". Why was his mother crying? The doctor came over to the bed and said: "Good morning, Ayad, how do you feel?" "Tell me what happened to me", replied the frightened boy. The doctor told him he had been hit by a car while crossing the road on the way home from school. "You lost consciousness and they brought you here. It's a miracle that things are not worse", he added. Ayad's entire body hurt and he asked the doctor how long it would be before he was better. The doctor said it would be some time because he would have to undergo surgery on his leg. Ayad said nothing but thought to himself that now he would not be able to take part in the bicycle contest and was very depressed at the thought…His depression deepened, he refused to eat or drink and when his friends came to visit him, he refused to talk to them. He had been obliged to give up his dream of winning the cup, so what was left to him in life?!

Ayad's parents and siblings tried to console him, and so did his friends, but without success. They brought him candy and gifts, and promised that he would be able to ride his bike again but nothing helped. Ayad cut himself off from the world. Then one day his teacher, Faten, of whom he was very fond, came to visit him. She asked him how he was and he told her that the doctors had inserted a plate in his leg and told him that he would never be back to his old self. Faten took out a copy of the Quran and asked his permission to read him the story about the Prophet Abraham: **"Tell them about the guests of Abraham… They said: "We give thee glad tidings in truth: be not then in despair!" He said: "And who despairs of the mercy of his Lord, but such as go astray?"** "Since I know you", she added, "and I know that you are not one of those who go astray, I am sure that you, like Abraham, will not despair. And I want to teach you one more thing. With determination you can achieve anything. If you want to, you can go back to being the way you were". For the first time since the accident, Ayad smiled.

Explanation: many people sink into depression when they are seriously ill, undergo surgery or are injured. When someone feels that their body is betraying them, they naturally tend to be depressed. This is true of people recovering from surgery. Relatives and friends can help and encourage the patients and their presence is vital to the convalescence process. However, when the crisis is great, as in the case of Ayad, whose dream has been shattered, convalescence can be even harder. In such cases, faith is a vital element which can endow the individual with strength and extricate him from his depressed state. Faten said it beautifully through a story from the Quran which made the point that only those without faith despair while true believers never lose hope. It is not surprising that Ayad smiled. His faith had been restored.

9. What can a child do if his parents don't listen to him?

{ أَوْفُوا الْكَيْلَ وَلَا تَكُونُوا مِنَ الْمُخْسِرِينَ * وَزِنُوا بِالْقِسْطَاسِ الْمُسْتَقِيمِ * وَلَا تَبْخَسُوا النَّاسَ أَشْيَاءَهُمْ وَلَا تَعْثَوْا فِي الْأَرْضِ مُفْسِدِينَ } (الشعراء: 181-183)

Give **just measure, and cause no loss (to others by fraud). And weigh with scales true and upright. And withhold not things justly due to men, nor do evil in the land, working mischief.** (The Poets: 181-183)

Samia is in the second grade in the school where her father teaches. She works hard, prepares her homework regularly and only then goes out to play with her friends. One day she was playing hide and seek with her friends in the neighborhood. A quarrel broke out with one of the other girls who threatened to tell her father untrue stories about Samia. Samia ignored her and went home. The next day, the other girl met Samia's father, seized the opportunity and said sarcastically: "You have a really well-behaved daughter. If you only knew what she said to me yesterday while we were playing..." Sama's father was angry and shouted at his daughter in front of all the children: "From now till the end of the month, you're not to leave the house!" Samia tried to defend herself but her father refused to listen.

She went and sat sadly in her room. Then she picked up the Quran, leafed through it and found what she was looking for. She took a sheet of paper and a pen and wrote to her father: **"Give just measure, and cause no loss (to others by fraud). And weigh with scales true and upright. And withhold not things justly due to men, nor do evil in the land, working mischief".**

When her father read her note, he came in to talk to her and realized that he had made a mistake. The next day, Samia found a note on her desk, reading: "I apologize, my dear daughter".

Explanation: it was wise of Samia to seek a way of explaining to her father through the Quran. It was this choice which enabled her to convey her message to him. He could not refuse to listen to the Quran. Samia was setting an example for many children who feel that their parents do not understand them and have treated them unfairly. Children should study the Quran and then they can quote it when they feel that nobody is listening to them or that they have been accused unfairly.

10. What can we say to someone who is mortally ill?

{ وَيَسْتَعْجِلُونَكَ بِالْعَذَابِ وَلَن يُخْلِفَ اللَّهُ وَعْدَهُ وَإِنَّ يَوْماً عِندَ رَبِّكَ كَأَلْفِ سَنَةٍ مِّمَّا تَعُدُّونَ } (الحج: 47)

Yet they ask thee to hasten on the Punishment! **But Allah will not fail in His Promise. Verily a Day in the sight of thy Lord is like a thousand years of your reckoning.** (The Pilgrimage: 47)

Nura is the mother of seven-year-old twins. Two years ago, she fell sick with leukemia and since then her life has been filled with pain, sadness, medication and chemotherapy. Her strength has drained away and she is weary of suffering. She even contemplated suicide but lacked the courage. It is hard for her to be unable to raise her children and she knows that she will not live to see them graduate from high school or to see grandchildren.

At night Nura sits alone on the porch and weeps. One day her husband heard her crying and went over to her. He held her hand and tried to encourage her and tell her that God would ease her suffering. He reminded her about Job, who had suffered so greatly and, in the end, had been rewarded by God. When she said that she could wait no longer and asked why God had not yet rewarded her. He told her not to forget the verse: **"Verily a Day in the sight of thy Lord is like a thousand years of your reckoning".** She must be patient, he said.

Explanation: hope is what we all want and need in life. We all struggle with difficulties and suffer and yearn for Allah to help us and for a better future. But often this future seems far distant. This is doubly true for Nura who is severely ill and feels that God is not helping her. Her husband did well to quote the Quran and explain that God's time span differs from hers and that her reward will come someday. He is giving her hope, which is so important for all of us, and in particular for the sick.

13 | Democracy and Society

1. Is it permissible to innovate?

{يَوْمَ تَأْتِي كُلُّ نَفْسٍ تُجَادِلُ عَن نَّفْسِهَا وَتُوَفَّى كُلُّ نَفْسٍ مَّا عَمِلَتْ وَهُمْ لاَ يُظْلَمُونَ}
(النحل: 111)

One Day every soul will come up struggling for itself, and every soul will be recompensed (fully) for all its actions, and none will be unjustly dealt with. (The Bees: 111)

Rim is a hard-working, good-hearted teacher who loves her pupils and invests great effort in them. One day, surprisingly, the principal summoned her for a talk, and Rim was uneasy because she didn't know the reason for the summons. She entered the principal's office, and sat down quietly.

Principal: Good morning, Rim. Let me speak straight out. I've heard that you are teaching by a different method to our accepted teaching method. The parents are complaining.

Rim: I know what I am doing.

Principal: But you don't have permission to do as you choose.

Rim: Yes, I'm aware of that but I'm not just doing what I fancy. I examine the class and decide what is suitable for them and that is what I do.

Principal: Listen, I want to call in the counselor. I like to consult other people – particularly the counselor.

They went into the counselor's office and she sat them down in her seating corner which was decorated with flowers and books.

Principal: I am torn between what Rim has to say and what the parents say.

Counselor: Tell me about it.

Principal: Rim is employing different teaching methods. She divides the into groups and relates to each group separately. The parents have complained about her method.

Counselor: What do you say, Rim?

Rim: I didn't choose this method at random. I chose it because I discovered that it is suitable because it stimulates the pupils' interest.

Counselor (to the principal): What are you going to decide?

Principal: I don't know. I believe Rim, and I identify with her but the parents are also part of the study process. I can't ignore them.

Rim: But I can explain my method to them.

Counselor (to the principal): If you are convinced by Rim's methods, I think you should accept responsibility and support what you believe in.

Principal: Yes, but I'm apprehensive.

Rim: There's nothing to fear. I'm ready to explain to the parents.

Counselor: Listen please, both of you. I want to read you a verse from the Quran: **"One Day every soul will come up struggling for itself, and every soul will be recompensed (fully) for all its actions, and none will be unjustly dealt with".**

Principal: Yes, as the Quran says, I have to face the parents with what I believe, and I believe that Rim is an excellent teacher who is employing new teaching methods in order to arouse the pupils' interest. Perhaps the parents are scared of any innovation. They are accustomed to the familiar methods they remember from the time when they were at school – the teacher stands at the center of the classroom and talks and everyone listens. But when you divide the children into groups, more children can take part and express their opinions. If it is done correctly, it is a very refreshing method. Thank you.

Rim: Yes, thank you.

Explanation: many important innovations fail because people are afraid of them and cling to what they really believe in. The principal had need of the Quran verse in order to accept Rim's different teaching method. The Quran explains that at the Day of Judgment every soul will struggle for itself and will be left with its own truth. The principal's truth, which the Quran helped him to uncover, is that it is permissible and necessary to seek new teaching methods so as to catch the pupils' interest. But in order to accept this, he needs to face the parents without fear and to explain the change and its significance. Perhaps he should invite the parents for a meeting and start by reading them the verse. Then each parent will discover within him what the principal has discovered – that it is permissible to try new methods, particularly if one believes in them.

2. What is the value of a human being?

{ وَآتِ ذَا الْقُرْبَى حَقَّهُ وَالْمِسْكِينَ وَابْنَ السَّبِيلِ وَلاَ تُبَذِّرْ تَبْذِيراً } (الإسراء: 26)

And render to the kindred their due rights, as (also) to those in want, and to the wayfarer: But squander not (your wealth) in the manner of a spendthrift. (The Night Journey: 26)

Sharif, a fourth-grader, is the oldest child of a rich family child, whose every request is granted. One day he traveled with his father to Jerusalem to pray at the al-Aqsa mosque. Sharif loves going to Jerusalem, buying in the market and boasting to his friends about his acquisitions. After the prayers, he and his father went into the market. He was struck by the many poor people in torn clothing selling small objects at very low prices.

He began to jeer at them and said to his father: "Look what they are doing?" His father replied: "My dear son, we have just been in the mosque and prayed that everyone should have money and happiness. Allah gives to some and to others he does not give. But we must respect those who are in want and not boast of our money and certainly not squander it on trifles. We must spend our money wisely as the Quran says: **"And render to the kindred their due rights, as (also) to those in want, and to the wayfarer: But squander not (your wealth) in the manner of a spendthrift".** That same day Sharif decided to respect the poor and help them and to stop squandering money on unimportant items.

Explanation: one of the most beautiful exhortations of the Quran refers to the value of human beings. It says that everyone is of value whether they are rich or poor and all deserve respect and help. This is the essence of the democratic approach of the Quran which preceded Western. Sharif's father is teaching him on the basis of that Quran verse and inculcating in him awareness of the value of humility. Moreover, he is also telling his son that if, in future, he should be impoverished he will still be a valuable human being. It may be hard to be poor but it is no disgrace, he says. Now Sharif understands that it is the individual who is important and not his property or wealth, that the inner essence is more important than the external trappings and that Sharif's value too will endure. What greater confidence could he give him?

3. What can we say to someone who interprets kindness as weakness?

{ وَإِذَا أَنْعَمْنَا عَلَى الإِنسَانِ أَعْرَضَ وَنَأَى بِجَانِبِهِ وَإِذَا مَسَّهُ الشَّرُّ كَانَ يَؤُوساً } (الإسراء: 83)

Yet when We bestow Our favours on man, he turns away and becomes remote on his side (instead of coming to Us), and when evil seizes him he gives himself up to despair! (The Night Journey: 83)

Amer, a fifth-grader, lost his father and brother in a shocking accident several months ago. His class teacher explained to his classmates that it would be difficult for Amer to endure the next few months without their help and since then they have been treating him with great consideration. But, surprisingly enough, Amer has begun to behave intolerably. At first, he displayed physical violence towards the weaker children in the class and now he interprets their treatment of him wrongly. He says that all the other children are afraid of him and that is why they buy him things and help him. For example, when Yusuf brought him candy, he claimed that Yusuf was afraid that if he didn't give it, Amer would take it from him anyway and hit him. This week Amer tormented Hilmi for refusing to copy material from the blackboard into a notebook for him.

His classmates decided that they were no longer ready to help him and they wanted to teach him a lesson. So, whenever he asked one of them for something, the other refused. When Amer reacted with insults or physical violence, the entire class rallied against him. The situation continued for a month till Amer began to understand that he had behaved badly and caused the group to reject him. He felt bad about himself, stayed home and did not go out to play. He began to be depressed.

Then, one day, someone knocked on the door of his room and Amer called out "Come in", in a weak, despairing voice.

It was Saber, his good friend. Amer turned on him: "What's wrong with you? Have you also stopped being my friend? Why don't you come any more?" Saber replied: "Because of the way you behave". When Amer said he didn't understand, Saber quoted: **"when We bestow Our favours on man, he turns away and becomes remote on his side (instead of coming to Us), and when evil seizes him he gives himself up to despair!"** He explained why Amer's classmates were treating him like that and what his mistake had been. Amer clutched his own head and muttered: "Oh, how bad I've been. Now I know how mistaken I was and how to change".

Explanation: Amer suffered a tragedy and his friends rallied to help him in the hope that he would appreciate their help and not interpret kindness as weakness, as people often do. This important Quran verse says that if we bestow favors on others, they sometimes turn away from us, and when something bad happens to them, they find it hard to understand that it may be connected to their behavior. Saber did well in explaining to Amer by means of this verse what his mistake had been, thereby enabling him to change his behavior.

4. Is it permissible to compel someone to be religiously observant?

فَلِذَٰلِكَ فَادْعُ وَاسْتَقِمْ كَمَا أُمِرْتَ وَلَا تَتَّبِعْ أَهْوَاءَهُمْ وَقُلْ آمَنتُ بِمَا أَنزَلَ اللَّهُ مِن
كِتَابٍ وَأُمِرْتُ لِأَعْدِلَ بَيْنَكُمُ اللَّهُ رَبُّنَا وَرَبُّكُمْ لَنَا أَعْمَالُنَا وَلَكُمْ أَعْمَالُكُمْ لَا حُجَّةَ بَيْنَنَا
وَبَيْنَكُمُ اللَّهُ يَجْمَعُ بَيْنَنَا وَإِلَيْهِ الْمَصِيرُ (الشورى: 15)

Now then, for that (reason), call (them to the Faith), and stand steadfast as thou art commanded, nor follow thou their vain desires; but say: "I believe in the Book which Allah has sent down; and I am commanded to judge justly between you. **Allah is our Lord and your Lord: for us (is the responsibility for)**

our deeds, and for you for your deeds. There is no contention between us and you. Allah will bring us together, and to Him is (our) Final Goal. (Ash-shura: 15)

Nabil has recently become extremely religious. He pores over the Quran and other religious works and asks the sheikh of the mosque many questions. Whenever he sees one of his friends doing something which he believes to be violating religious tenets as he understands them, he becomes angry and begins to argue with him. His friends are keeping their distance because he keeps criticizing them and quoting Quran verses. He has changed greatly recently and has made several new friends who are also extremely orthodox, and they discuss religious issues together. Nabil's family also find him hard to live with as he criticizes them constantly, and checks whether his sisters are dressing modestly. He does not like to see them leaving the house and has even begun criticizing his mother. His father recently called him for a talk and read him a Quran verse: **"Allah is our Lord and your Lord: for us (is the responsibility for) our deeds, and for you for your deeds. There is no contention between us and you."** He asked Nabil if he understood the verse. It was the first time in months that Nabil had fallen silent and listened. "I was wrong", he said. "According to the Quran I must not put pressure on people and quarrel with them. Each of us is judged according to his own deeds. I may be pained by your behavior but I can't help you". His father hugged him and said that he liked that answer.

Explanation: it is permissible for Nabil to choose how to express his religiosity but, according to the Quran, he must not force his views on others. The Quran recommends avoiding pointless. Each individual is responsible for his own actions and in the end, Allah will judge all of them. Nabil's father did well in choosing this verse for his son. In this world, where disputes regarding religion are rife, this verse is of vital importance.

It reminds us that we should not force our views on others whether we advocate extreme orthodoxy or extreme secularism. It reminds us that God enjoins us to take responsibility for ourselves, and not to attempt to take responsibility for others by forcing our views on them.

5. Is it permitted to litter the streets?

{ إِنَّ الَّذِينَ آمَنُوا وَعَمِلُوا الصَّالِحَاتِ إِنَّا لَا نُضِيعُ أَجْرَ مَنْ أَحْسَنَ عَمَلًا }
(الكهف: 30)

As to those who believe and work righteousness, verily We shall not suffer to perish the reward of any who do a (single) righteous deed. (The Cave: 30)

Sami bought a frozen popsicle in the grocery store, tore off the wrapping and threw it down on the ground. Ahmed saw him and said: "Pick up your litter. Remember, the street is the place where we walk and play and it's like a second home. Remember the verse: **"As to those who believe and work righteousness, verily We shall not suffer to perish the reward of any who do a (single) righteous deed."** Sami bent down, picked up the wrapper and threw it in the garbage can. Since then, whenever he sees someone littering without consideration for his friends and his surroundings, he reminds him of the verse.

Explanation: both children and adults should be taught to respect and preserve the environment. Many people throw litter in the streets because they feel that that outside their home they can do as they choose. They have no consideration for others. The Quran teaches us that those who do good deeds will be rewarded. To preserve a clean environment is a good deed because it implies that care for others so that all of us can enjoy the places where we work, study and live. Ahmed did well to find that particular verse and use it to teach his friend a lesson.

6. Is everyone able to read and understand the Quran?

{ فَإِنَّمَا يَسَّرْنَاهُ بِلِسَانِكَ لِتُبَشِّرَ بِهِ الْمُتَّقِينَ وَتُنذِرَ بِهِ قَوْماً لُّدّاً } (مريم: 97)

So have We made the (Qur'an) easy in thine own tongue, that with it thou mayest give Glad Tidings to the righteous, and warnings to people given to contention. (Mary: 97)

Fifteen-year-old Samahar is always arguing with her mother about clothes. "I want to buy new clothes, something more revealing, more modern, like my friends do. I don't want to be different", she says. "I want to present myself in the best possible light. Why do all the mothers permit their daughters to buy clothes like that and only you make difficulties?" Her mother is constantly seeking verses from the Quran about the importance of modesty and showing them to Samahar. "Allah loves girls who dress modestly and not those who wear revealing clothes", she explains. "We have certain customs". But Samahar continues to argue and the verses do not persuade her to change her ways.

One day Samahar visited the counselor and told her about the arguments at home. The counselor opened the Quran and read her the verse: **"So have We made the (Qur'an) easy in thine own tongue, that with it thou mayest give Glad Tidings to the righteous, and warnings to people given to contention".** "Do you understand what this verse is saying?" she asked. Samahar replied that the Quran was written in Arabic so that everyone would understand. "True", said the counselor. "You too can read any verse in the Quran and decide to let it guide your behavior. It is simple". From that day on the arguments at home ceased.

Explanation: this important verse says that every individual can read the Quran and understand it. It is indeed a guide for life which can be understood with relative ease. Parents and teachers should encourage children to read the Quran regularly, to raise questions about what they read and to find the answers to many of their queries. In the end, the Quran gave Samahar the strength to resist her friends and to dress as she saw fit.

7. What are the basic elements of healthy nutrition?

{ كُلُوا مِن طَيِّبَاتِ مَا رَزَقْنَاكُمْ وَلَا تَطْغَوْا فِيهِ فَيَحِلَّ عَلَيْكُمْ غَضَبِي وَمَن يَحْلِلْ عَلَيْهِ غَضَبِي فَقَدْ هَوَى } (طه: 81)

(Saying): "Eat of the good things We have provided for your sustenance, but commit no excess therein, lest My Wrath should justly descend on you: and those on whom descends My Wrath do perish indeed! (Ta-Ha: 81)

The school educational counselor gives health lessons. She goes from classroom to classroom and explains to the pupils how important it is to eat healthy food: large quantities of fruit, vegetables and milk. She explains the damage to the body of an excess of sugar and food coloring as well as how to check their ideal weight according to their body types. She stresses the importance of physical activity and the dangers of nicotine, drugs and alcohol. She starts and concludes each lesson with the Quran verse: **"Eat of the good things We have provided for your sustenance, but commit no excess therein, lest My Wrath should justly descend on you: and those on whom descends My Wrath do perish indeed!"**

Explanation: it is indisputable that our modern lifestyle demands considerable discipline with regard to eating habits. Sweetmeats and even dishes which appear healthy are often filled with harmful additives such as food coloring, synthetic materials etc. Young people are also exposed to cigarettes, drugs and alcohol which can be very harmful, and the verse is referring to this as well. The counselor was right to teach the children from an early age the important rules of nutrition, with the aid of the Quran.

8. What can we say to parents who live in the past and force their customs on their children?

{ وَلَقَدْ آتَيْنَا إِبْرَاهِيمَ رُشْدَهُ مِن قَبْلُ وَكُنَّا بِهِ عَالِمِينَ * إِذْ قَالَ لِأَبِيهِ وَقَوْمِهِ مَا هَذِهِ التَّمَاثِيلُ الَّتِي أَنتُمْ لَهَا عَاكِفُونَ * قَالُوا وَجَدْنَا آبَاءَنَا لَهَا عَابِدِينَ * قَالَ لَقَدْ كُنتُمْ أَنتُمْ وَآبَاؤُكُمْ فِي ضَلَالٍ مُّبِينٍ } (الأنبياء: 51-54)

We bestowed aforetime on Abraham his rectitude of conduct, and well were We acquainted with him. Behold! he said to his father and his people, "What are these images, to which ye are (so assiduously) devoted?" They said, "We found our fathers worshipping them." He said, "Indeed ye have been in manifest error - ye and your fathers. (The Prophets: 51-54)

Maryam, who is in the eighth-grade, told her teacher that she was betrothed and would be marrying in the summer so that she would not be returning to school next year. The teacher was surprised and tried unsuccessfully to persuade Maryam that it was not a good idea to leave. The teacher referred her to the principal, who invited her for a talk. Maryam told him that her mother was forcing her to marry, saying that she too had been married young, at thirteen.

The principal explained to Maryam that not everything our parents do and say is necessarily right. He told her that study is very important for our development and our children's future. "You must complete your studies first and only then marry", he said. "There is a time for everything and now is the time for study and when you are older it will be time to marry". Then he took out the Quran and read her the verse: **"We bestowed aforetime on Abraham his rectitude of conduct, and well were We acquainted with him. Behold! he said to his father and his people, "What are these images, to which ye are (so assiduously) devoted?" They said, "We found our fathers worshipping them." He said, "Indeed ye have been in manifest error - ye and your fathers".** He went on to say: "The previous generations were in error when they married off their daughters at a very early age. Today we know that it is not a good thing to do. I recommend that you talk to your parents and read them this Quran verse. I am ready to visit your home and talk to your parents to explain to them how important it is to study".

Explanation: the generation gap to which this important verse refers is a painful issue. The world is changing and many parents do not succeed in adapting to the new world because they were raised in a different world. Among those parents are some who force their children to adopt their accustomed way of life even though it is not suited to the new reality. They have good intentions but often the outcome is not good. Maryam's mother does not understand the importance of study in today's world. The principal did well to use that particular verse to persuade Maryam and her parents. The Quran teaches us that often it is the children and not the parents who are right and sometimes parents should accept their children's stand point even if it clashes with their own traditions.

9. Why should we make peace?

{ إِنَّ هَٰذِهِ أُمَّتُكُمْ أُمَّةً وَاحِدَةً وَأَنَا رَبُّكُمْ فَاعْبُدُونِ } (الأنبياء: 92)

Verily, this brotherhood of yours is a single brotherhood, and I am your Lord and Cherisher: therefore serve Me (and no other). (The Prophets: 92)

In the seventh-grade class, many of the squabbles between pupils develop into violent clashes. There are rivalries between boys and girls, between town-dwellers and villagers and between Bedouin and fellahin. The class teacher initiated a project in order to calm down the class and encourage the pupils to be good friends, cooperate and help one another. She copied onto the blackboard the Quran verse: **"Verily, this brotherhood of yours is a single brotherhood, and I am your Lord and Cherisher:**

therefore serve Me (and no other)". Then she asked the pupils what they thought it meant. They talked about the need to respect one another, the importance of unity and of mutual forgiveness. She organized activities aimed at encouraging better contact between the pupils (games, contests etc). In conclusion, she reminded them again that they were all brothers and sisters believing in one God and read out the verse again.

Explanation: the power and authority of God unites all His believers into one nation. This important verse can bring peace to a classroom, peace between quarreling families and hamoulas and between nations who believe in the same God. Similarly, the authority of the paterfamilias brings siblings closer together and encourages them to take responsibility and to care for one another. The teacher found the appropriate verse which exhorts us to live in peace because we are all brothers.

10. What can we say to someone who demands preferential treatment for a relative?

{ فَإِذَا نُفِخَ فِي الصُّورِ فَلَا أَنسَابَ بَيْنَهُمْ يَوْمَئِذٍ وَلَا يَتَسَاءلُونَ * فَمَن ثَقُلَتْ مَوَازِينُهُ
فَأُوْلَئِكَ هُمُ الْمُفْلِحُونَ * وَمَنْ خَفَّتْ مَوَازِينُهُ فَأُوْلَئِكَ الَّذِينَ خَسِرُوا أَنفُسَهُمْ فِي
جَهَنَّمَ خَالِدُونَ } (المؤمنون: 101-103)

Then when the Trumpet is blown, there will be no more relationships between them that Day, nor will one ask after another! Then those whose balance (of good deeds) is heavy,- they will attain salvation: But those whose balance is light, will be those who have lost their souls, in Hell will they abide. (The Believers: 101-103)

Today was the new science teacher's first day of teaching in a school. As she entered the classroom, her head buzzed with questions: "What will the pupils think of me? What will they ask? How will they treat me?" She tried to recall what she had learned about teaching methods and found herself hesitating about which method to use, which theory to follow. She tried to reassure herself: "First I must get to know them in order to know how to start. Then I will decide on the best method..."

"Good morning, pupils", she said with a pleasant smile and waited for an answer. "Good morning, teacher. You're the new teacher, aren't you, the science teacher?" "Yes", she confirmed. "And your name is Yasmin?" "Yes", she said and added: "How nice of you to ask my name and take an interest. I want to get to know you as well". They started telling her their names, and when they reached one of the boys, he added: "My name is Yusuf and I'm the son of the principal" "Glad to know you", she said, and went on to the next pupil.

In a few days' time, Yasmin was already familiar with her pupils. She tested them to discover their abilities and discovered that there were differences between them and that the class was heterogeneous. She decided to divide the class into groups and to teach each group according to their natural pace on the basis of the marks she gave them and projects. At the end of the lesson, one of the pupils stood up and said: "I'm sorry, teacher but you've put me in the second group and I don't want to be there". It was Yusuf, who had been assigned to the lower group. She explained how she had divided the class and added that in two months' time she would change the classification on the basis of their achievements.

The next day the principal summoned Yasmin: "Do you know what you've done?" he asked. She was surprised at his tone. Without waiting for her reply, he said: "Why didn't you put Yusuf in the first group? Didn't you know he's my son?" Yasmin explained that she knew who Yusuf was but had divided the pupils by grades and test results and not by family affiliation. The principal was surprised: "You are arguing with me instead of promising me that my son will be in the first group??" Yasmin replied: "I can't transfer him because that would harm him and not help him make progress. I will work with each pupil at his or her pace. Believe me, I am working according to a plan which will ensure that each pupil makes progress and I believe the results will be positive". "I am the principal and I decide", he said. "I have the final word. From tomorrow, Yusuf is in the first group".

"With your permission, sir! This year you can look after your son and choose which group he will be in. But next year he will be in a different school and he won't be the principal's son there. Imagine what that will do to him! Let him be equal to the others so that he can make progress in his own right". Yasmin took out a copy of the Quran and read him a verse: **"Then when the Trumpet is blown, there will be no more relationships between them that Day, nor will one ask after another! Then those whose balance (of good deeds) is heavy,- they will attain salvation: But those whose balance is light, will be those who have lost their souls, in Hell will they abide".**

"Good for you, Yasmin!" said the principal. "Your words are worth gold. Go back to your class and I support your decision. Continue with your plan".

Explanation: preferential treatment and concessions for family members are a common phenomenon. Who does not want to help his family? But such conduct can cause great damage. First, society loses because it is not the best and brightest who win the important positions but those who have good connections. Moreover, sometimes it is the beneficiary of the preferential treatment who suffers. For example, if Yusuf is assigned to a group which is too advanced for him, he will suffer because he will not understand the material. He will learn that his father arranges things for him and that he does not need to make an effort for himself. Yasmin answered the principal well when she asked him what would happen to Yusuf in another school where his father was not the principal. The Quran, with its great authority, combats this phenomenon which can destroy a society. Yasmin did well to use this verse in order to convince the principal.

11. How can we foster a democratic approach to others?

{ وَالْمُؤْمِنُونَ وَالْمُؤْمِنَاتُ بَعْضُهُمْ أَوْلِيَاءُ بَعْضٍ يَأْمُرُونَ بِالْمَعْرُوفِ وَيَنْهَوْنَ عَنِ الْمُنكَرِ وَيُقِيمُونَ الصَّلاَةَ وَيُؤْتُونَ الزَّكَاةَ وَيُطِيعُونَ اللّهَ وَرَسُولَهُ أُوْلَـئِكَ سَيَرْحَمُهُمُ اللّهُ إِنَّ اللّهَ عَزِيزٌ حَكِيمٌ } (التوبة: 71)

The Believers, men and women, are protectors one of another: they enjoin what is just, and forbid what is evil: they observe regular prayers, practise regular charity, and obey Allah and His Messenger. On them will Allah pour His mercy: for Allah is Exalted in power, Wise. (The Repentance: 71)

During the local election campaign, the atmosphere is tense because politics infiltrate the school. Pupils from various families and hamoulas often argue as to the most suitable candidate for council head. In the last elections there were several cases of violence among pupils within the school. One of the worst incidents occurred in the ninth grade. Salim argued with classmates who were related to one of the candidates while he was related to another one. Salim claimed that his hamoula was smaller but that his candidate was better educated and that was what was important. The argument soon deteriorated into a shouting and cursing match. His classmates attacked him and beat him. He yelled with pain but there was no teacher in the vicinity. The other boys defaced his belongings, insulted him, told him he didn't understand a thing and warned him that if he mentioned his candidate again, he would be in trouble. Similar incidents occur during each election campaign. Parents support their warring children and encourage them to be violent, and the violence spreads outside the school.

Since the election date was approaching, the school principal decided to hang a large poster at the entrance to the school, quoting the verse: **"The Believers, men and women, are protectors one of another: they enjoin what is just, and forbid what is evil".**

Explanation: there can be no doubt that the ability to be a positive participant in democratic elections is not self-evident and calls for suitable psychological preparation. The ability to argue in such a manner that each insists on his own views but respects the opinions of others requires guidance and practice. In the West as well, the democratic process evolved slowly and people had to be taught to combine assertiveness with empathy. Assertiveness enables the individual to have his say without fear but also without aggression. Empathy enables him or her to understand the viewpoint of the other without necessarily agreeing. These two emotional stances are vital for democracy. It is recommended, therefore, that each parent and each teacher teach children how to be assertive yet empathetic. For example, a teacher can raise various questions and organize debates where both sides present their views but listen to the other view and respect it. The Quran suggests this path and recommends that we treat one another with respect. People are permitted to express different views and are enjoined to defend one another's right to express personal opinions. It proposes that this be achieved through social cohesion whereby each participant feels it his obligation to defend the other.

Letters of appreciation

A letter from Yuli Tamir, Minister of Education

MINISTER OF EDUCATION
Jerusalem
29.4.2008
Reference: 14608142

Dear Dr. Grosbard,

Re: "The Quran: a Guide for Education"

Many thanks for sending me a copy of this book. It is a very impressive work as is the Quranet[1] project - the bidirectional social network: between Islam and the West.
Dr. Shlomo Alon, the Chief Inspector for Arabic and Islamic studies, has also expressed his admiration for the book and for the educational project which you carried out with a group of Bedouin students studying for graduate degrees in educational counseling at the Oranim College. The students were recipients of study grants from the Ministry of Education.
The selection of your project for the exhibition: "Tomorrow's Space" is particularly gratifying.

Yours sincerely,
Yuli Tamir
Minister of Education

Cc: Ms. Shlomit Amihai, Director-General
Professor Anat Zohar, Chairperson, Pedagogic Secretariat
Ms. Leah Rosenberg, Deputy Director-General and Director, Pedagogic Administration
Dr. Shlomo Alon, Chief Professional Inspector, Arabic Studies

---

1 www.quranet.net

A letter from Sheikh Muhammed Omari

IN THE NAME OF GOD, THE MERCIFUL THE COMPASSIONATE

The Quran, in the eyes of Muslims, is the greatest of guides. It is the word of God which is inimitable and it is granted to the last of the Prophets, Muhammed, peace and blessings upon him. The word of the Quran accompanies Muslims in their everyday life. They listen reverently to its verses and attribute to them great sanctity, both during and after prayers. Muslims frequently memorize the Quran and quote from it in various circumstances and it has great impact on the molding of the Muslim character as regards beliefs, prayers, customs and culture. A Muslim who is in close affinity with the Quran, which is the source of morality and ethics, preserves for himself thereby a place close to God, close to his religion, to the Prophet and to Paradise.
Aisha, wife of Muhammed, was asked what were Muhammed's moral qualities. She replied that his moral qualities were the word of the Quran. Thus, the Quran serves in many spheres: as a source of guidance for purposes of preaching and peacemaking, physical and spiritual healing and for judgment and rulings. Scholars, educators and experts on the behavior of the individual and Islamic society adopted this book as their guide. They were aware of its vast positive influence on ways of dealing with educational and social problems in the life of the Muslim individual and the rectification of such negative conduct as violence, rebellion, envy, hatred and various customs originating in the pre-Islamic period (jahaliya). These customs include drinking of wine, drug taking, dishonorable behavior, licentiousness, prostitution, sodomy, theft, obscene language, lying etc. Thus, the leadership of the society could invest efforts in the right direction in order to amend and improve a situation. For there is no more reliable source than the Quran, which declares in this context: *"By the Soul, and the proportion and order given to it;"* (Surah 91, Verse 7)

It is only natural that we should derive benefit from the knowledge of scientists and experts in various spheres of human and social science, apart from those matters which are irreconcilable with the basic elements of the supreme religion based on the Quran, the Sunna and

Islamic culture. It would not be wise on our part to disregard the greatest source in the life of Muslims.

The present project seeks to create a link between the Quran, which serves as the basis of faith and culture in our lives, and modern sciences and research in the sphere of the healing of the soul. The stories provide examples of problems encountered in everyday life in our society. The solution, which is illustrated by a Quran verse, demonstrates how to deal with such problems and serves as clear guidance and as a beacon of light. The reader then reads an educational explanation, which clarifies the Quran response from the psychological viewpoint.

In many cases we could undoubtedly find other verses which offer guidance on solution of the problem. These verses can influence and speak to the heart and soul of any Muslim who is sanctifies and reveres the word of the Quran and strictly observes its commands in order to do the will of God and his Messenger and to be counted among the good Muslims.

Dr. Ofer Grosbard, a clinical psychologist by profession, has labored with his students to implement this impressive project. The students, all Muslims, who are studying for graduate degrees in educational counseling, are keenly aware of the importance of the link between psychology and the Quran in the effort to help schoolchildren and their families. The readers will easily locate the Quranic and educational answers to their questions and will be able to derive great benefit. This is a worthy enterprise which deserves encouragement and admiration. In future it will be possible to add to the quoted Quran verses, the sayings (Hadith) of the Prophet Muhammed, peace and blessings upon him, because the deeds and conduct of the Prophet are, in effect, the beginning of the Quran: *It is He Who has sent amongst the Unlettered a Messenger from among themselves, to rehearse to them His Signs, to sanctify them, and to instruct them in Scripture and Wisdom, - although they had been, before, in manifest error;* (Surah 62, Verse 2).

I must emphasize that this work is a blessed project, the first of its kind in this country, the fruit of cooperation between a teacher and his students. This initiative deserves gratitude, appreciation and attention. It inspires fresh ways of thinking and encourages initiative for creativity and innovation in this and other spheres. The researcher who links modern science with the Quran and Islamic culture, is making a valuable contribution for the benefit of mankind as a whole. As the Quran says: *"Verily this Qur-an doth guide to that which is most right (or stable), and giveth the glad tidings to the Believers who work deeds of righteousness, that they shall have a magnificent reward; (Surah 17, Verse 9). And as the Prophet, peace and blessings on him, has said: The best among you are those who study the Quran and teach it to others."*

Sheikh Muhammed Omari,
Lecturer, al-Qasami College,
Deputy Chief Inspector of Islamic Religious Teaching,
Ministry of Education and Culture.

A letter from Sheikh Abdullah Nimer Darwish

CHILDREN ARE GIVEN TO US AS A SACRED TRUST

Children have rights even before they are born. They are entitled to loving parents who respect one another, a reasonable economic status, the right to inherit etc. After birth, the infant is entitled to be suckled by his mother, and to be under the care of an adult. Sometimes infants exploit their developing skills in order to damage objects in the home. They want our attention and not only in order to fulfill basic needs such as food, clothing, hygiene and sleep. Therefore, it is incumbent on us to establish a connection with our children, to buy them suitable toys and to concern ourselves with their development. The objective of educating children is to do the will of God. Hence it should be recalled that a child is not a plant, which needs nothing but nutrition. The education of children entails far more that providing basic needs. The objective is, among other things, to inculcate in the child the basic tenets of faith from early infancy. One should not underestimate the importance of the early years for education, and parents who dismiss this period in the life of the child will later regret it.

In the pre-school period, the child asks many questions and takes an interest in the world around him and sometimes seems to argue a great deal. He can differentiate between what is forbidden and what is permitted, between good and bad. This being so, in this period it is possible to build the child's personality in all spheres (faith, science, culture, conduct, social skills, psychology, emotions, taste and love of beauty and creativity). These realizations led the scholar Ahmed Suleiman to claim in his book: "The Muslim child in light of the Quran and the Suna" that it is possible to educate a child in the early years to be capable of responding to and obeying the command of Allah: *"Preserve your souls and the members of your household from fire."* It is also possible to explain to a child the meaning of the verse: There is no God but Allah and Muhammed is the Messenger of God."

It is advisable to learn from the way in which the Prophet educated children and delved profoundly into the values of the faith with them. Thus, the child will grasp the essence of the stories which connect him to God and will appreciate God and his Messenger, the Prophet Muhammed.

In order to achieve this aim, it is recommended to encourage the child's positive actions or diligent study by granting prizes and gifts.

The child's manners and conduct develop through emulation of the conduct of his or her parents. When parents speak courteously and exhibit self-control during anger, the child will behave similarly. He should be taught to treat adults with respect, to greet them and ask permission before acting on his own initiative. It is important to teach him to treat animals properly and to explain that he should have mercy on them and not torture them. Children should be brought to the mosque and should be taught to love it. Beyond this, it is incumbent on parents to endeavor to understand the child and his feelings and to be aware of his needs. Care should be taken not to insult him in front of strangers and to ensure that he goes to bed each night with a light heart. He should be distanced from frightening things (as Professor Liz Elliot of Chicago University has pointed out).

I do not wish to write at length, but merely to offer an introduction based on the wisdom of scholars who have studied childhood. I have read the work of Bushra and the group of graduate students in educational counseling who are studying under Dr, Ofer Grosbard and my impression is that this pioneering experiment can serve as effective material for study. But, at the same time, I recommend refraining from expanded interpretation of the Quran verses, particularly those verses which reflect the concepts of the basic tenets of the faith.

In any event, I welcome this good idea and I wish every success to the team which is carrying out the project. I recommend profound study of Islam so that those interested can discover for themselves how mighty this Islam is and what power it contains on questions of education and raising children. To raise a child is a task for human beings while education requires the hand of Allah and the will of Allah.

Sheikh Abdullah Nimer Darwish
Founder of the Islamic movement
November 25, 2007

A letter from Sheikh Musa Admani

THE QUR'AN IS THE GUIDE FOR ALL HUMANITY

The Qur'an is not meant exclusively for Muslims, as some Muslims and non-Muslims believe. The book is meant for anyone who is prepared to adopt its principles and its philosophy. Those who do so will be enriched and will constitute a living example of its ideals and ideas. This is what the Qur'an says: *"O mankind, instruction has been given to you by your Lord, and healing for anything that troubles your hearts, and guidance and mercy for the believers."* (Sura 10, Verse 57). In this verse God addresses the human race in general and exhorts it to listen to His message.

Negative human nature is the source of all our problems. We thus have to be aware of the destructive forces concealed within us, and take the appropriate protective measures. The Qur'an is both the protection against our illness and the remedy for curing it. We as individuals and as collective communities are capable of reaching great heights and accomplishing record-breaking achievements in the material world, because we are endowed with the intellectual capacity to learn and to apply our knowledge and experience. We have failed, however, in applying this knowledge for constructing ourselves, and we have shied away from any shouldering of responsibility. Sometimes, we ourselves are the source of the problem. It is then difficult to identify it, and we tend to look for various excuses, are quick to blame the other and ever ready to punish him. Few are prepared to take responsibility and to start putting things right. Shouldering responsibility requires courage, maturity and the ability to rise above mankind's negative traits.

The Qur'an and the holy books that preceded it explained at length the issue of constructing the self and the individual's capacity for taking responsibility. A positive and responsible character is not constructed in order to gain an advantage over the other. On the contrary, the price for constructing this character is to renounce the advantage and the status that the individual acquires as a father, a brother, or a highly acclaimed person. This renunciation is done in order to further truth, justice, compassion, respect, conciliation, and consideration toward others, even if they dislike me. When we try to be nice to those around us, we usually do so from our point of view and not from theirs. The Qur'an suggests that we should be the upholders of justice and its defenders, even if this goes against our desires or those of our parents or relatives. It is easy to preach this to others, but difficult to apply it to ourselves and to those close to us. What the Qur'an teaches us is a love of humanity; what it teaches us to avoid is selfishness.

We know that everyone is responsible for his actions. But are people also responsible for their feelings and their motives? The answer, unequivocally, is yes! External laws will not help in this case. We have to activate our internal alarm clock to awaken us before we sleepwalk into inappropriate behavior. Bear in mind that the human being will only be victorious once he ceases to use his knowledge as an instrument for profiting at the other's expense. Knowledge has to guide us in many areas, and particularly regarding our internal and most intimate feelings. Then, and only then, can we declare that victory is ours. Until then, we have to continue the struggle against ourselves. We need to concentrate and give attention to our positive characteristics, and learn to block our negative characteristics. The Qur'an gives us a list of negative characteristics that any person can identify. Our recent history offers us many reasons to be proud, as well as much that we need to continue to improve. But it has also exposed our dark side, of which we have to take heed.

The following is a partial list of negative human characteristics. People tend to be hasty, unjust, ignorant, mean, argumentative and pessimistic. Despite these weaknesses, people are God's emissaries on earth. Human beings have been granted this status because they are capable of overcoming these barriers with the help of knowledge, faith, and good deeds. We cannot allow ourselves to behave like Joseph's brothers whose envy got the better of them and caused them to sell their brother. We have to behave like the prophet Job who, despite losing everything, did not allow despair to overwhelm him. We need to behave like Joseph who did not waste his time lamenting what his brothers had done to him, but rather helped the Egyptians to survive the famine.

All this reminds us that the age-old problem of balancing our desires with the needs of others requires unflagging commitment and constant education. We have to further our knowledge, including the knowledge directed toward developing character, so that instead of becoming slaves to our culture, our history and our tradition, we will realize what our lives mean and strive for better lives for us all, thereby leaving the next generations with a better world than the one we inherited. As God's creations we have to assist each other to bear the burden, and to remind one another of the need to take care of others and do good deeds.

I have had the privilege of meeting Dr. Ofer Grosbard and becoming familiar with some of his work. When Ofer asked me to write a foreword to his wonderful book, which deals with treating people's difficulties with the help of the Qur'an, I saw this as a great honor. I must admit that as a student of the Qur'an for the past twenty years, I was fascinated by Ofer's work. For me it is a demonstration of the authenticity of the Qur'an's claim to be a guide for all humanity. The book is exceptionally clear in the manner in which a wide range of difficulties that people experience can be solved by means of the Qur'an. For example, when a person is told, with the help of a verse from the Qur'an, that he does not have to feel guilty about things that are beyond his control, this extricates him from his depression. In another case progress was achieved because the parents were told, with the help of a verse from the Qur'an, that their children have the right to a certain amount of freedom, and that they should respect their children's decisions. These are clear and proven examples of how studying the Qur'an can improve the condition of humanity. I hope and pray that the reader will make use of this book, and benefit from the wealth of knowledge it contains. I would urge all students of the Qur'an, irrespective of their religion, belief or culture, to read this book.

I will conclude with a quote from Sura 103: *"The human being is utterly lost, except those who believe and lead a righteous life, and exhort one another to uphold the truth, and exhort one another to be steadfast."* It is the continuous search for truth, tolerance, belief and doing the right work that will help us to avoid the loss and the hopelessness.

Sheikh Musa Admani
Imam of London Metropolitan University
Head of the Luqman Institute of Education and Development

A letter from Dr. Khwaja Iftikhar Ahmed

To whomsoever it may concern

After having met Professor Ofer Grosbard in the presidential conference, held in the Holy city of Jerusalem, Israel; I believe that persons of his caliber, understanding and background are the real treasure for all those people among Muslims and Jews who by conviction believe in cultivating a mutually beneficial relationship among the two very significant members of the Family of Abraham.
We the Muslims believe in Moses as much as we believe in Mohammad (PBUT). In fact, for us denial of Moses is denial of Mohammad and this very belief makes our bonds with Jews absolutely eternal. Strengthening this God gifted tie among the followers of Judaism and Islam is our joint responsibility.
We, in the Foundation(IFHFI) accord top priority to building a strong and sustainable relationship with Jews around the world and any effort that pushes this process towards its logical conclusion is more than welcome at our end. Honesty, integrity and credibility are the hallmarks of any relationship and I am sure that these are going to be the guiding and governing principles for all the future actions and initiatives taken by Ofer.

The great work that Ofer has done on Holy Quran needs to be translated in English and thereafter perhaps in all the languages which are spoken by Muslims. This work by a Jewish brother can act as a wonderful bridge to achieve the aforesaid goal. This effort needs to be appreciated and supported both morally and materially. The work that he has done is of immense value and does possess the potential to tremendously boost the fraternal bonds among the two major communities of the world.

With utmost regards,

Dr. Khwaja Iftikhar Ahmed,
Founder President, IFHFI, New Delhi, 19-05-2008

www.ingramcontent.com/pod-product-compliance
Ingram Content Group UK Ltd.
Pitfield, Milton Keynes, MK11 3LW, UK
UKHW022002190726
13853UKWH00004B/1684

9 789659 282906